NEW STUDIES IN POST-COLD WAR SECURITY

New Studies in Post-Cold War Security

Edited by
K.R. DARK

Dartmouth

Aldershot • Brookfield USA • Singapore • Sydney

Published by
Dartmouth Publishing Company Limited
Gower House
Croft Road
Aldershot
Hants GU11 3HR
England

Dartmouth Publishing Company
Old Post Road
Brookfield
Vermont 05036
USA

British Library Cataloguing in Publication Data
New studies in post-Cold War security
  1.Security, International 2.World politics - 1989-
  I.Dark, K.R.
  327'.09049

Library of Congress Cataloging-in-Publication Data
New studies in post-cold war security / edited by K.R. Dark
      p.   cm.
   Includes index.
   ISBN 1-85521-728-7
   1. World politics–1989- 2. Europe–Politics and government-
-1989- 3. Security, International. I. Dark, K.R. (Ken R.)
D860.N39   1996
327'.0'04–dc20   96-16535
                                                                     CIP

ISBN 1 85521 728 7

Printed and bound in Great Britain by Hartnolls Limited, Bodmin, Cornwall

Contents

Preface

This book is unusual in two respects: most recent studies of post-Cold War security have been works by well-established scholars, whose careers span both the Cold War and its aftermath. They have, understandably, tended to be somewhat retrospective in tone - emphasising the ending of the Cold War - rather than the emerging security environment. Unlike such works the contributors to this volume are 'newer', and for the most part 'younger', scholars and adopt a prospective approach befitting the first 'post-Cold War' generation of security analysts. It must be stressed that the papers included are not the outcome of a single research programme or of a coordinated series of individual investigations, rather they are the product of independent studies undertaken within a range of theoretical and methodological frameworks, although the work included here shares a historical, rather than for instance philosophical, approach.

It is neither the intention to present a series of chapters arguing through a single theme or adopting a single approach, nor to offer a comprehensive treatment, either thematically or geographically, of all aspects of a wide-ranging topic. Many important areas and themes have, of course, been excluded or discussed only in passing. Rather, the aim is to provide studies examining specific themes that can form the basis for further discussion and analysis.

The contributions here are mostly based on completed postgraduate research or postdoctoral study and consequently the views expressed by any of the contributors cannot be taken as those of the others, or of the editor. The same point applies to the geographical coverage of the papers, the emphasis is on case-studies rather than on attempting global coverage.

This being said, there is a clear structure to the book. The first two contributions concentrate on a central theme in post-Cold War security - the question of changes in relative utilities in the post-Cold War world of Cold War strategy and weapons. The following five papers examine regional issues, offering detailed studies of some key areas for Western security that pose wide-ranging questions. Finally, there is a more polemical piece on security dilemmas facing Britain in the post-Cold War world, written by David Higginbottom, who was a British army officer for thirty years.

Likewise, despite the independence of the work represented, and the differing approaches and backgrounds of the authors, common themes and similarities can be noted. These include some which might seem surprisingly 'traditional' aspects of security studies. For example, the contributors, not all of whom would consider themselves 'realists', share a common interest in using the state as *a* (in some cases rather than *the*) unit of analysis in international security. There is a shared trend to analyse security primarily in terms of military threats to the interests of the West and its allies, rather than, for example, ecological issues. Several contributors also stress the continuing importance of NATO and the political and military relationships established within the Atlantic Alliance during Cold War period as a means of providing for Western security in the post-Cold War period.

Yet there are also less traditional themes which can be found in common, notably the importance assigned to unconventional and low-intensity warfare and to the dangers of terrorism. Perhaps this mix of long-standing problems and changed forms of warfare is itself an indication of the character of the post-Cold War security situation.

Whether or not the reader agrees with the interpretations offered, I hope that this volume will stimulate further discussion of the issues raised and prompt more work on the themes incorporated here. In the fast-changing political and technological environment of the 1990s, these are possibly among the most important achievements that any examination of contemporary international security can hope to produce.

1 The changing form of post-Cold War security

KEN DARK

Introduction

The end of the Cold War has brought about fundamental shifts in the nature of international security (for recent discussions, see McInnes, 1992a; Buzan *et al*, 1990). These affect both the form and the means of warfare, and the meaning of security itself. In the Cold War, most analysts, whether they were academics or practitioners, saw security in terms of the state, and war in terms of conventional or nuclear, biological and chemical weapons (NBC) threats (discussed in its context by Dunbabin, 1994). In such a situation, the purpose of ensuring security was to protect the state and thereby its citizens, and to endeavour to ensure the absence of inter-state warfare. The means of ensuring security was the maintenance of such conventional and other forces as were deemed necessary by planners to prevent direct threats to the state turning into military action. There was also a political, diplomatic, economic and cultural dimension to security in that the conflict was between two opposing worldviews and economic ideologies as much as between opposing forces. Communist political and economic beliefs and interests had, therefore, to be 'contained' as part of the overall strategy to ensure Western security.

In the post-Cold War world, there is widespread recognition that neither security nor its provision can any longer be understood in these terms alone, although states still form one important source of security problems, and an important unit of analysis in examining international security (for example, Kolodziej, 1992; Tickner, 1995; Buzan, 1991; Brown, 1994). Communism no longer constitutes a serious global threat to Western interests and the Marxist-Leninist worldview has been conclusively defeated worldwide. New threats have been identified, however - such as ecological change and the development of intensified economic competition - that represent more serious problems for the constituent populations of states ('the people') than perhaps they do for the survival of states themselves (Mathews, 1994; Bunch and Carillo, 1994; Dark, 1996). The threats posed by intrusions into individual and corporate privacy, and by terrorism, often for reasons unrelated to inter-state conflicts, are also examples of problems now to the fore. Many of these threats are not easily countered by a single state nor even military alliance, and their control lies beyond the scope of national defence-forces or even intelligence services (for instance Pirages, 1994).

It can be said, therefore, that post-Cold War threats to Western security have acquired a transnational character. They have also moved away from areas traditionally seen as the preserve of military forces and strategists (for example, Cable, 1995). The constraints increasingly imposed by the spread of liberal democracy may also have limited the scope of military forces, and the global network of media communications has made their actions increasingly visible throughout the developed world (compare Taylor, 1992).

The risk of inter-state war has changed, too. Instead of 'superpower confrontation', there is a new emphasis among military planners on low-intensity and mid-intensity inter-state conflict (Booth, 1991). The perceived threats here, therefore, are not from 'great powers' or blocs of technologically-advanced and politically-expansionist states, but instead include regional and local invasions by small and medium-sized states outside of the immediate geographical environs of the Western states, mostly in the southern hemisphere (the 'South') or in Asia (Kegley and Wittkopf, 1995, pp. 434 and 461). In addition to the danger of war resulting from the activities such less-technologically developed aggressor states, there is also a threat posed by state-sponsored terrorism against Western interests and this may partially overlap with, or be combined with, terrorist campaigns by non-state groups (Wilkinson, 1990).

A particular problem of international security in the post-Cold War period has also come to be the rise of civil, and other intra-state, factional warfare and such conflicts could easily be combined with direct threats against Western interests, or be aggravated by (and have a negative impact on) ecological and economic changes detrimental to Western populations (Horowitz, 1994). Obviously, from the point of view of non-Western states, these problems may be more pressing, and these types of threat far more likely to emerge in close proximity to their own borders.

The long-standing North-South division in global wealth and technological capabilities has to some extent been eroded by the emergence of new, globally-important, economies in South East Asia and elsewhere, but there are still regional and hemispheric tensions of this sort (Homer-Dixon, 1994; Ferraro and Rosser, 1994). These are now no longer aggravated by the Cold War ideological conflict, but even this still persists in two isolated instances: Cuba and North Korea. Clearly, if ecological change adversely affects the South more acutely than the North, then this too might aggravate international tensions, either by provoking large-scale migrations or by intensifying feelings of injustice in the global economy (on the implications of population change, see Freedman and Saunders, 1991).

As many critical economic resources of key importance to the West lie in the southern hemisphere, or in other areas susceptible to such anti-Western tendencies, this must be an important issue for Western planners (Bearman, 1995, pp. 139-53). Likewise, it will be of key importance to ensure that the South and the Asian states cooperate with the West to limit the environmental impacts of rapid economic change (see Camilleri and Falk, 1993; Lundestad and Westad, 1993).

Elsewhere in this volume I shall consider the impact of economic and political change in Southeast Asia and East Asia and its effects on global security, but the questions raised in relation to the South overall must also be of pressing concern to those hoping for international political and economic stability. Here, I wish to concentrate on the implications for the USA and Europe - that is, for the NATO partners - and to approach the question of post-Cold War security from the viewpoint of the West. My aim is not to look at specific military and strategic changes in these areas in detail, examining every aspect of their security problems and possibilities after the end of the Cold War, but to analyse some common themes in regard to regional and global security arising from changes resulting from two factors (for further discussions, see Bluth *et al*, 1995; McInnes, 1992a). First, the end of the Cold War itself and second, the impact of technology on the form of war (and of international security) in the post-Cold War world (McInnes, 1992b). It will be argued that, by changing the character of warfare itself, these two factors have changed global strategic and military capabilities and ranking, most fundamentally affecting the NATO states and the former Soviet Union, although many of the points made have a wider relevance to global security.

This approach requires one to ask, of course, what were the implications for the character of warfare resulting from the end of the Cold War? That is, apart from the obvious cessation of the threat of 'superpower' war and global nuclear exchanges, which may seem somewhat obvious.

First, there seems general agreement among both scholars of International Relations and military planners, that the end of the Cold War has reduced the utility of massed conventional land forces of the sort facing each other across the German border in the 1960s and 70s. These large conventional forces are expensive to maintain and difficult to transport over long distances. They are suited to specific forms of warfare, especially the waging of pitched armoured battles of the type exemplified in the post-Cold War period by the Gulf War (Freedman and Karsh, 1992). Such equipment is most effective in relatively flat and open terrain: the folly of employing tanks and other armoured vehicles in mountain passes is, perhaps, the most well-known example of their failings.

The reduced utility of large-scale artillery and battlefield missile forces has also been highlighted. Problems of rapid transport and relative effectiveness against a dispersed (for instance, guerilla) force have been shown by the related difficulties faced by gunners in the former Yugoslavia (on the conflict in the former Yugoslavia see, for instance, Gnesotto, 1994; Zametica, 1992). Heavy artillery and battlefield missile forces seem at their most effective in opposing static or 'dug-in' opponents: that is, opponents offering fixed (or at least relatively large) targets rather than fast-moving, dispersed, infantry forces operating in broken terrain.

This realisation of the limitations of the types of weapons upon which Western land commanders relied in the Cold War, and the likelihood that the scene of future conflicts may be both distant from Europe (and at least as distant from the USA) and far less suitable for such weapons than was the Gulf (Freedman, 1994, pp. 357-63), suggests that the force-size and structure of the USA, Russia and China may exceed present expected utility value, given the nature of the potential threats as outlined above (note also Herring, 1991). The most likely battlefields of the near future are the very types of terrain to which these types of weapons are most ill-suited - mountains, jungles, forests and built-up areas containing non-combatant civilians (Freedman, 1994, pp. 357-63). The most likely opponents are terrorists, guerillas, local militia and the small armies of civil wars. So, a potential post-Cold War aggressor against Western forces is more likely to be an un-uniformed and guerilla-style force of local infantry with conventional (possibly out-dated) weapons and a detailed knowledge of the terrain within which operations must be conducted, rather than a regular army equipped with heavy armour and static positions (Heydte, 1986). A further consideration affects not only the utility of conventional land forces, and nuclear weapons, but airforces and navies.

The post-Cold War pattern of warfare seems characterised by

combatants who act within and among civilian, non-combatant, populations (Kegley and Witkopf, 1995, pp. 454-7). These may be terrorists or guerillas operating within 'friendly' territory, or local irregulars whose quarters and equipment may be positioned in civilian areas. Still worse, such opponents may be more inclined to take hostages or to deliberately use civilians as 'shields' (on terrorist warfare, see Hanle, 1989). The forces of Western liberal democracies, operating under the gaze of their own and foreign media, have very limited opportunities for employing air-power in such situations. Losses in terms of public relations and propaganda victories for enemy forces may outweigh any military gains of such action, even setting aside the serious ethical and legal problems that it poses.

If the utility of massed air-power has been reduced in a post-Cold War situation, the role of Western navies has been changed even more drastically. While it is clear that the West must retain a capacity to engage enemy airforces and navies in direct warfare, the technological advantage held by Western forces is likely to be such that far fewer aircraft and ships will be required to sustain this capacity in future. The primary purpose of navies, in particular, may increasingly become logistic (although navies may take on new functions to accommodate new technologies, see: *Defense News*, 21-27 August 1995, pp. 1 and 28). That is, the threats faced in the post-Cold War period are unlikely to include large-scale naval battles: so far, most post-Cold War conflicts have been essentially land-based. Navies continue to play a vital role in maintaining communications and in transporting troops and equipment in such conflicts, and in keeping forces supplied once in location. So there is still, of course, a need for the maintenance of both airforces and navies by the Western states, but, once again, current force-levels in the USA far exceed any possible post-Cold War need. Like nuclear forces, a large navy and airforce may be an expensive luxury for the USA after the Cold War.

The defence cuts proposed in the USA are, therefore, going to be most effective if they trim force sizes and reduce acquisition policies in these areas (Neaman, 1994, pp. 13-21; Neaman 1995, pp. 13-23). What seems to be needed for the next decades are highly flexible and highly mobile armed forces, with an emphasis on improved training, especially in fighting guerilla-style and jungle-warfare, rather than on mechanisation and means of intensive bombardment. More attention must be given to anti-terrorist (and perhaps low-intensity urban) operations and less to the development of large airforces and navies (on anti-terrorist approaches, see Smith, 1990).

The declining utility of nuclear weapons

While nuclear weapons could be seen as the basis for global security in the Cold War, many of the same arguments apply to them as to other costly weapons systems (for nuclear strategy in the Cold War, see Freedman, 1989). It has to be asked whether they are suitable for the type of conflicts liable to be prevalent in the post-Cold War period (Freedman, 1994-95; Witney, 1994-95; Yost, 1994-95; Krass, 1994; Karp, 1991). The global bipolar confrontation, with its vast arsenal of nuclear (and 'NBC') weaponry, was closely linked to the development of theories of nuclear strategy, the value of which can also be doubted in relation to the post-Cold War period (McGwire, 1994). The non-use of these forces was one of the great achievements of Cold War military and political leaders, superseding even the prevention of direct conventional conflict. Unless we recognise that the utility of strategies designed to counter Cold War threats may be reduced - perhaps even to zero - in the post-Cold War period, then we are in danger of 'preparing for the last war', rather than preparing for the new international situation. This does not mean to say that all aspects of Cold War strategic thinking are redundant, but that the new situation, itself, requires new strategic thinking.

The end of the Cold War has greatly lessened the threat of large-scale NBC war, and so it has brought into severe doubt the value - even in political terms - of large nuclear arsenals, of the type held by the USA and Russia (McGwire, 1994). Of surviving nuclear states, only two

(Russia and China) have any capacity to engage the West in nuclear war on a large scale. Of these, Russia is hardly likely to enter into a nuclear conflict with the West. China is possibly less clearly committed to non-proliferation and non-expansionist policies, and could be seen as more likely to engage in a nuclear conflict. But Chinese nuclear arsenals and delivery systems both are, and are likely to remain, few and technically poor compared to those of the West (Neaman, 1994, pp. 165 and 170). It is inconceivable that China could hope to 'win', or even gain advantage from, even a limited nuclear exchange with any of the NATO states. Even the limited nuclear arsenals of France or the UK could wreak terminal damage to the Chinese state (Neaman, 1994, pp. 36-7, 45 and 69). The Chinese are well aware that no country, even China, is big enough to withstand a large-scale nuclear attack.

Nor, of course, is there more than a hypothetical military threat posed to the West in this way by either Russia or China. There is no evidence that strongly suggests that either Russia or China intend to develop such a strategy in the near future, or have inclinations toward war with the West. Even if Russia was governed by a more authoritarian or nationalist government this would not necessarily make it militarily threatening to Western interests.

No other nuclear state could conceivably gain from a nuclear attack on the West, so, unless (once again) one envisages a terrorist group using a nuclear device, the direct nuclear threat to the West is far reduced from 1980s levels (on nuclear terrorism, see Leventhal and Hoenig, 1987; Schelling, 1985; Jenkins, 1985). Clearly, this is a question to which many of the arguments on the utility of 'Cold War' armed forces, already discussed, can be seen to relate. There is no point in attempting to deter a small and mobile terrorist group with a massive force of ICBMs or SLBMs - it simply will not work.

Although the variability in global, and Western, non-proliferation strategies may mean that the West is likely to be faced with more nuclear states in the twenty-first century (Navias, 1990a; Hackett, 1990; Mahnken, 1990; Davis, 1994), none of these are likely to hold sufficient stocks of nuclear weapons, and have technically advanced enough delivery systems, to present a serious threat of global nuclear war with the NATO allies. Except in the case of Middle Eastern and North African states, geographical factors also make it unlikely that, with the available delivery-systems technologies which they could obtain, any new nuclear state could pose a direct threat to European or North American states able to call upon NATO nuclear deterrent forces (on potential nuclear states and the available technologies see: Navias, 1990b). Although there may well be other more advisable solutions to this problem, even if non-proliferation strategies fail, deterrence against hostile states in the Middle East or North Africa with small nuclear forces would still require the availability of very few nuclear weapons, especially if delivery systems included SLBMs stationed beyond the range of potentially hostile missiles and undetectable by technologies available to those states.

The minimum deterrent, in terms of warheads and delivery systems, to counter these much smaller-scale threats and to render a Russian or Chinese nuclear attack too costly a strategy to contemplate (and it is very doubtful whether such a strategy would be contemplated in the post-Cold War world) is all that is required by the Western states in the new international circumstances. It is inconceivable that any new state, other than China, will develop 'Cold War'-scale nuclear forces prior to the mid-twenty-first century, if current non-proliferation strategies succeed even partially (Neaman, 1994, pp. 256-61). So, the threat of nuclear war is not only much diminished but the requirement for the West to maintain large nuclear forces is effectively eliminated, provided that political change does not render Russia hostile to the West once again.

The small scale of the nuclear threat posed by states to the West after the Cold War has perhaps not been appreciated fully (for instance, Barnaby, 1990, seems excessively pessimistic). Assuming that Russia does not collapse into nationalistic anti-Western rule, the Russian nuclear arsenal can effectively be eliminated from our consideration, except insofar as it is vulnerable to non-state subversion or illegal proliferation without state backing. It is inconceivable that a democratic Russia with strong Western economic links, and institutional connections, would pose any military threat to the West. If one makes this evaluation of the absence of direct threat from Russia, there is no potential nuclear threat to the NATO allies anywhere in the world, aside from 'nuclear terrorism', that cannot be countered by very small deterrent forces on the scale of those of Britain or France.

This, in turn, means that the end of the Cold War reduced the utilities of the forms of military might with which it had been most closely associated: nuclear forces (the same arguments apply to both chemical and biological weapons) and the use of massed armies, especially those relying on heavy weapons. Similar arguments can be applied to other aspects of Cold War armed forces, such as bomber forces, which carry similar criticisms of the scale of the airforces and navies of the West. Unlike the end of World War II, it did not enable a new role to be found for forces established to meet a beaten foe, due to the fundamental changes which had occurred in the range and character of possible threats and theatres of war. The end of the Cold War meant the end of 'Cold Warfare', by which I mean global nuclear confrontation combined with middle-scale conventional war involving heavy armour and bomber fleets. The last such conflict may well prove to have been the Gulf war of 1990/91 (Freedman and Karsh, 1992).

Consequently, given the high costs of maintaining such forces in their present form, it may be advisable to reform their current sizes and structures, at least in the USA and Russia. In both of these states there seems to be no military justification for maintaining current force-sizes, and national and UN security commitments could probably be met with forces closer in scale to those held by the major European states such as Germany and France. Such forces would be capable of meeting any conceivable direct land, or air-, strike against Russia or the USA, and maintain a safe level of nuclear deterrence at a far reduced cost (on current US views, Cambone and Garrity, 1994-95). Plainly, the development of anti-ballistic missile systems and other counter-measures, alongside further developments in satellite-based and aerial surveillance, will even further reduce the utilities of deterrent forces similar in scale to those maintained by the USA and USSR in the Cold War (this is not to suggest a return to costly SDI-style defences, on which see Bulkely and Spinardi, 1986; Carter and Schwartz, 1984; Reiss, 1992). They will also enable nuclear states to hold fewer weapons and delivery systems at lower costs: a few nuclear weapons may be sufficient to deter any possible early-mid twenty-first century aggressor if the possibilities of undetected preparations for a hostile launch can be reduced to near zero.

This raises the question of the technological changes taking place in the West and elsewhere, which have potential impacts on strategic issues and international security (the current impact is discussed in Bearman, 1995, pp. 33-4). These hold out the probability of the development of new types of weapons and, with them, new types of strategies for the post-Cold War period.

The changed utility of elite forces

What, then, are the types of 'warfare' that will be developed as a result of this change in relative utilities? It might be supposed that the reduction in 'massed force' and 'NBC' utilities will profit only airforces, navies and highly-mobile and 'unconventional' army units, of an otherwise principally 'Cold War' type: such as marines and airborne forces. But this may well be an illusion.

Although the utility of small, mobile, well-trained, and especially experienced, military units specialising in anti-terrorist and low-intensity warfare may be increased in the new international situation, this will be so only in specific circumstances. Such units have a great capacity for using their skills to counter small-scale and guerilla-warfare threats (Smith, 1990). If they are to do so they must, however, in a post-Cold War situation, be capable of deployment behind enemy lines very rapidly, and they must have the capacity for operations in, at least, the desert, mountainous terrain or the jungle, and in combined operations. The reluctance of non-NATO states, not now threatened by the Soviet Union or its allies, to be used for Western bases must also be anticipated, so any such forces have to be capable of being deployed from bases which are within the NATO area, or from aircraft or ships close to their targets.

The model for such units can be seen as the UK's SAS and the USA's Delta Force, and these have shown their use in many forms of warfare, including against terrorist opponents. Such units require, however, that Western governments must be prepared to develop new modes of operation and the ability for rapid engagement in the new situation. These operations may require the redesignation of 'legitimate' targets for military operations to unfamiliar fields. Future 'legitimate' targets for military action may be the originators of transnational threats. These could include international criminals, such as illegal drug-producing cartels and other groups currently the responsibility of crime-fighters rather than military forces (Bearman, 1995, pp. 25-33). It must be remembered that such groups may well have the capacity to wage terrorist or guerilla campaigns against Western interests themselves, and could gain access to weapons of mass-destruction, perhaps of a chemical or biological, rather than nuclear, type (Jenkins, 1985; Schelling, 1985; Leventhal and Hoenig, 1987).

To combat these threats, there will also be a need to employ intelligence-gathering and surveillance functions alongside the use of direct action. Yet to achieve this in a constitutionally and politically acceptable fashion, in what are (without exception) liberal democratic countries, will require cautious, political handling of sensitive issues and increased responsiveness to public concerns.

The political and ethical implications of using such troops, especially in regard to relations between the West and the 'Developing World', must be reconsidered also. These are especially relevant to policy, given the potential risk of political damage both at home and overseas. To avoid political problems, it seems essential that such units should only be deployed - and still less sent into action - as a last resort after non-military means have failed, not merely as a means of promoting Western interests. If this safeguard is lost, then the West stands a risk of being branded as a sponsor of illegal intervention and subversion by potential allies in the South, and governments may face serious political consequences from their own electorates. The end of the Cold War has not disengaged military action from a matrix of political, cultural, economic, legal and ethical factors and constraints - it may have intensified the importance of all of these, at least in relation to the West.

Yet, the use of small 'elite' units may be the most credible type of direct force in a situation in which the pattern of warfare is itself fragmented (Booth, 1994, p. 119). We have already noted that, in such a situation, the opponents may be geographically dispersed among the civilian population, in civilian clothes and superficially indistinguishable from the non-combatants surrounding them. To avoid the danger of so-called 'atrocities' being committed by Western troops, or the danger of being seen to engage in 'state-sponsored terrorism', any such military action will require much more public explanation than has been usual in the past. The risk of subsequent international diplomatic problems means that the direct use of force against an 'integrated' enemy of this sort (that is, one which uses intermingling with civilians as a means of camouflage) must be able to be closely validated on detailed argument: simple diplomatic rhetoric may cause more problems than the application of direct force.

For instance, if one employed troops of this sort to enter a sovereign state to eliminate drugs production or the terrorist development of nuclear, biological or chemical weapons, this would require detailed and thorough justification in political, legal, moral and other terms in order to prevent serious political damage to the interests one was attempting to protect. Such action could even prompt a military response from the state affected. In this respect, the unilateral use of military force may be in decline in the face of the internationalisation of political and economic affairs and the formulation of international legal norms, however often these may broken.

Consequently, while the relative utility of such elite forces has been enhanced by the end of the Cold War, their use presents very significant problems in contemporary international politics. These problems are not entirely of a military type, rather they are principally political and diplomatic. In this sense, such types of military action are not 'a continuation of policy by other means' (Clausewitz, as translated by Michael Howard and Peter Parret, reproduced in Freedman, 1994, p. 207), so much as a response to the failure of diplomatic means, and can only be conducted through the diplomatic and legal construction of a matrix of complex justification. So, the utility of small elite units has been increased but the constraints on their use are also enhanced.

If direct military action is less useful for 'resolving' international disputes in the post-Cold War period and nuclear weapons have lost much of their value as deterrents, then it is clear that fundamental changes in the character of warfare itself have been occurring and, with this, in the character of international security. These necessitate the downscaling of forces to achieve economic cost-effectiveness and a move from nuclear-based to non-nuclear strategies. In the post-Cold War period, deterrents comprising a few nuclear weapons would suffice against any conceivable opponent, especially if targeting concentrated on the preemptive destruction of enemy NBC arsenals, combined with efficient and detailed information-gathering capable of detecting preparations for a nuclear attack.

A new role for nuclear weapons

Combined with enhanced satellite and airborne surveillance systems, and efficient computer-based and conventional intelligence-gathering systems, a minimum deterrent may, in the post Cold-War period, be very small in numbers of warheads and delivery systems (Mazarr, 1995, notes that it may even be possible to hold some of these in reserve, disassembled). Consequently, the West European nuclear states (France and the UK) could cost-effectively maintain sufficient deterrents to counter all potential nuclear threats, unless there were to be drastic political changes in Russia, while the nuclear forces of the USA and Russia are, by this analysis, far too large and un-cost-effective (force-sizes are reviewed in Neaman, 1994, pp. 15-16, 22-3, 108 and 111-12).

The need for improved abilities to monitor and collect data about enemy troop-movements, NBC arsenals and capabilities, armoured vehicles and airforces is a crucial aspect of international security in the 1990s, and is likely to remain so into the twenty-first century. The need for maintained naval- and air-logistic capabilities in the West is also shown: rapidity of movement and speed of information acquisition may be more important in the new situation than total troop numbers or the firepower of tanks. These are areas which major European states might seek to develop rather than reduce.

These changes, therefore, suggest in themselves that we might afford much greater attention than at present to information- and intelligence-gathering. They enable a reallocation of resources to new areas, while maintaining a 'realistic' conventional warfighting capability. This brings us back to the effects of technological change on post-Cold War security.

There is a further reason why nuclear force reductions may be possible, and why drastic conventional force reductions may also be feasible. This is by employing existing collective security agreements in new, post-Cold War, ways. NATO and other alliance-structures may be a safeguard against the shift to such forms of defence rendering a state vulnerable to conventional or nuclear threats (on NATO after the Cold War, see, for instance, Kinkel, 1992; Sloan, 1995). Within the NATO framework a direct attack on Europe seems inconceivable in a post-Cold War situation, as it would meet with insuperable opposition from the combined might of the allies. Maintaining this alliance can, therefore, provide a safety-net for a revised security structure for the NATO allies.

Further safeguards can be provided by the intensification of non-proliferation contacts and the linkage between economic and other forms of 'aid' and the demilitarisation of regions and economies (Spector, 1995). Such moves may reduce external threats and control their character to levels which are easily met.

Coordination between NATO allies can also enable a new attention to be paid to increasing the mobility and flexibility of existing conventional forces, so as to pay greater attention to both rapid out-of-area deployment and multiple terrain capabilities. Here, a move to helicopter transportation and combined operations capabilities may be advisable for the armies of all NATO states, given the character of the threats potentially posed in the next decades.

Likewise, more attention to preparing troops for operation under bacteriological and chemical attacks and in combating guerilla and terrorist opponents may be required (on the 'advantages' of these to an unethical but cost-conscious enemy, see Dando, 1994), while 'pitched battles', such as those seen in the Gulf War of 1991, are increasingly unlikely. Here, the significance attached to intelligence and counter-measures may again be highlighted.

Switching priorities from armour, large numbers of combat aircraft and ships, and nuclear weapons, would free funds for investment in the emerging areas of special significance. These areas can be defined partly in conventional terms, but for the most part comprise new forms of 'warfare', unlike those seen prior to the twentieth century.

The implications of new forms of warfare

Technological developments have led to the emergence of new types of 'warfare' since the end of the Cold War (see Toffler and Toffler, 1993; Arquilla and Ronfeldt, 1993; De Landa, 1991). Some of these are based on developments begun in the Cold War period or even before, but their development has been accelerated by technological advances since the late 1980s (De Landa, 1991). These include: information war, electronic war, communications-systems and intelligence-gathering. All of these areas have already attracted attention from strategists but, so far, not much progress has been made toward realising a shift in the importance attached to these that is commensurate with their new centrality to international security (for a non-Western view, see Fitzgerald, 1994).

The range of issues covered is wide. Electronic warfare ranges from computer security and offensive 'hacking' to counter measures against enemy command and control systems (Cohen, 1995). The somewhat related area of 'information warfare', ranges from the inducement of information-overload to the disruption of computer-based command and control systems. Communication-systems are being transformed from conventional radios to field computer-based systems and satellite navigation (for example, see Lambakis, 1995; Blair, 1985). Intelligence-gathering is moving from conventional means to employing the above techniques, alongside computer-enhancement and remote sensing (for example, Zimmerman, 1990).

All of these areas will transform the form of warfare in the next decades, if current trends persist. It will be possible to close down enemy command and control systems, and to disrupt enemy communications beyond those of a most basic type (this includes civilian media, on the problems of which, see Rosenblum, 1993). Such approaches may also be capable of destroying incoming missiles and 'grounding' aircraft prior to take-off, using electronic means alone. Combined with these, more conventional counter-measures (such as anti-ballistic missiles) should enable a massive reduction in the utility of missile-based weapons systems of all types, of almost all guided weapons, and of battlefield computers by less technologically-developed opponents. They may also prevent aircraft and ships dependent upon computers or telecommunications from operating.

Although there remains a risk of attack by terrorists and criminals operating outside of a state structure, and the question is clouded by the potential use of mercenaries with relevant expertise and equipment in information warfare, the West has a significant advantage in this area (for recent developments, see, for example, *Defense News*, 12-18 June 1995, pp. 1 and 66; and 4-10 September 1995, pp. 4 and 36). With the possible exception of the Asia-Pacific region it is hard to envisage any non-Western governments gaining technological superiority in these areas over the NATO allies. Recent developments in the USA, Britain and elsewhere suggest that the Western advantage is already so great as to be unassailable in these areas if current progress is maintained, and the threat posed by terrorists, criminals and international mercenaries has to be set against the rapidly developing expertise in information warfare within NATO. It shows, however, that effective defences against information warfare attack must be developed as retaliation against individuals, who may be operating from widely-dispersed locations and in a wide range of ways, and may be impossible. Deterrence is unlikely to work in this new situation.

The use of 'information war' methods and improved communications can both confuse and render far less formidable an opponent. Combined with the inducement of 'information overload' by the massive 'bombardment' of enemy command and control centres with data, confusion and/or the inability to convey even simple instructions to tactical units may be induced (*Time*, 21 August 1995, pp. 27-32). At the most basic level, these approaches will render the soldier, sailor or airman in the field, confused and isolated from their command structures and information-gathering capabilities.

When one combines this with more conventional types of information-war, such as telecommunications-jamming, then the effect on the tactical capabilities of opponents could be devastating. Such methods also have a deterrent effect.

The combination of these methods has a potentially dramatic effect on the pace of warfare (on the early stages of its impact, see Campen, 1992). They may speed up response times and the pace of engagements, while rendering sophisticated surveillance and weapons-systems invalid or of limited use. They may effectively prevent missile attacks and airborne cover and they could cause serious problems for any type of sophisticated, but less technologically developed, naval warfare. If they are combined with the increased use of interception against missiles and, in extreme cases, conventional preemptive strikes against enemy ammunition, fuel and against any NBC capabilities, they can render even medium-scale war against the West 'unwinnable' by a less technologically-advanced opponent.

As such, these methods enable the West to reduce the scale both of their own forces and of threats, and to necessitate that opponents adopt low-technology, 'dispersed', guerilla methods or terrorist techniques (on these, see Asprey, 1995). The existence of 'elite' units, specially trained in combating these types of warfare and aided by enhanced intelligence and information-gathering capacities, may deter opponents from guerilla or terrorist campaigns. That is, the West can effectively use such means to force an opponent - equipped to fight on a larger scale - into the forms of warfare for which Western forces have become especially thoroughly prepared, and to make an aggressor doubt the utility of employing even these, low-intensity, forms of warfare. With improved scanning of potential entry into the West of NBC weapons by terrorist groups (the cases discussed by Bearman, 1995, pp. 17-25, are worrying in this respect), and an active non-proliferation strategy, these approaches can render a massive reduction in the scale of armed conflict.

In favour of developing greater 'information warfare' and electronic warfare capabilities are the factors of cost, of required 'manpower', of location (such defences can be based anywhere), and of public relations (*Time*, 21 August 1995, p. 31). 'Information warfare' and electronic warfare may even prove popular concepts with the more pacifistic elements of Western populations - these means of defence depend, at their core, on stopping (rather than perpetrating) acts of violence!

The European states and NATO in the new security environment

Such methods of ensuring Western security are likely to be most effective if NATO members work together to maintain a credible lead in the relevant technologies and cooperate freely in their willingness to transfer information about relevant developments between, for instance, Germany, the USA and the UK. Yet the level of cooperation already achieved by NATO, and the overall 'closeness' of the allies and their interests, makes it likely that the organisation of technological interchange can be established. The shared interests inherent in adopting such an approach and sharing the costs of its maintenance are too clearcut to avoid.

This may, then, be the future form of warfare, and one which has profound implications for the twenty-first century roles of the USA and the European partners in NATO (for a discussion of this point, see

Goldstein, 1994). Not only will it enable the survival and enhanced unity of the alliance in the post-Cold War period but it can also facilitate a reallocation of roles, giving the European states a greater part in paying for and providing for Europe's (and the USA's) defence (on Europe and the USA after the Cold War, see Gebhard, 1994). Elite forces might be seen as a current strength of the armed forces of both the UK and France, and NATO could be a useful structure for the development of highly-mobile specialist forces: the Rapid Reaction force could be seen as a first move in this direction.

Such a shift in responsibilities would free the USA to concentrate on the Asia-Pacific region, and reduce its spending on European defence without endangering either NATO or European security (Kerr, 1994). As the Asia-Pacific is the area in which the only credible technological rivals to the West - if it adopts this strategy - exist (not that these states show any present indication of hostility toward the NATO allies), US concentration on building Asia-Pacific security will favour the whole alliance. It will permit the European states to play an enhanced role, as they have since the end of the Cold War, in the maintenance of European regional security (although Wallace, 1995, may overstate Germany's potential role, on this see also Bluth, 1993b).

These changes also have implications for the future role of the major European states, especially Britain, France and Germany, outside Europe. The changed form of warfare, the reduced utility of massed forces and nuclear weapons, and the cessation of the constraints of the Cold War, will permit the European states to play an enhanced global role. Elite forces are more easily transported over long distances and may not require US logistical support to deploy, while information warfare is even more easily deployable and, to a great extent, can be based in any part of the globe.

Consequently, the new form of warfare may hold significant implications for both NATO and the West in general, which may act in favour of Western interests, if prompt action is taken. If not, there is a danger of the West being in a similar position to that of a medieval kingdom having large numbers of mounted knights (in this case: tanks, armoured vehicles and heavy artillery - as well as nuclear weapons) but no guns (here technologically-based 'information-', and electronic-, warfare capacity) when its opponents have cannon. Plainly, this is a situation to be avoided.

Bibliography

Arquilla, John and Ronfeldt, David (1993), `Cyberwar is coming!', *Comparative Strategy* 12.2

Asprey, Robert B. (1995), *War in the Shadows*, 2nd edn., Little Brown and Co, Boston, Mass.

Barnaby, Frank (1990), *Weapons of Mass Destruction: A Growing Threat in the 1990s?*, RISCT, London

Bearman, Sidney (ed.) (1995), *Strategic Survey 1994/95*, Oxford University Press, London

Blair, Bruce G. (1985), *Strategic Command and Control*, Brookings, Washington DC

Bluth, Christoph (1993a), *Germany and the Future of European Security*, Brassey's, London

Bluth, Christoph (1993b), *The Future of European Security*, Centre for European Studies, University of Essex, Colchester

Bluth, Christoph, Kirchner, Emil and Sperling, James (eds) (1995), *The Future of European Security*, Dartmouth, Basingstoke

Booth, K., `Strategy', in Groom, A. and Light, M. (eds), *Contemporary International Relations: A Guide to Theory*, Pinter, London

Brown, Seyom (1994), `World interests and the changing dimensions of security', in M. T. Klare and D. C. Thomas (eds), *World Security*, St Martin's Press, New York

Bulkely, Rip and Spinardi, Graham (1986), *Space Weapons- Deterrence or Delusion?*, Blackwell, Oxford

Bunch, Charlotte and Carillo, Roxanna (1994), `Global violence against women: the challenge to human rights and development', in M. T. Klare and D. C. Thomas (eds), *World Security*, St Martin's Press, New York

Buzan, B. *et al* (1990), *The European Security Order Recast: Scenarios for the Post Cold War Era*, Pinter, London

Buzan, B. (1991), *People States and Fear*, 2nd edn., Harvester Wheatsheaf, Hemel Hempstead

Buzan, Barry (1995), 'Japan's defence problematique', *The PacificReview* 8.1

Buzan, Barry and Segal, Gerald (1994) 'Rethinking East Asian security', *Survival* 36.2

Cable, Vincent (1995), `What is international economic security?, *International Affairs* 71.2

Cable, Vincent and Ferdinand, Peter (1994), 'China: enter as a giant', *International Affairs* 70.2

Cambone, Stephen A and Garrity, Patrick J. (1994-95), `The future of US nuclear policy', *Survival* 36.4

Camilleri, J. A. and Falk, J. (1993), *The End of Sovereignty? The Politics of a Shrinking and Fragmenting World*, Edward Eiger, Aldershot

Campen, Alan D. (ed.) (1992), *The First Information War*, AFCEA International Press, Fairfax, VA.

Carter, Ashton B. and Schwartz, David N. (eds) (1984), *Ballistic Missile Defence*, Brookings, Washington

Cohen, Frederick B. (1995), *Protection and Security on the Information Superhighway*, John Wiley, New York

Dando, M. (1994), *Biological Warfare in the 21st Century*, Brassey's, London

Dark, K. R., 1996, 'Ecological change and political crisis', in Holden, B. (ed.), The *Ethical Dimensions of Global Change*, Macmillan, London

Davis, Zachary S. (1994), 'Nuclear proliferation and nonproliferation policy in the 1990s', in M. T. Klare and D. C. Thomas (eds), *World Security*, St Martin's Press, New York

De Landa, Manuel (1991), *War in the Age of Intelligent Machines*, Zone Books, New York

Ferraro, Vincent and Rosser, Melissa (1994), 'Global debt and Third World development', in M. T. Klare and D. C. Thomas (eds), *World Security*, St Martin's Press, New York

Fitzgerald, Mary C. (1994), 'Russian views on information warfare', *Army* 44.5

Freedman, Lawrence (1989), *The Evolution of Nuclear Strategy*, Macmillan, London

Freedman, Lawrence (1994-95), 'Great powers, vital interests and nuclear weapons', *Survival* 36.4

Freedman, Lawrence (ed.) (1994), *War*, Oxford University Press, Oxford

Freedman, Lawrence and Karsh, Efraim (1992), *The Gulf War 1990-91*, Faber and Faber, London

Freedman, L. and Saunders, J. (eds) (1991), *Population Change and European Security*, Brassey's, Oxford

Gebhard, Paul R. S. (1994), *The United States and European Security*, Brassey's, London

Gnesotto, Nicole (1994), *Lessons of Yugoslavia*, WEU Institute for Security Studies, Paris

Goldstein, Walter (ed.) (1994), *Security in Europe: the Role of NATO after the Cold War*, Brassey's, London

Hackett, James T. (1990), 'The ballistic missile epidemic', *Global Affairs* 5.1

Hanle, Donald J. (1989), *Terrorism: The Newest Face of Warfare*, Pergamon-Brassey, Washington

Herring, E. (1991), 'The decline of nuclear diplomacy', in K. Booth (ed.), *New Thinking About Strategy and International Security*, Harper Collins, London

Heydte, Friedrich August (1986), *Modern Irregular Warfare in Defense Policy and as a Military Phenomenon*, New Benjamin Franklin House, New York

Homer-Dixon, Thomas (1994), 'Environmental scarcity and intergroup conflict', in M. T. Klare and D. C. Thomas (eds), *World Security*, St Martin's Press, New York

Horowitz, Donald L. (1994), 'Ethnic and nationalist conflict', in M. T. Klare and D. C. Thomas (eds), *World Security*, St Martin's Press, New York

Jenkins, Brian M. (1985), 'Nuclear terrorism', *Orbis* 3

Karp, R. C. (1991), *Security with Nuclear Weapons? Different*

Perspectives on National Security, Oxford University Press, Oxford

Kegley, Charles W. Jr and Wittkopf, Eugene R. (1995), *World Politics,* 5th edn., St Martin's Press, New York

Kerr, Pauline (1994), 'The security dialogue in the Asia-Pacific', *The Pacific Review* 7.4

Kinkel, Klaus (1992), 'NATO's enduring role in European security', *NATO Review* 7

Kolodziej, E. A. (1992), 'What is security and security studies?, *Arms Control* 13.1

Krass, Allan S. (1994), 'The second nuclear era: nuclear weapons in a transformed world', in M. T. Klare and D. C. Thomas (eds), *World Security,* St Martin's Press, New York

Lambakis, Steven (1995), 'Space control in Desert Storm and beyond', *Orbis* 39.3

Leventhal, Paul L. and Hoenig, Milton (1987), 'The hidden danger: risks of nuclear terrorism', *Terrorism* 10.1

Lundestrad, G. and Westad, O. A. (eds) (1993), *Beyond the Cold War: New Dimensions in International Relations,* Oxford University Press, Oxford

McGwire, Michael (1994), 'Is there a future for nuclear weapons?, International Affairs 70.2

McInnes, C. (ed.) (1992a), *Security and Strategy in the New Europe,* Routledge, London

McInnes, Colin (1992b), 'Technology and modern warfare', in Baylis, John and Rengger, N. J. (eds), *Dilemmas of World Politics,* Clarendon Press, Oxford

Mackerras, Colin, Taneja, Pradeep and Young, Graham (1994), *China Since 1978,* Longman Cheshire, Melbourne

Mahnken, Thomas G. (1990), 'The spread of missile technology to the Third World', *Comparative Strategy* 9.3

Mathews, Jessica T. (1994), 'The environment and international security', in M. T. Klare and D. C. Thomas (eds), *World Security,* St Martin's Press, New York

Mazarr, Michael J. (1995), 'Virtual nuclear arsenals', *Survival* 37.3

Navias, Martin (1990a), *Ballistic Missile Proliferation in the Third World*, Brassey's, London

Navias, Martin (1990b), 'Is there a Third World ballistic missile threat to Europe?', *RUSI Journal* 135.4

Neaman, Rachel (ed.) (1994), *The Military Balance 1994-1995*, Brassey's, London

Neaman, Rachel (ed.) (1995), *The Military Balance 1995/1996*, Brassey's, London

Pirages, Dennis (1994), 'Demographic change and ecological insecurity', in M. T. Klare and D. C. Thomas (eds), *World Security*, St Martin's Press, New York

Reiss, Edward (1992), *The Strategic Defence Initiative*, Cambridge University Press, Cambridge

Rosenblum, Mort (1993), *Who Stole the News?* , John Wiley, New York

Schelling, Thomas C. (1985), 'Thinking about nuclear terrorism', *International Security* Spring

Sloan, Stanley R. (1995), 'US perspectives on NATO's future', *International Affairs* 71.2

Smith, G. Davidson (1990), *Combating Terrorism*, Routledge, London

Spector, Leonard S. (1995), 'Neo-nonproliferation', *Survival* 37.1

Taylor, P. M. (1992), *War and the Media*, Manchester University Press, Manchester

Tickner, J. Ann (1995), 'Re-visioning security', in K. Booth and S. Smith (eds), *International Relations Theory Today* , Polity Press, Cambridge

Toffler, Alvin and Heiddi (1993), *War and Anti-War*, Little Brown and Co, Boston, Mass.

Wallace, William (1995), 'Germany as Europe's leading power', *The World Today* 51.8-9

Wilkinson, Paul (1990), *Terrorist Targets and Tactics: New Risks to World Order*, Research Institute for the Study of Conflict, London

Witney, Nicholas K. J. (1994-95), 'British nuclear policy after the Cold War', *Survival* 36.4

Yost, David S. (1994-95), 'Nuclear debates in France', *Survival* 36.4

Zametica, John (1992), *The Yugoslav Conflict,* Brassey's, London
Zimmerman, Peter D. (1990), 'Remote sensing satellites, superpower relations and public diplomacy', *Space Policy* 6.1

2 Nuclear weapons and territorial integrity in the post-Cold War world

RICHARD J. HARKNETT

Introduction

The global competition between the United States and the Soviet Union paralleled the emergence of a new phase in international political history. The progression of the Cold War occurred simultaneously with the evolution of the nuclear era. The presence of nuclear weapons in the international system and the superpower competition were two separate phenomenon. Although this may seem to be rather obvious at face value, a strong link between the role of nuclear weapons and the Cold War has been maintained in academic perceptions. This results from the fact that the strategy of nuclear deterrence served as an important support for the overall US foreign policy approach of 'containment'. Since containment policy is now seen as having served its purpose, consideration is being directed toward moving away from its strategic foundations as well. Thus, one of the tangible manifestations of the end of the Cold War has been major reductions in the size and deployment of nuclear weapons worldwide.

It would be a mistake, however, to view nuclear weapons as purely by-products of the Cold War competition. The Cold War and US containment policy helped determine the levels of weapons needed and the strategies for their employment, but it did not drive the weapons' initial invention. The Cold War affected the role to be played by nuclear weapons in the international system, but the fact remains that as the Cold War fades into history nuclear weapons endure.

Our thinking about nuclear weapons, therefore, must be informed by the idea that they are a permanent and prominent feature of international security relations. They are not merely military tools that support the policy of containing aggression but rather represent a conditioning factor in the overall structure of inter-state relations. While international relations remains, at its essence, a struggle for power, it is a struggle that is constrained by the fact that direct territorial aggression against a nuclear state is an extraordinarily risky venture; so steeped in risk as to eliminate it as a rational option.

The self-help dynamic produced by the anarchical structure of international relations focuses states' attentions toward relative gains (Waltz, 1979). While the international system remains anarchical, the possession of nuclear capabilities forces greater attention to be directed toward the potential of absolute losses (Baldwin, 1993). The shift from relative to absolute calculations increases the possibility of resolving conflicts of interest without resorting to military force.[1] In terms of military security relations, the impact of nuclear possession is profound. To support this assertion, I suggest that we may focus on the relationship between weapon capability and the concept of state territoriality.

The main argument presented in this chapter stands in stark contrast with the underlying assumptions guiding current nuclear non-proliferation policy in the United States (Perry, 1991; McNamara, *New York Times*, 23 February 1993, p. A1; Nitz, *Washington Post*, 16 January 1994, p. C1; Allan, 1994). That policy assumes that the further spread of nuclear weapons will lead to greater instability in world politics and to an increased possibility of actual use. The argument presented is that 'the more nuclear weapons that are held within different political jurisdictions, the greater the probability that political turmoil or technological faults can lead to their loss or unauthorized use' (Nye,

1992).[2] The United States 'seeks to cap, reduce and, ultimately eliminate' the capability of emerging nuclear states and 'prevent' any new nuclear powers (The White House, 1994, p. 11). This non-proliferation focus has been connected to an increasingly popular call to reduce the overall role played by nuclear weapons in national and international security relations.

However, there is a growing discrepancy between how nuclear weapons are conceived of by American defence strategists and the impact nuclear weapons are perceived to have had during the Cold War (Mueller, 1989; Schlesinger, 1993; Mearsheimer, 1993; Waltz, 1993; Gaddis, 1982).[3] Faced with evidence that nuclear weapons place limitations on the use of force, it is becoming more difficult to argue that nuclear possession is harmful to national security and thus should be avoided.[4] Here, I shall attempt to draw attention to the theoretical questions with which post-Cold War nuclear policy must increasingly grapple by examining the linkage between individual state territorial integrity, system stability, and nuclear possession, and argue that nuclear weapons are likely to remain prominent features of international security relations because of their effect on territoriality.

Following a brief overview of the contemporary view of nuclear strategy, the discussion is divided into four principal sections. The first section examines the concept of territoriality and how it has been treated in 'security studies' academic literature. The second section develops the argument that nuclear weapons fundamentally alter state security relations. The third section delineates the strategic implications of a future in which nuclear weapons remain prominent in international politics. I conclude by assessing the connection between nuclear prominence and territoriality.

Nuclear Strategy and the end of the Cold War

In his final State of the Union address, President Harry Truman articulated the foreign policy approach to be followed by the United

States for the next forty years:

> 'As we continue to confound Soviet expectations, as our world grows stronger, more united, more attractive to men on both sides of the iron curtain, then inevitably there will come a time of change within the communist world. We do not know how that change will come about...but if the communist rulers understand they cannot win by war, and if we frustrate their attempts to win by subversion, it is not too much to expect their world to change its character, moderate its aims, become more realistic and less implacable, and recede from the Cold War they began.' (Allinson and Treverton, 1992, pp. 102-3)

Truman's statement makes clear that nuclear weapons were fundamental to the superpower competition between the United States and the Soviet Union. Reliance on nuclear deterrence was to eliminate armed aggression as an option for the Soviet Union if they wished to challenge the status quo. The success or failure of the containment approach rested to a great extent, according to Truman, on whether the Soviet leaders could be convinced that they could not achieve their international objectives by initiating war. Containment policy essentially rested on the premise that, everything else being equal, the United States had the political and economic strength to outlast the Soviet regime.

Throughout the Cold War, therefore, deterrence of armed aggression through reliance on the threat of nuclear response prevailed as the core conceptualisation that drove Western strategic thinking about nuclear weapons (Freedman, 1989). Deterrence matched well the overall United States foreign policy approach of containment. Reliance on nuclear threats allowed the United States to extend its protection over a vast array of vital interests. This, of course, was accomplished with a significant amount of discord and debate over the twin issues of rationality and credibility. Most of the critical literature on nuclear deterrence focused on the incredibility of extending it beyond one's own territorial protection. Would an American president be willing to risk Washington to protect Bonn?, was a familiar sceptical query. The problem of linking the protection of one's own territory with the territory of allies under a 'nuclear umbrella' was never satisfactorily resolved by the United States and its NATO allies. In fact, the uncertainty surrounding the question of nuclear response actually came to serve as the focal point of extended nuclear deterrence. The unpredictable nature of a potential conflict between the nuclear superpowers was highlighted with the hope of raising enough uncertainty along with risk to make a potential aggressor hesitant and cautious (Schelling, 1966, p. 121).

The success of containment and the end of the Cold War has led to two somewhat contradictory stances with regard to the role of nuclear weapons in international politics (Treverton and Bicksler, 1992).[5] Nuclear weapons have been included as a variable in most explanations of why the Cold War stayed 'cold'. Given this general recognition that nuclear weapons may have had a stabilising impact, one would expect that post-Cold War nuclear strategy debates would be focused on highlighting and expanding upon those stabilising attributes. Instead, the collapse of the Soviet Union has been seen as an opportunity to significantly constrict the role nuclear weapons will play in the twenty-first century. This constriction is a natural outgrowth of the fact that while nuclear weapons might have had a role in de-escalating crisis situations, Americans were never very comfortable with them for their presence ultimately eliminated the United States' ability to independently secure itself. This desire to contract the role of nuclear weapons is manifested in the emerging post-Cold War emphasis on extended conventional deterrence.

Secretaries of Defense Les Aspin and William Perry have both argued that the United States must stay engaged in the protection of its overseas interests and do so without heavy reliance on nuclear weapons (Aspin, 1993; Perry, 1991). This approach is supported by the belief that 'conventional weapons are or will soon enough be, nearly perfect substitutes for nuclear weapons in terms of military effectiveness, deterrent value, and reassurance' (Millot, Molander and Wilson, 1993). The movement toward reliance on conventional capabilities is further justified by noting that nuclear threats will lack credibility in the most likely regional crises that the United States will face over the next decade (Nitz, *Washington Post*, 23 February 1994, p. C1). Most advocates of extended conventional deterrence recognise that such a strategy might be less durable over time than its nuclear counterpart and argue that occasional use of force may be necessary to 'rejuvenate the credibility of deterrence' in order to produce periods of stability (Guertner, Haffa and Quester, 1992, p. 3). The overwhelming victory in the Desert Storm operation is pointed to as an exemplary use of force that should sow caution in the minds of prospective aggressors for the immediate future.

The movement away from extended nuclear deterrence to extended conventional deterrence strategy rests on a fundamental shift in attitude concerning the use of force. The Cold War conception of deterrence was founded on the necessity to avoid war. In its post-Cold War manifestation, deterrence allows for (and may necessitate) the occasional use of force (Haffa, 1992). For extended conventional deterrence to be viable, however, three conditions must persist: conventional superiority (better capabilities), conventional dominance (better ability to project force), and a willingness to use force if necessary. Although the strategy of extended conventional deterrence is open to direct criticism on a variety of levels, the following sections will challenge the basic premise that it rests upon; namely, that it promises to be a more stabilizing strategic alternative than a reformulated reliance on nuclear weapons. The basic assumptions held by advocates of conventional deterrence about the impact of nuclear weapons on the territoriality of the nation-states are questionable.

Territoriality and military force

The basic unit of the modern international system is the territorially defined, mutually exclusive and fixed nation-state (Gottman, 1973; Mellor, 1989). It is this system of rule that, in modern times, has been considered best at fulfilling the twin objectives of physical protection and promotion of a general population's welfare. The essence of the nation-state is its territoriality, that is, its defensibility against hostile outside forces. Although the stability of the state rests on other factors such as internal and external legitimacy (Herz, 1976, p. 31)[6] as well as relations with other states (for discussions on the idea of reciprocity as a basis for international relations, Gulik, 1955, pp. 3-24; Morgenthau, 1985), the fundamental rationale for organising within the nation-state unit is its potential ability to protect.

The territorial state is not the only system of rule under which political-social organisation has been accomplished. There have been systems of rule that were not territorial at all (kinship), where territory was not fixed (nomadic), and where territory was a basis for political-social organization and was fixed, but was not mutually exclusive (medieval Europe) (Ruggie, 1993, pp. 149-50). However, 'it is the case that the modern state has succeeded in driving out substutiable alternatives more effectively than any other prior form' (Ruggie, 1993, p. 167). Whether the territorial state will continue to be considered the best alternative and remain the primary unit of international relations has been a central topic of debate in the study of international economics and in relation to research into technological revolutions in communications and transportation (Krasner, 1985; Krasner and Thomson, 1992). Discussions over global issues such as population growth, pollution, ozone depletion, and health have centred on questions concerning the appropriateness and limitations of the territorially-bounded nation-state international system (Keohane and Nye, 1989, 1992). The relationship between twentieth century developments in military capabilities and territoriality has not received much attention.[7] This is curious to note for two reasons: first, most studies of the development of the modern state have emphasized the linkage between military advancements and state consolidation (McNeill, 1982); and second, the dominant theoretical tradition in the study of international relations - realism - posits state security as a central driving dynamic.

In the field of international security studies, the best analysis of territoriality is found in the work of John H. Herz (Herz, 1957, 1959,

1968). Herz specifically analysed the relationship between nuclear weapons and the power of protection. He argued that protection was the basic rationale supporting the creation of the territorial state. The development of nuclear weapons called this protective function of the territorial state into question because even the most powerful units were now vulnerable to utter devastation. Herz conceptualised pre-nuclear territoriality as a 'hard shell' of defence that was relatively impermeable. Within this hard shell, an internal order could be constructed and the promotion of the general welfare conducted. Nuclear weapons created a 'new condition of permeability' (Herz, 1976, p. 121). The protective function of the territorial state was overwhelmed by a technical achievement. Herz concluded that this loss of protective power would produce incentives and pressures to move away from the modern state-system. According to Herz, the extension of superpower influence and control over opposing blocs of nations could be viewed as the first manifestation of this movement. The locus of defence and protection was shifted away from the nation and towards the bloc. Herz pointed out, however, that such extension did not change the fundamental condition of vulnerability created by nuclear weapons. He advanced the idea that the pressures on territoriality created by nuclear weapons would promote incentives to move toward an alternative universalist system of international order and argued that, as the number of 'nuclear weapon states' multiplied, the degree of vulnerability and the potential for use would increase as well. Proliferation would generate additional pressure to reject the territorial state system.

The literature on nuclear non-proliferation has generally accepted Herz's position. 'Most people believe that there is a common global interest in slowing the spread of nuclear weapons' (Nye, 1992, p. 8). This belief, manifested in the signature of over 140 countries to the Nuclear Non-proliferation Treaty (NPT), rests on the proposition that there is a direct correlation between the number of nuclear weapon states and potential systemic instability (Dunn, 1982; Davis and Donnelly, 1990, 1993). The increasingly popular call in the United States to reduce the overall role played by nuclear weapons in its national defence posture also flows naturally from the Herz analysis. If nuclear weapons both threaten the essence of the individual territorial state and destabilises the system of states, prevention of both horizontal and vertical proliferation seems an appropriate response. Current policy trends accept Herz's assumptions and logic but diverge in the proposed solution to the nuclear age. In rejecting Herz's universal alternative, current American nuclear policy can be seen as an attempt to restore the viability of the territorial state by containing, reducing, and potentially reversing the condition of permeability created by nuclear weapons. In July 1994, the Clinton administration released what it called a 'new national security strategy for [a] new era', which outlined a policy of 'non-proliferation and counter-proliferation.' The strategy calls for a capability not simply to deter the use of nuclear weapons, but to **prevent** their use. Such a capability would include enhanced defensive capacity as well as improved ability to 'locate, identify, and disable arsenals of weapons of mass destruction, production and storage facilities for such weapons, and their delivery systems' (The White House, 1994, pp. 11-12). An aspiring nuclear state is thus to be faced not only with attempts to deny access to the necessary components of a nuclear programme (non-proliferation), but with the prospect that at any time during the development of a nuclear programme or after its completion, the United States might use military force to destroy the programme (counter-proliferation). In the context of territoriality, current American non-proliferation and nuclear policies are nothing more than efforts at restoration. Where Herz identified incentives for movement beyond the territorial state,[8] current policy taken to its logical end presages a return to an international system of relatively impermeable states. In such an environment, the varying conventional abilities of states to provide for self-protection would be relevant. The distribution of these capabilities would once again reflect those territorial units that tended to dominate over international politics. Current efforts at non-proliferation and to reduce reliance on nuclear weapons are policies that promote the *status quo ante bellum*: that is, before 1945. They would produce an international system dominated by traditional power politics and capabilities. Whereas Herz suggested a universalist solution to the permeability problem, the Clinton administration is embarking on an attempt to 'turn back the clock' and to restore the condition of territorial impermeability.

But what if the basic assumptions of both restorative and universalist solutions to the nuclear era are incorrect? What if the relationship between territoriality and nuclear possession is positive? What if the enhancement of individual territorial integrity bolsters the stability of the territorial state system?

The empirical record does not support the thesis that the protective function of the territorial state has been overwhelmed by nuclear weapons, or that international stability has been lessened as more states acquired the technology. Although the relevant time-period is short in historical terms, and the number of relevant states small, it is still true that no two nuclear weapon states have gone to war with each other.[9] This is an interesting observation, despite the noted limitations, because a serious potential for war has existed between all of the nuclear weapons states. In fact, during the first 49 years of the nuclear age, wars have been fought between these states when at least one did not possess nuclear weapons (USA-China in Korea; India-Pakistan; India-China) but not after mutual possession. The absence of war can not be explained away by a lack of pretext. During the Cold War, the United States and Soviet Union had a number of actual military incidents and crises that in every case led to de-escalation rather than war. In 1969, a territorial dispute between the Soviet Union and China led to actual skirmishing but again de-escalation was the outcome. Since 1987, when Pakistan first began hinting at its nuclear capability a number of serious crises between Pakistan and India have 'fizzled out' rather than 'exploded'. Although it is difficult to prove the cause of a non-event, the unmistakable trend in 'nuclear weapon state' security relations is toward war avoidance.

Can this avoidance of war be related to a positive relationship between territoriality and nuclear weapons? In contrast to the accepted Herz analysis, I offer two hypotheses:

1. Nuclear weapons enhance territoriality by creating deterrent power. The presence of nuclear weapons does not eliminate the protective function of the territorial state but requires its adaptation. The hard-shell wall of defence, which was never impenetrable, has been replaced by the soft-shell of deterrence. In the pre-nuclear age, the protection of a state's territorial integrity rested on the ability to repulse an attack (as we see in the case of the Spanish Armada). After World War II, that same protective function is served by the ability to convince another state not to initiate an attack in the first place. The territorial state still retains the power of protection in the nuclear age through the dissuasive influence of nuclear possession. The nuclear era does not require a change in the basic functions performed by nation-states. The existence of nuclear weapons simply requires an alteration in how states perform those functions. The concept of a hard-shell of defence implies that state investment in the power to defend is an appropriate strategy for pursuing the protective function of the state in a conventional weapon environment. The soft-shell of deterrence, in contrast, assumes that power rests in capability to deter, which is an appropriate state response, (although not necessarily the only one as will be discussed later) to a strategic environment conditioned by nuclear possession.

2. Military power projection over extended interests will decrease as the possession of deterrent power by individual states increases. Reduced power projection will reduce instances over which military conflict may occur.

During the first phase of the nuclear age the superpowers responded to their increased vulnerability by expanding the territory that they wished to protect (Herz, 1959, p. 169). Extended nuclear deterrence was a particular response to the recognition of assured destruction capability and the bipolar distribution of power. The major weakness that extended nuclear deterrence suffered from was a credibility gap. There was a disbelief that the United States would risk destruction of its own cities by responding to an attack on its allies' territory. In essence, the problem with extended deterrence was a difficulty in being able to think in terms of extended territoriality.

With the collapse of the Soviet Union, the structural imperative behind extended nuclear deterrence has waned, while the protective function of the state remains. One possible response to this situation might be the individuation of deterrent power. Where the first phase of the nuclear era focused on extended deterrence, the second phase, initiated with the end of the Cold War, may well be defined by increased reliance on central deterrence. The ability of 'great powers' to project beyond their borders - which is their distinguishing characteristic - will be hampered by the possession of deterrent power by smaller powers (Kennedy, 1987; Morgenthau, 1985; Waltz, 1979).[10] In order to begin to address the above hypotheses the dynamics associated with nuclear possession must be examined.

Nuclear weapons and international security relations

Neo-realist thought holds that anarchy - the absence of any centralised international governing authority - creates the structural imperative of relying on oneself for ultimate security.[11] The distribution of power throughout the system, which reflects the relative positions of individual states, conditions state relations. In their pursuit of ensuring their basic objective of national security, states must be concerned with their relative position in the international system. Joseph Grieco has argued that states, therefore, are best described as 'defensive positionalists'. In order to remain secure and independent, states must be forever aware of where they stand relative to both potential opponents and allies. Allies deserve attention because, 'minds can be changed, new leaders can come to power, values can shift, new opportunities and dangers can arise'.[12]

This focus on relative position leads to a concern about relative gains that may be produced by state interaction. Kenneth Waltz has argued that the relevant question traditionally asked by state policy makers is not whether their state will gain through a particular interaction with another state, but rather who will gain more? Waltz argues that this raises a significant obstacle to achieving international cooperation, even when cooperative behaviour represents a mutually beneficial option. When coordinating international activity over time, states must be concerned with the gaps that may arise in gains achieved between themselves and other states even when that activity produces absolute gains for all parties. While two states may benefit from coordinating their actions, producing an overall gain, the distribution of the gains is unlikely to be symmetrical.

Liberal, regime, and neo-liberal institutional theories all assume that the prospect of cooperation will be enhanced as the assurance of benefits increases (Krasner, 1983; Keohane, 1984; Kegley, 1995). The reduction of uncertainty and the expectation of iteration are considered critical for cooperation under anarchy (Oye, 1986). The problem, according to neo-realists, is that relative calculations still remain. The gains made relative to another state may be used to the advantage of a state and, most importantly, to the disadvantage of other states. The prospects for international cooperation are more problematic than liberal theorists recognise because they fail to allow for the continued relevance of relative calculations. Where gaps produced in gains intensify focus on relative calculation, the probability for cooperation diminishes.

The pessimistic outlook of realist theory ultimately rests on the supposition that a focus on relative calculation tends to dominate across most issue areas of importance. Robert Powell has suggested that states' concern for relative gains is best explained in the context of constraints rather than preferences (Powell, 1991, p. 1317). It is the structural imperative of self-help created by anarchy that necessitates a focus on relative power. Powell suggests, however, that while anarchy creates the general structure within which states must conduct themselves, the presence of certain sets of constraints will affect the latitude states have to conduct their relations. The most significant of these constraints is the prospect of military force. When the use of force is at issue, the focus on relative calculations becomes more intense and the possibility for cooperation diminishes. But if the cost of war is sufficiently high, states will tend to focus more on the prospect of absolute gains and losses. In line with liberal theorists, Powell concludes that the potential for cooperation will rise when state calculations are conceived of in absolute terms (Powell, 1991, p. 1314).

Powell's formalised model supports his hypothesis only by assuming that there is certainty about the cost of war. Joseph Greico suggests that Powell has produced a model that may allow for the possibility of absolute calculations more than it should. While not directly attacking the thesis that when the cost of war is too high, relative thinking will give way to absolute calculations, Greico argues that uncertainty works to support continued relative calculation. Greico's reasoning is sound when applied to the traditional battlefield. In a military environment dominated by conventional weaponry, where certainty about the cost of war does not exist, the intensity of relative assessments is at its highest. It is a concern for security that necessitates relative calculations. This concern is most relevant when the possibility of war is being contemplated, either by an initiator or defender. The act of going to war ultimately challenges a state's ability to act independently. If a state is deciding to initiate a war, relative assessments must be carefully made concerning, among other factors, the opponent's military defences and retaliatory capabilities, political stability, natural resources, potential allies, and economic strength. A state fearing an attack must engage as vigorously in a similar set of calculations. It should be assumed that an extremely intense focus on relative power guides states in assessing the potential costs of going to war and makes cooperation in avoiding armed conflict all the more difficult.

This assessment, however, can be constrained or exacerbated depending on the type of strategic environment in which the states find themselves. This environment is greatly influenced by the weapons relied upon for deterrence of war.[13] What Greico and Powell fail to do is explicitly distinguish between conventional and nuclear environments and their respective effects on state security calculations. States relying on a strategy of conventional deterrence will tend to have an intense focus on relative power because the retaliatory costs that they can threaten are ultimately contestable.

With conventional deterrents, there exists the potential for finding technical, tactical, and operational solutions that may reduce or completely circumvent the threatened level of retaliatory costs (for more detail of this discussion, see Harknett, 1994). This prospect fuels the intensity of relative calculations since both the state considering the initiation of war and the one trying to deter it know they must counter each other's moves. While the costs of modern conventional warfare may be extremely high, the concept of winning still endures. The calculation driving the decision to go to war is not necessarily whether a state will be better off in absolute terms (given the destructive rather than constructive nature of war this has been rare in history). The critical question is whether a state will be in a better position after fighting than before fighting *vis-a-vis* other states in the system. Contest on the conventional battlefield is the ultimate arbiter in the distribution of power across the international system.[14] A conventional military environment does nothing to moderate the tendency to make relative calculations. In the end, conventional war determines whose relative assessments were more correct.[15]

The calculation of gains and losses is constrained considerably in a nuclear deterrence environment. The retaliatory costs associated with nuclear weapons approach a degree of certainty concerning the capability to inflict those costs, which is unobtainable by conventional weapons. Military threats simply represent promises of future action. There is a reasonable degree of uncertainty that can be attached to conventional threats. Whether the level of destruction threatened can actually be reached is suspect. The costs to be inflicted by a conventional deterrent capability can be contested by an opponent. In a nuclear environment, the capability is not open to circumvention. If used, the level of destruction threatened can be reached. Uncertainty exists only at the level of whether the weapons will be used, not whether they can actually inflict the damage they threaten. This is a much less vexing problem than has typically been thought of in the literature. When it comes to the issue of national security, states are likely to be risk-averse in their calculations, erring in the direction of worse case planning (Grieco, 1993, pp. 301-38). The type of strategic environment states find themselves in will affect their risk averse behaviour. In a conventional military environment, where relative calculations dominate, risk-averse states will find cooperation difficult. While it may be viewed as a mutual gain, agreeing to avoid war in one instance may produce an uneven outcome overall. War avoidance might be sought only to obtain the time necessary to build the needed forces or find the appropriate strategy that will make the use of force an attractive option in the future. However, in a nuclear environment in which certainty exists about the absolute loss that would result from a use of the capability, the cautious calculus of a risk-averse state should incline that state to cooperate on avoiding such action. In a conventional environment relative calculations are intense and small differences may make a significant impact. It is appropriate for states to 'assume that there is at least some chance that force' could be used (Grieco, 1993, p. 314). The overwhelming power of nuclear weapons, however, tends to overshadow small differences. Potential gaps in power, which may translate into relative advantage, are not sufficient in a nuclear environment to provide military opportunity. Once a secure second strike force is available the focus of assessments becomes political will rather than capabilities. Here, risk aversion leads a state considering the use of force to assume that there is a chance that the other side will use its nuclear deterrent as it has threatened to do. Since nuclear retaliation would outweigh any conceivable benefit, war initiation is likely to be avoided. The slight chance of a response involving a certain unacceptable level of destruction is more likely to produce war avoidance than a greater chance of response involving a high but suspect level of destruction. This is the difference between state security calculations in nuclear and conventional deterrence environments. This is not to say that relative calculations have not driven the development of nuclear forces. They have. But when it comes to actual use of nuclear forces, states are faced with a strong sense of absolute loss. The difference in framing is significant. Whereas conventional warfare can be discussed in terms of relative gains, nuclear war must be conceived of in the context of absolute loss.

Greico's defensive postionalist state is concerned with maintaining independence. Nuclear weapons provide unconditional support for state territorial integrity. While gaps in gains and power may be exploited in non-military areas and extended military environments, national territorial security is enhanced by central nuclear deterrence.[16]

Anarchy creates structural incentives for states to act as if 'relative gain is more important than absolute gain' (Waltz, 1959, p. 198). Nuclear weapons, however, place significant constraints on the effects of this anarchical structure. While viewed as unit-level attribute (enhancements to military power), nuclear possession must also be recognised for its structural impact. The strategic interaction between states armed with nuclear weapons is fundamentally different from that of conventionally-armed states. While still attempting to better themselves relative to other states, nuclear opponents must make their calculations without the recourse to war as a viable option. In a nuclear context, the question guiding decisions concerning peace and war is 'How can I achieve my objectives, without provoking a military response from my opponent?'. This differs significantly from the question that can be asked in a conventional environment. There, the possibility of achieving objectives exists even after an opponent responds militarily. In the former situation alternatives are constrained by a focus on the possibility of absolute losses; in the latter, relative gains remains relevant.

The avoidance of military engagement when conflicts of interests arise requires some degree of coordination, if not cooperation. International security relations can be viewed as a on-going bargaining process. Cooperation on the objective of avoiding war, while still seeking the best results in the competition for gains, is supported by the absolute nature of nuclear conflict. Competition is not eliminated but rather channelled away from the military battlefield.

In part, Cold War history supports this assertion. The major competition between the United States and the Soviet Union was contested primarily through the arms-race and in extended interest areas. The two states came to manage central security issues with great care, particularly after 1962. While analysis of the Cold War is important, it is necessary to keep in mind that it was simply the initial stage of the nuclear era, the end of which has not arrived. As Robert Malcolmson has suggested, 'the perils and dilemmas of the nuclear age are sure to be much more enduring than the animosities of the Cold War'. This ominous tone may be tempered by recognising that, as with any initial stage, the learning curve tends to be at its steepest early on. This first phase may be remembered most for the development of greater crisis management sophistication and a focus on the problems of extended deterrence.[17] Nuclear weapon-states enter the post-Soviet stage of the nuclear era with a formidable knowledge of many of Malcolmson's perils and dilemmas.

The era of nuclear prominence

When states care about absolute gains and losses, cooperation becomes easier. On the issue of war avoidance, nuclear weapons focus the attention of states on the prospect of absolute loss. Relative gain can only be attained if the resort to nuclear weapons is avoided. While accepting the basic realist explanation of international behaviour, this view of nuclear weapons sees them as constraining a particular state activity - international war - by creating an incentive structure that promotes cooperation on the issue of war avoidance.

The hypothesis being presented here is that nuclear weapons represent intervening variables in the structure of international anarchy. The presence of nuclear weapons places significant de-escalatory pressures on states as the possibility of war becomes acute. Their impact is not to produce resolution of conflicts of interests, but rather to channel energies towards non-military solutions. As we move away from the Cold War strategies of containment and extended nuclear deterrence, new strategic possibilities will emerge for the avoidance of war.

In September 1991, President George Bush announced a series of initiatives to reduce the size and nature of US overseas nuclear deployments (NATO, 1991, pp. 11-12). The effect of these withdrawals of ground-launched theatre nuclear weapons and sea-based tactical nuclear weapons was to signal the initial movement on the part of the United States away from reliance on nuclear weapons to protect extended vital interests. Although the American nuclear umbrella still remained open over its allies through reliance on its strategic arsenal, a key component in America's extended nuclear deterrence strategy was removed. Tactical nuclear weapon deployments, while providing some denial capability, were primarily made to enhance the credibility of the United States' commitment. One must assume that the credibility issue is not solved by the removal of these weapons and in fact should be exacerbated. The only way, therefore, to contend with reduced deployment is to reduce actual reliance from a policy standpoint. This is the underlying reasoning behind the movement on the part of the Clinton administration towards greater reliance on extended conventional deterrence. While it is possible that this shift in strategy will reduce the influence of nuclear weapons on international politics, the opposite possibility must also be considered. The contraction of extended nuclear deterrence, in the long run, may lead to an increase in the prominence of nuclear weapons worldwide. This increased prominence will be manifested in the rise of central nuclear deterrence and the emergence of new innovations in nuclear strategy.

Central deterrence and power projection

The superpowers' willingness to extend their deterrence strategies to protect allied territory served as a strong counterweight to the further spread of nuclear weapons. In cases where the credibility or reliability of extended deterrence was questioned - France and China - independent forces were sought. The nuclear option was developed in Israel, India and South Africa, where significant security threats were perceived, no explicit extended deterrent existed, and the technical/material base was present. While much focus is placed on the possibility of nuclear development in renegade states like Iran, Iraq, and North Korea, the ease at which states like Germany and Japan might adopt a nuclear posture can not be overlooked. Although constitutional and domestic opinion constraints exist, the emergence of a viable external threat (an 'Imperial' Russia or a 'nuclear' North Korea) combined with suspicion concerning continued American reliability quickly could lead to nuclear status.[18]

The move away from American extended nuclear deterrence and toward a more minimal central reliance will create incentive structures for a number of states to acquire independent nuclear forces. The irony in this case is that by reducing the role to be played by nuclear weapons in its national security approach, the United States may increase the importance of nuclear weapons globally.

This incentive structure will also be bolstered by the continued existence of the Russian nuclear force. Russia's nuclear status will have an impact on the national security decision-making of its neighbours. If nuclear weapons provide confidence against external infringements on one's territorial integrity, stability would be served if such confidence was held by each potential side.[19] In the case of Russia's major neighbours - Germany, Poland, Ukraine - indigenous independent nuclear forces do not exist.[20] The extended nuclear umbrella of the United States used to counter the Russian force covers only Germany (on the shortcomings of the Clinton administration's plan 'The Partnership for Peace', see Kissinger, *Time*, 14 March 1994, pp. 73-7). Warsaw, Kiev and Berlin are quite aware that in any confrontation with Moscow they lack the central deterrent which the Russians possess. This is not to say that the presence of Russian nuclear weapons mandates future development by Poland, Ukraine or Germany. It does suggest that in future affairs their strategic (military and economic) calculations must assume the presence of a regional nuclear hegemon. Focus on nuclear forces will be exacerbated by the increasing uneasiness of the United States to continue to extend or to broaden its nuclear deterrent to protect others. Whether continued Russian possession will promote eventual proliferation around its borders is unknown, but it will remain prominent in the minds of Moscow's non-nuclear neighbours.

The potential increase in central deterrents worldwide may not be limited to aspiring great powers alone. 'Middle' and 'minor' powers may find nuclear possession attractive. If they do, the potential effect of emerging central deterrents worldwide would necessitate reconsideration of one of realist theory's classical pillars, the concept of power politics. The principle of power politics - that, 'the standard of justice depends on the equality of power to compel and that in fact the strong do what they have the power to do and the weak accept what they have to accept' - is drawn from the historian Thucydides in his famous account of the Athenian assault on the island of Melos during the Peloponnesian War (Thucydides, *The Peloponnesian War*, p. 402). The residents of Melos, we are told, reject this line of reasoning and find themselves destroyed by the more powerful Athenian forces. But what if the Melians had possessed nuclear weapons? Would the prospect of retaliation against their own city-state have made the generals of Athens more cautious in their action toward Melos. Would nuclear possession, in fact, have produced an equality of power that would have required the Athenians to limit their demands or to exercise a different type of diplomacy. Could a 'great power' brazenly threaten the existence of a weaker power, if that weaker power possessed the capability to threaten massive destruction?

Weak states, such as ancient Melos, can not hope to compete with 'great powers' in the general struggle for power across issue areas. However, if they can attain equality in the power to hurt they may fundamentally alter the traditional dynamic that has existed between weak and 'great powers'. Realist logic holds that the independence of weaker states is primarily based on exogenous factors such as the distribution of power, the presence of a 'great power' benefactor or great power disinterest (the classic treatment of 'great power'/small power relationship is found in Morgenthau, 1985, pp. 193-6). Nuclear possession by weaker powers may serve as a sufficient equaliser to secure state territorial integrity and thus, basic independence.[21]

Kenneth Waltz, who once rejected the idea that nuclear weapons facilitated entry into the 'great power' club, recently asserted that 'because nuclear weapons widen the range of economic capabilities within which great powers and would-be great powers can effectively compete, the door to the great-power club will swing open' if those states only knock (Waltz, 1993, p. 54). For states like Germany and Japan who have most of the attributes of a 'great power', save the military component, Waltz sees the nuclear option as securing that status for them. Where Waltz does not extend his argument is to the impact nuclear possession might have on 'great power'-minor power relations. While 'great powers' will still remain the actors who most influence the conduct of international affairs, nuclear possession by minor states will intervene to provide a very different structure to their relations than has historically been the case.

Both consistency and change can be identified in future 'great power'-minor power relations. The significant change will come in the limitations or constraints placed on the behaviour of 'great powers', who will no longer have available the option of threatening the existence of smaller powers in order to influence their actions. What will remain consistent with the past is the inability of minor powers to engage effectively in the advancement or protection of peripheral or extended interests. While nuclear weapons can support defensive independence, they are less effective in offensive compellence situations.[22] By definition and necessity, minor powers are less concerned with extended interests, but most concerned about basic independence. Since nuclear weapons facilitate the latter, while adding little to the former, it can be surmised that nuclear possession will remain of interest to minor powers.

The preceding discussion is tied together by the common thread of central deterrence. The dissuasive power of protection - the soft shell of nuclear deterrence - will remain attractive for actual and potential nuclear states alike. As the nuclear era transitions from a period defined by extended deterrence to one of central deterrence, international security relations will tend to become more constrained. Traditional power politics centred around exploitation of military capabilities will diminish in a world of nuclear prominence. Competition will be funnelled towards other aspects, such as economic trade and development, and conventional military conflict will be likely to occur only in peripheral non-nuclear interest areas. The issues, debates and dynamics associated with nuclear weapons are also likely to be different in a world dominated by multiple central deterrents. For example, as the number of states adopting central nuclear deterrence postures increases, the focus of international security analysis and policy will need to shift away from primary concern over external aggression to fear of internal collapse. The internal stability of nuclear-capable states, from Russia to North Korea, will increasingly become a significant issue. Nuclear chaos will be as important as nuclear war. In most states of the world, the transition of power is far removed from the staid and ritualised process instituted in America. Much analysis will need to be done to develop policies to deal with contested power grabs, economic collapse, and internal unrest within nuclear states. It is also likely that deterrence, as conceived during the Cold War, will not be the only rationale for nuclear possession. In fact there is already evidence that one possible strategy, which I distinguish as nuclear insurance, has been developed by some emerging nuclear states.

Nuclear insurance

The central objective of nuclear possession - securing territorial integrity - has been served during the Cold War through deterrence. Nuclear deterrence rests on the presumption that the integration of an invulnerable force structure with credible employment tactics will ultimately influence the potential behaviour of an adversary to the point of precluding offensive actions against the homeland and/or extended vital interests of one's country. Most people accept the axiom Bernard Brodie pointed to nearly 50 years ago: the military utility of nuclear weapons is their influence in promoting the avoidance of war rather than the actual fighting of war.[23]

An alternative to deterrence that still seeks the principal objective of state security exists in what might be distinguished as 'nuclear insurance'. Instead of adopting deterrence theory's focus on influencing opponent's behaviour, nuclear insurance posits the assumption that the main purpose of nuclear possession is to influence a potential ally's behaviour. Nuclear insurance is not to be confused with the idea of blackmail, which, like deterrence, assumes that the interaction between the involved parties is adversarial. Nuclear insurance assumes a collaborative relationship between the principal actors. It is most likely to be considered as a national security approach when secure second strike deterrence is not an available option. Under such circumstances, the point of nuclear possession might not be to ward off an adversary directly but rather to influence a third party, one who is concerned by the potential use of nuclear weapons in a crisis, to intervene on your behalf.

Conditions for nuclear insurance

There seem to be three basic conditions that support a strategy of nuclear insurance:

1. small/regional nuclear power facing an imminent internal and/or external threat to national security;
2. a 'great power' with a perceived stake in avoiding the international use of nuclear weapons;
3. some basis of expectation on the part of the small power that coordination with the 'great power' is possible (perhaps a formal or informal alliance; traditional friendly relationship; regional interest in the survival of a particular state).

If a vulnerable nuclear power can assume that a larger benefactor exists, it need not develop a full-fledged nuclear force structure or a deterrence posture. In fact, the need to explicitly announce oneself as a nuclear power prior to any crisis disappears. If the goal is not primarily to deter but to influence third party behaviour when facing a threat, keeping the 'bomb in the basement' is appropriate. By not 'going nuclear' in an explicit manner (and so foregoing the establishment of a public deterrence posture), an emerging nuclear state would avoid the possible sanctions and disruption of friendly relations that might follow such action. The ability to influence a great power's behaviour during a crisis might actually be enhanced by the surprise produced in a direct acknowledgement of nuclear possession at the height of a conflict (this would be true even in such cases like Israel, where they suspect that we suspect they have the bomb).

Steven E. Miller, among others, has argued that the formidable requirements of nuclear deterrence strategy - a developed and expensive force structure, sophisticated command and control, an explicit political commitment - may prove too daunting and serve to discourage some states from acquiring nuclear capabilities (see the debate between Miller and Mearsheimer in *Foreign Affairs*, 1993). The possibility of adopting a strategy of nuclear insurance rather than nuclear deterrence, however, should alter our thinking about emerging nuclear states. The threshold for being considered a 'viable' nuclear state is much lower than traditional analysis would lead us to believe. Emerging nuclear states may be able to develop an approach that couples nuclear possession with defence and foreign policy objectives without constructing a traditionally-conceived deterrence force posture.

Nuclear insurance functions on the basis of leverage against the growing norm opposing the next use of nuclear weapons. The superpower's avoidance of wartime use of nuclear weapons established a pattern of behaviour that is leading to a convergence of expectations around the idea that these weapons simply should not be used. In his discussions concerning regimes, Oran Young has noted that 'patterns of behavior that persist over extended periods are infused with normative significance' (Krasner, 1983, p. 9). The calls for adoption of a no-first use extended deterrence posture for NATO in the early 1980s are finding greater resonance now as extended deterrence becomes less critical. The mutual public recognition by Ronald Reagan and Mikhail Gorbachev, that nuclear war cannot be fought because it cannot be won, lends support. The developing norm, however, is not limited to opposing military use. The initialling of the Comprehensive Test Ban (CTB) after the 1995 Non-proliferation Treaty (NPT) extension conference is becoming increasingly likely. Previously, both the United States and the United Kingdom have been unwilling to commit to CTB in the NPT context. The Clinton administration's heavy emphasis on non-proliferation principles may signal a change on the testing issue. While not yet fully accepted, what might be termed a norm of 'No-next use' seems to be gaining strength.[24] Paradoxically, the stronger the norm against use of nuclear weapons becomes, the more insurance leverage is created.

How might nuclear insurance be practised as a national security strategy?

Nuclear insurance and external threat

Both South Africa and Israel serve as illustrations of how nuclear insurance might work.[25] While evidence is anecdotal, it can be proposed that this is the strategic rationale followed by both countries. In March, 1993, the government of South Africa revealed that, despite 115 international inspections, it had manufactured six 10-18KT fission weapons. The main focus of attention at the time of the announcement and since has been on the claim that the entire nuclear programme was dismantled; an assertion of which some intelligence services and International Atomic Energy Agency officials are sceptical. What has not received sufficient analysis is the unique nuclear strategy that South Africa had reportedly devised. According to the few officials that have spoken out about their programme, the South African nuclear strategy closely resembled the approach I have defined as 'nuclear insurance' (Mark Hibbs, 1993 and *Washington Post*, 12 May 1993, p. 1A).

The nuclear capabilities were not to be acknowledged unless the country found itself under attack from one of its northern neighbours (e.g., Angola, Mozambique). With its back against the wall, the South African leadership planned to force the United States to pressure the Soviet Union to reign in its clients. The leverage to be used with the USA was the discovery that South Africa had the bomb and was about to use it. If the American president was sceptical, the South Africans planned to explode one device at their test-site at Kalahari and let it be known that they had at least five more, and were prepared to use them.

What is intriguing about this strategy is that it seems to be a more developed and sophisticated extension of the supposed Israeli nuclear approach during the 1973 Yom Kippur War. Many non-proliferation analysts have long pointed to possible technical cooperation between South Africa and Israel. It is not out of the question that the South African strategic rationale for its nuclear weapons was informed by the Israeli experience and strategic thinking.[26] According to some, the main reason the American airlift of supplies to Israel began, after the Israeli Defence Forces' (IDF) initial setback, was the indication from the Israeli leadership that they were prepared to use tactical nuclear weapons against Egyptian forces. The evidence is not concrete. However, if true, the incident implies that Israel did not see the primary utility of its nuclear capability to be deterrence (otherwise a public deterrent threat would have been directed at the Sadat government) but rather, influencing American behaviour.[27]

What is most significant about these two examples is that the threat to use nuclear weapons sent a signal not primarily to the adversary, but to a third party 'great power'. While there might have been some deterrent effects on the adversary, this was not the underlying strategic goal. Influencing the behaviour of a potential ally was the primary mission assigned these small nuclear arsenals.

The explanatory power of the concept of nuclear insurance may be significant. For example, understanding the possible dynamics associated with nuclear insurance may be important for analysing both Pakistani and Ukrainian thinking. These emerging nuclear states share the common problem of facing an adversary that will for the foreseeable future retain a position of conventional and nuclear superiority. Even if both Pakistan and Ukraine were to become explicit nuclear powers, their arsenals would be comparably small and highly vulnerable to the nuclear arsenals of India and Russia respectively. A traditional deterrence strategy might suffer from questions about credibility given the disproportionate destruction that could be inflicted on these smaller powers. If one assumes that deterrence is the primary strategic rationale for possessing a nuclear force, continued Pakistani and Ukrainian pursuit of nuclear capabilities must be explained away by prestige/domestic political interests or military naivete. However, if the possession and possible use of nuclear forces is viewed by these countries primarily as levers to effect third party support (USA and China in the case of Pakistan; the USA, France, Germany and Great Britain in Ukraine's case), a military strategic rationale emerges.

Nuclear insurance and internal threats

Even more speculative, but just as intriguing, is the case of North Korea. Much of the debate during the North Korean nuclear crisis of 1993-94 has focused on whether North Korea possessed a bomb. The nuclear possession debate along with discussions concerning appropriate US and IAEA responses have dominated the press and journal accounts of this story.[28]

While such analysis is important, the essential question of why North Korea would opt for nuclear possession has received scant attention. This may be a consequence of the fact that determining the motivations that drive the secretive regime of Kim Jong Il is near impossible. Although such analysis is fraught with difficulty, it is, at the same time, imperative. The choice of policy options ('carrots and/or sticks') and policy goals (continuing inspections/right of special inspections) is difficult for it must be based on some assumptions concerning the values and interests of Pyongyang. It is for this very reason that a broader and more intense focus of attention should be directed towards assessing the determinants of North Korea policy.

Three general rationales can be suggested. First, Pyongyang may want nuclear weapons to deter outside attack. If this is the case, then we are dealing with a paranoid regime that can not correctly determine that US-Republic of Korea (ROK) forces are aligned defensively. Second, the

North Koreans may wish to attack South Korea. In this case, we are dealing with an irrational regime that can not correctly assess the overwhelming air and sea power that the US possesses. Third, Kim Il Sung, and now his son, may have been taking out 'regime insurance'. In this case, we are dealing with a regime suffering from economic failure and worried about internal collapse. Kim Il Sung may have viewed nuclear possession as an insurance policy against his most pressing problem - regime collapse.

When analysing North Korea our unit of analysis should not be the nation-state, but rather the elite leadership. It is not national survival that concerns Kim Jong Il, but personal regime survival. (In fact, one could assume that he equates the two.) No-one wants a nuclear detonation on the Korean peninsula, or anywhere else for that matter. The North Korean leadership may anticipate that Seoul, Tokyo, and Beijing will view collapse from internal revolt very differently if it involved the possible loss of control over nuclear devices. A chaotic transfer of power in a nuclear-capable state could not be ignored. If the regime was convinced that it was nearing internal collapse, possession of a nuclear device could be used to guarantee support from neighbours. The message is simple: 'come save us or we don't know what might happen in all of the confusion'.

Kim Il Sung and his son may have drawn a great many lessons from the quick collapse of East European communist regimes, most particularly Romania. Highly isolated, and lacking any bargaining levers, Nicolae Ceausescu paid the ultimate price in front of an angry firing squad, while the West stood on the sidelines. It is not incredible to believe that some of Kim Jong Il's present thinking is informed by the death of this other isolated authoritarian. Such a possibility should inform our own thinking as well.

If one assumes that the primary concern of the elite regime of North Korea is personal survival, then opening up to the West may be the last thing the regime wishes to do. Any new integration with the West might increase the awareness of the highly isolated and controlled population of North Korea to how badly off they are relative to the rest of the world.[29] Such a recognition might precipitate the type of internal discord that could lead to a 'firing squad' transition of power, like the kind that ended Ceausescu's rule. The promise of better relations with the West if IAEA inspections and continued monitoring are allowed assumes a regime that can adapt to the domestic changes such relations might bring. This may not be an adaptable regime. As Paul Bracken suggests, offers of Western trade and relations may be 'poisoned carrots' (Bracken, 1993, p. 150).

So, from Pyongyang's perspective, nuclear possession could, if things worsen, be used to influence Chinese and, indirectly, American behaviour. Aid funnelled through the regime could be requested by suggesting that the alternative is nuclear chaos. Ultimately, if conditions greatly worsen, 'The Button' might be traded for a Duvalier- or Marcos-type departure from power - two dictators who managed to use their alignments with the West to secure themselves after regime-collapse. The point is that Kim Jong Il may be more concerned with influencing the behaviour of a potential ally (for instance, China), rather then dissuading the actions of an opponent (read IAEA/US). Nuclear possession may be the only effective lever available. Thus, threats to prevent possession may be ineffectual with those who are already convinced that they have no other alternative. It is not far-fetched to suggest that an isolated elite would make national decisions based on personal concerns. The idea that nuclear possession is being driven by the need for personal regime insurance is worth consideration. Such an assumption may prescribe very different policy options than have previously been debated.

Implications

The Clinton Administration has made reducing the international role played by nuclear weapons a national security priority. In preparation for the 1995 conference on the NPT, non-proliferation advocates, both inside and outside the administration, sought to strengthen internationally accepted norms not only against proliferation but against the 'next use' of nuclear weapons. The aim was to ban not only first use deterrent responses but all testing as well.

Efforts at promoting non-proliferation and No-Next Use generally assume that deterrence is the central strategy guiding nuclear force structures and operational planning. While political motivations of prestige and domestic interest group pressure might encourage the spread of nuclear weapons, the military rationale assumed to be supporting possession is the hope that potential adversaries will be convinced that risks are too high to justify offensive military action. When the possibility of creating a viable nuclear force structure is remote, as in the case of many emerging nuclear states, the main motivation driving the desire to acquire nuclear weapons must be considered political rather than military. Such reasoning implies that the strategic rationale - that possession might induce some caution in an adversary - is a weak argument for proliferation and can be dismissed by threats of ruptured diplomatic relations and strategic isolation. Thus, much of the effort in support of a non-proliferation regime is directed at undercutting the political/prestige-driven motivations. As more nations place political importance on the maintenance of an international regime in which non-proliferation and no-next use are the accepted norms, nuclear weapons will play an ever-diminishing role in international relations.

This line of reasoning is what nuclear insurance hopes to exploit. Again, the strength of the international norm against the next use of nuclear weapons, paradoxically, is key. In order to create a climate in which military use is unacceptable, one must create the image that equates next use with the opening of 'Pandora's Box'. Such an argument suggests that the international system the morning after the next use of nuclear weapons will be very different; the potential instability is unthinkable. This unfortunately creates a 'house of cards' dilemma. If international non-proliferation policy is predicated on the principle of no-next use, and such use occurs, the entire non-proliferation regime may come crashing down. In terms of the analysis above, however, it is most important to recognise that efforts that place a premium on thwarting the next use of nuclear weapons may increase the incentive to adopt a nuclear insurance strategy. Placing paramount importance on preventing nuclear use produces leverage for those nuclear powers convinced that such use is necessary to save either their country or particular regime. Heavy emphasis on no-next use may be exploitable by emerging nuclear powers.

There are three important implications of nuclear insurance. First, in the case of potential nuclear states, nuclear insurance, while certainly risky, presents a sufficiently valid strategic rationale that may give greater leverage to those domestic elements arguing for nuclear development. The strategy presents a vulnerable state with an option when deterrence and other foreign policy alternatives must be rejected, given force structure limitations and the superiority of potential adversaries or given international isolation and potent internal threats.

Second, the efforts to promote a norm of no-next use, must be developed with the understanding that it may be an exploitable concept. The international community would have to raise the norm to the highest level if its exploitation is to be prevented. This, however, raises the possibility of making territorial aggression by conventional means safer for the militarily superior state. In this case, the international community would be establishing a rule of conduct that implies that world opinion will line up against a state under attack, if such a state resorted to nuclear weapons. Or opening up the possibility of simply living with a chaotic internal collapse in a nuclear state without an attempt at stabilisation.

The third implication of nuclear insurance relates to alliance/alignment behaviour in international relations. The problem of traditional alliance drag - where ties to weak states eventually force 'great powers' into conflicts where their vital interests are not directly engaged - highlights the potential problem of nuclear insurance. A 'great power', supportive of the norm of no-next use, might have to choose between support of the norm and abandonment of an ally or friend. Nuclear insurance potentially creates a new dynamic in alliance behaviour. Ties to emerging nuclear states may carry greater significance than the basic interests that underlie the friendly relationship. Where support for weak governments in the past held out the danger of over-extended commitments, adherence to the norm of no-next use and traditional interests that might encourage continued ties with emerging or suspected nuclear states (for example, the US-Israeli relationship) presents a dangerous potential for forced commitments. If the potential for dragging an outside benefactor in exists, the pursuit of such a nuclear strategy would become appealing for emerging vulnerable nuclear states.

Nuclear prominence, territoriality and proliferation

The spread of nuclear weapons will be supported by the growing recognition that they can enhance the territorial state's primary role - protection. The soft-shell of central deterrence constructed exclusively around the borders of a state represents territoriality in the nuclear age. In the role as central deterrents, nuclear weapons force states to calculate decisions about war and peace in terms of absolute losses, enhancing the prospect for agreement on the mutual goal of war avoidance. When nuclear deterrence is extended to cover peripheral interests, uncertainties about the political will necessary to retaliate will emerge. This will lead to an increased focus on relative calculations of intentions and make agreement on war avoidance slightly more difficult (the potential costs of reading intentions wrong will still dampen the intensity of relative calculating). Trends supporting movement toward central rather than extended deterrence are evident.

In 1990 we witnessed the end of a competition, not the end of an era. While the presence of nuclear weapons certainly impacted on the behaviour of the two superpowers, the competition itself overshadowed the structural change in security relations the weapons had begun to advance. In the post-Soviet world now emerging, the role and impact of nuclear weapons will grow in prominence.

The soft-shell of deterrence is a solid basis upon which to construct national security approaches. Rather than thinking of deterrence and reassurance as opposing policies, they should be integrated into a sophisticated approach. By limiting the options available to disaffected states, nuclear possession gives greater definition and impetus to the negotiating process of accommodation. By eliminating the option of all-out confrontation, while at the same time highlighting the enormous risk involved in allowing disagreement to develop over time or internal instability to spiral, nuclear possession can serve as a basis for accommodating solutions. It is this final prospect to which analytical attention should be directed. Rather than serving as a model for moving forward to Herz's universalist ideal or back toward Clinton's restorative solution, the soft-shell of deterrence power may support a modern reconceptualisation of the territorial state.

Notes

1.   For the purposes of this paper it is assumed that nuclear states are secure from preemptive pressures.

2.   Nye is currently an assistant secretary of defence for international security in the Clinton administration.

3.   This paper assumes that nuclear weapons had a stabilising effect on cold war politics. Of course this is a debated point. The most formidable critique is Mueller, 1989. However, for a perspective similar to mine, see Schlesinger, 1993, p.4; Mearsheimer, 1993; Waltz, 1993.

4.   The now infamous comment of an Indian army general that the true lesson of the Persian Gulf war was to avoid combat with the United States until you have completed your nuclear programme captures an important sentiment.

5.   Although it took longer then expected, one can not argue with the fact that the stated objectives of containment policy were achieved. For a similar argument on the 'success' of containment, see Treverton and Bicksler, 1992.

6.   Internal legitimacy rests on whether those who rule within the

state fulfil the functions of protection and promotion of welfare and external legitimacy, on whether the population believes it does not need to be integrated into a larger structure or split into smaller ones (Herz,1976, p. 31).

7.   Ruggie argues that the work of John H. Herz is the only 'serious' attempt by an international security specialist to address territoriality (Ruggie, 1993, p. 143).

8.   Herz argued for true universalist movement rather than for collective security, which he saw merely as 'an attempt to maintain, and render more secure, the impermeability of what were still territorial states'. (Herz, 1976, p. 113).

9.   Michael Doyle's thesis concerning the absence of war between liberal democratic states has also been criticised over time-line and number of cases problems, yet the observation still holds. See in particular Doyle, 1983.

10.   The ability to project power beyond one's border as a basic characteristic of any great power is implicit in the work of Paul Kennedy.

11.   For the original development of the neo-realist perspective, see Waltz, 1979. Further analysis of the perspective can be found in Keohane, 1986 and Buzan, Jones and Little, 1993.

12.   Robert Jervis cited in Greico, 1993, p. 314.

13.   I focus on deterrence rather than defence because of the simple fact that no impenetrable defence has ever been created historically. Defence implies a competing offence and focuses on limiting the damage caused by aggression.

14.   For war as a mechanism of change and distribution, see Gilpin, 1981, p. 15. For a more recent non-realist analysis that views war as an 'allocation mechanism', see Vasquez, 1993, p. 46.

15.   George Simmel writes, 'to be sure, the most effective presupposition for preventing struggle, the exact knowledge of the comparative strength of the two parties, is very often only to be attained by the actual fighting out of the conflict' (Simmel, 1904, p. 501).

16. Central deterrence focuses on the relationship between vital national objectives and the necessity to protect them. Extended deterrence deals with interests beyond what can be considered absolute central interests (Bobbitt, 1988, p. 9).

17. John Lewis Gaddis points to the development of great power mechanisms for deterring aggression during the Cold War (see Gaddis, 1991; see also Bobbitt, 1988 for a similar reference to phases).

18. With regards to Japan's and Germany's renunciation of nuclear weapons and the United States' guarantee, 'it is important to draw the line connecting these two facts'. (Bobbitt, 1988, p. 211).

19. The idea of the 'stability paradox', that is the argument that greater stability at the nuclear level may make for greater instability at the conventional or tactical nuclear level, is less vexing when we are talking about central deterrence. Even though a mutual assured destruction situation might exist, thus making it irrational for either side to employ nuclear weapons, to attack the territory of a nuclear state would be extremely risky. If the attack were to threaten the existence of the state than a spasm response may become more likely given the organisational breakdown and psychological stress that would be present in such a scenario. On the stability paradox, see Snyder, 1961.

20. To date Ukraine has not gained independent positive operational control over the nuclear weapons on its soil. On the difficulties of doing so see Miller, 1993, pp. 67-80.

21. Kissinger alludes to nuclear weapons as 'the great equalizer' (Kissinger, *Time*, 14 March 1994, p. 76).

22. Speaking of the superpowers, Kissinger wrote that 'thermonuclear capability enables them to avoid defeat but not to achieve a meaningful victory'. For minor powers, this type of stalemate might be a maximum objective. Kissinger, *Nuclear Weapons*, p. 129.

23. The fundamental link between nuclear strategy and deterrence explicated by Bernard Brodie in 1946, while occasionally

questioned during debates on preventive war, strategic defence, and preemptive windows of vulnerability, has never been seriously challenged.

24.   I use the term no-next use to include disapproval of both military first use and testing.

25.   A recent article independently comes to a similar conclusion although the term used to describe the strategy being used by Israel and South Africa is 'catalytic deterrence'. This term seems to cover only external threats. The idea being put forward in this section includes the possibility of taking out regime insurance against internal collapse (Howlett and Simpson, 1993).

26.   According to a South African Defence official recently interviewed South Africa had decided to follow Israel's lead and use its bomb 'to get a security guarantee from the United States' (Hibbs, *Washington Post*, 12 May 1993, p. 9).

27.   French official Francis Perrin is quoted as saying, 'We thought the Israeli bomb was aimed against the Americans, not to launch it against America but to say, "if you do not want to help us in a critical situation we will require you to help us, otherwise we will use our nuclear bombs"'. Cited in Howlett and Simpson, 1993, p. 173 fn. 40.

28.   In the Fall of 1994, the Clinton administration offered a deal to North Korea that, among other things, would provide alternative energy resources in exchange for a phased dismantling of the North Korean nuclear programme. The following analysis focuses only on the underlying motivations that may have led to a decision to begin a nuclear programme and does not assess this prospective deal.

29.   One should note that the Clinton administration plan essentially allows for contact to be fully controlled by the North Korean government and that Pyongyang continues, at the time of this writing, to refuse an opening of trade relations with the South.

Bibliography

Allan, C. T. (1994), 'Extended Conventional Deterrence: In From the Cold and Out of the Nuclear Fire?', *The Washington Quarterly* 17.3

Allison, G. and Treverton (eds) (1992), *Rethinking America's Security: Beyond the Cold War to New World Order*, W. W. Norton, New York

Art, R. and Jervis, R. (1992), *International Politics: Enduring Concepts and Contemporary Issues*, 3rd edn., Harper Collins, New York

Aspin, L. (1993), The Bottom-up Review: Forces for a New Era, Department of Defense, Washington D.C.

Baldwin, D. (ed.) (1993), *Neorealism and Neoliberalism: The Contemporary debate*, Columbia University Press, New York

Bobbitt, P. (1988), *Democracy and Deterrence: The History and Future of Nuclear Strategy*, St. Martin's Press, New York

Bracken, P. (1993), 'Nuclear Weapons and State Survival in North Korea', *Survival*, 34.3

Buzan, B., Jones, C. and Little, R. (1993), *The Logic of Anarchy: Neorealism to Structural Realism*, Columbia University Press, New York

Committee on Foreign Affairs, US House of Representatives (1993), 'Nonproliferation regimes: policies to control the spread of nuclear, chemical, and biological weapons and missiles', *Congressional Research Service Report*, March

Davis, Z. and Donnelly, W. (1990), 'Non-Proliferation: A compilation of basic documents on the international, U.S. statutory and U.S. executive branch components of non-proliferation policy', *Congressional Research Service Report to Congress*, 18 December

Doyle, M. (1983), 'Kant, Liberal Legacies and Foreign Affairs, Part 2', *Philosophy and Public Affairs* 12.4

Dunn, L. (1982), *Controlling the Bomb*, Yale University Press, New Haven

Freedman, L. (1989), *The Evolution of Nuclear Strategy*, St. Martin's Press, New York

Gaddis, J. L. (1982), 'The Long Peace: Elements of Stability in the Postwar International System', *International Security* 10.4

Gaddis, J. L. (1991), 'Toward the Post-Cold War World', *Foreign Affairs* 70.2

Gilpin, R. (1981), *War and Change in World Politics*, Cambridge University Press, Cambridge

Gottmann, J. (1973), *The Significance of Territory*, University Press of Virginia, Virginia

Greico, J. (1993), 'Understanding the Problem of International Cooperation', in Baldwin, *1993*

Guertner, G., Haffa, R. and Quester, G. (eds) (1992), *Conventional Forces and the Future of Deterrence*, Strategic Studies Institute, US Army War College, Carlisle Barracks, PA

Gulick, E. V., *Europe's Classical balance of Power*, Norton, New York

Haffa, R. (1992), 'The Future of Conventional Deterrence: Strategies and Forces to Underwrite a New World Order, ' in Guertner, G. *et al*, 1992

Harknett, R. J. (1994), 'The Logic of Conventional Deterrence and the End of the Cold War', *Security Studies* 4.1

Herz, J. H. (1957), 'Rise and Demise of the Territorial State', *World Politics* 9.4

Herz, J. H. (1959), *International Politics in the Atomic Age*, Columbia University Press, New York

Herz, J. H. (1968), 'The Territorial State Revisited - Reflections on the Future of the Nation-State', *Polity* 1.1

Herz, H. J. (1976), *The National-State and the Crises of World Politics*, David McKay, New York

Hibbs, M. (1993), 'South Africa's Secret Nuclear Program', *Nuclear Fuel* 24 May

Howlett, D. and Simpson, J. (1993), 'Nuclearisation and Denuclearisation in South Africa', *Survival* 35.3

Kegley, C. W. (ed.) (1995), *Controversies in International Relations Theory: Realism and the Neoliberal Challenge*, St. Martin's Press, New York

Kennedy, P. (1987), *The Rise and Fall of Great Powers*, Vintage Books, New York

Keohane, R. O. (1984), *After Hegemony: Cooperation and Discord in the World Political Economy*, Princeton University Press, Princeton

Keohane, R. O. (1986), *Neorealism and its Critics*, Columbia University Press, New York

Keohane, R. and Nye, J. (1989), *Power and Independence* 2nd edn., Harper Collins, New York

Keohane, R. and Nye, J. (1992), 'Protecting the Global Environment', in Art and Jervis, 1992

Kissinger, H. (1994), 'How to achieve the new world order', *Time*, 14 March

Krasner, S. (1983), *International Regimes*, Cornell University Press, Ithaca

Krasner, S. (1985), *Structural Conflict: The Third World Against Global Liberalism*, University of California Press, Berkeley

Krasner, S. (ed.) (1983), *International Regimes*, Cornell University Press, Ithaca

Krasner, S. and Thomson, J. (1992), 'Global Transactions and the Consolidation of Sovereignty', in Art and Jervis, 1992

McNeill, W. H. (1982), *The Pursuit of Power: Technology, Armed Force and Society since A.D. 1000*, University of Chicago Press, Chicago

Mearsheimer, J. (1993), 'The Case for a Ukrainian Nuclear Deterrent', *Foreign Affairs* 72.3

Mellor, R. E. H. (1989), *Nation, State and Territory*, Routledge, London

Miller, S. (1993), 'The Risks of Nuclear Proliferation', *Foreign Affairs* 72.3

Miller, S. E. and Mearsheimer, J. (1993), *Foreign Affairs* 72.3

Millot, M. D., Molander, R. and Wilson, P. (1993), 'The Day After', Study: Nuclear Proliferation in the Post-Cold War World, vol.1, Summary Report. RAND MR-266-AF, Santa Monica, CA,

Morgenthau, H. J. (1985), *Politics Among Nations: The Struggle for Power and Peace*, 6th edn., Knopf, New York

Mueller, J. (1989), *Retreat from Doomsday*, Basic Books, New York

NATO (1991), *Nato Review*, 5 October

Nye, J. S. (1992), 'The Cause for Concern: Is Non-proliferation policy mistaken?', *Harvard International Review* 14.3

Oye, K. (ed.) (1986), *Cooperation Under Anarchy*, Princeton University Press, Princeton

Perry, W. J. (1991), 'Desert Storm and Deterrence', *Foreign Affairs* 70.4

Powell, R. (1991), 'Absolute and Relative Gains in International Relations Theory', *American Political Science Review* 85.4

Ruggie, J. G. (1993), 'Territoriality and Beyond: problematizing modernity in international relations', *International Organization* 47.1

Schelling, T. C. (1966), *Arms and Influence*, Yale University Press, New Haven

Schlesinger, J. (1993), 'The Impact of Nuclear Weapons on History', *The Washington Quarterly* 16.4

Simmel, G. (1904), 'The Sociology of Conflict, I', *American Journal of Sociology* 9.4

Snyder, G. H. (1961), *Deterrence and Defense: Toward a Theory of National Security*, Princeton University Press, Princeton

Treverton, G. and Bicksler, B. (1992), 'Getting From Here to Where?', in Allison and Treverton, 1992

Vasquez, J. A. (1993), *The War Puzzle*, Cambridge University Press, New York

Waltz, K. N. (1959), *Man, the State, and War: A Theoretical Analysis*, Columbia University Press, New York

Waltz, K. N. (1979), *Theory of International Politics*, Random House, New York

Waltz, K. N. (1993), 'The Emerging Structure of International Politics', *International Security* 18.2

White House (The) (1994), *A National Security Strategy of Engagement and Enlargement*, Government Printing Office, Washington D.C.

3 Russian foreign policy in the 'Near Abroad'

SALLY N. CUMMINGS

Introduction

Sergei Stankevich, one of President Yeltsin's hand-picked state advisors, has argued that much of the instability on Russia's borders derives from 'ballroom diplomacy': that is, a policy based not on considerations of power, but on smiles and good wishes. Russia's foreign policy intentions in the 'New World Order' are the subject of intense controversy. In the wake of the failed coup of August 1991, the Soviet Union disintegrated. Centripetal forces induced the fifteen successor states to begin the arduous tasks of state- and nation-building, at whose heart lies the definition of a community's *raison d'etre* and interests, which, in turn, serves to shape a country's foreign policy. This chapter concentrates on the case of Russia, and on its foreign policy towards the other states of the Former Soviet Union (FSU), dubbed in January 1992 as the 'Near Abroad'.

The 'Near Abroad' provides the 'litmus test' of how Russian foreign policy has developed. Contiguous to the Russian landmass, the successor states are politically vulnerable, economically dependent, and militarily defenceless. So far as the wider world is concerned, relations with Russia will continue to shape the foreign policy of the successor states.

I shall adopt the following approach. Section I provides a brief theoretical approach to foreign policy formation in general, together with its historical context in Soviet and post-Soviet Russia; section II explores Russia's redefinition of its interests since dissolution of the Soviet Union; and section III proceeds to outline how these interests have been translated into practice (assuming a link between intentions and actions), whilst a conclusion assesses some wider implications. I intend to provide an overview of the main trends in Russian foreign policy at the time of writing in December 1994, rather than speculate on future developments.

Section I: Theory and context of Russian foreign policy formation

A country's foreign policy - by which I mean the sum of a state's intentions towards the outside world - is determined by the interplay of its own properties; history, geography, population, society, polity, economic power and military posture, and the international environment. The two act in a symbiosis. From the point of view of the domestic political system, a strong state, possessing the required resources, time and cohesion, is more likely to exhibit a coherent, clearly defined and consistent foreign policy. By way of further example, an unstable international environment limits the autonomy of any single state from outside shocks.

Up to 1985 and the coming to the fore of Mikhail Gorbachev, the main Soviet foreign priorities - which had been evolving since the end of the 1960s - were basically twofold: competition with the United States and containment of China in Asia. Additional objectives included the undermining of the NATO alliance, the maintenance of (albeit largely unchallenged) Soviet dominance in Eastern Europe, support of regional opponents of China, the enhancement of Soviet conventional military preponderance in Europe and the Far East, the extension of naval and air forces overseas, and the endeavour to 'catch up with' and, if possible, to overtake the United States in the strategic, and space, arms race, juxtaposed by arms control and detente negotiations (Arbatov, 1993, p.3).

Gorbachev engaged in a far-reaching domestic transformation from above. Ideology became less restrictive. In 1989 and 1990, the first competitive elections under Soviet rule saw the widespread rejection of official candidates and the 'establishment'. In at least six of the former Soviet republics, overtly nationalist administrations were elected. The Communist Party lost members and influence and in March 1990 it surrendered Article 6, its constitutionally-guaranteed leading role.

After the attempted coup of August 1991, the Party was itself suppressed. Like the other 'transitional' economies, Russia began to experience hyperinflation, an unprecedented fall in output, a decline in income, spiralling unemployment, and a loss in gold reserves, conditions which all served to place the country in a position of extreme dependence on the West for economic stabilisation. Russia's geopolitical space was revolutionised, adopting the boundaries of the Russian multinational Federation of 1922. The Russian empire's collapse was rapid and unexpected, and the fact that most Russians saw it not as an Empire but as a 'country' meant that there was, therefore, very little political or psychological preparation for the Soviet Union's dismemberment. After the initiative for its creation was announced on 8 December 1991 (by leaders of Belarus, Russia and the Ukraine) on 21 December 1991 an ill-defined 'Commonwealth' of Independent States (CIS) replaced the USSR. To Russia's West and South now lie independent former Union republics, marked by a high degree of internal instability, very much open to external influences, and in conflict with each other. Post-communist patterns of politics began to develop in what were now 15 independent states (White, Gill and Slider, 1993, esp. Ch. 1).

Not all of the 15, however, joined the CIS. Whilst on 21 December 1991, the leaders of Armenia, Azerbaijan (Azerbaijan technically remained an observer until September 1993), Kazakhstan, Kyrgyzstan,

Moldova, Tajikistan, Turkmenistan and Uzbekistan joined the three Slavic states in signing the founding Commonwealth treaty, the three Baltic republics and Georgia had already declared independence. Although the former declared that it would not join the Union, the latter eventually joined in October 1993 (Georgia had consistently sent observers to the CIS meetings). These discrepancies foreshadowed the type of political entity that the CIS proved to be. It was, from its outset, viewed as a transitional body. Devoid of parameters prescribing the degree and extent of cooperation, free from supranational institutions (even if its capital was to be in Minsk), members joined with disparate aims. Few commentators supposed that it would have a long life.

Russia itself annulled the purpose of the CIS by considering itself a 'continuer', as opposed to a 'successor state', as oft-repeated by President Yeltsin and Foreign Minister Kozyrev. These concepts have important ramifications for Russia's relations with the rest of the CIS republics, since, as a 'continuer state', Russia would exert exclusive rights over the global privileges of the former Soviet Union, whilst also assuming former liabilities, including the USSR's international debt and adherence to nuclear arms cuts and disarmament measures. In Margot Light's words, 'as the recognized legal heir to the USSR and a permanent member of the UN Security Council, Russia immediately enjoyed prominent international status' (Light, 1994, p. 64).

Russia enjoyed an additional and distinct advantage over other successor states in that the institutional framework for foreign policy-formation was already in place. Initially there was talk of establishing a separate ministry for the successor states, on the lines of the old British Colonial Office, but this would have made the other states suspicious. Even if knowledge of neighbouring states was superficial, the Russian Ministry of Foreign Affairs (RMFA) was able to hire specialists from the Institute of Ethnology and Anthropology and from the former CPSU Central Committee sub-department on nationality affairs. When it was decided that FSU affairs would be handled by a department within the RMFA rather than by a separate body, the RFMA simply took over the Soviet Ministry of Foreign Affairs, including its buildings and most of its personnel, who were mainly Russian. It also laid claim to Soviet embassies around the world.

Section II: Russia's redefinition of its interests

Despite the initial framework, however, foreign-policy making institutions in Russia became nebulous when the Presidential Council and the Russian Ministry of Defence and Security Services became involved. The President plays an influential role in foreign policy formation. Moreover, interests came to not reflect institutions. In many ways, this is indicative both of the creation of Russian foreign policy and the analysis of this. Interests are mainly expressed by individuals and foreign policy-making institutions. The views of a leading individual do not always reflect that of his/her institution. Institutional checks and balances are still too weak to absorb the statements and changes of personalities. Nor do individuals in one institution necessarily share the same viewpoint. Moreover, the original intentions of individuals/institutions are often not implemented. In short, it is important to note that these emerging parameters are official trends taking shape within the official establishment of Russian foreign policy. The non-official positions may be similar or deviate from these official trends but they usually find some common ground within the official lines.

The first eighteen months after Soviet dissolution were characterised by a wide-ranging debate over the fundamental direction of Russia's policies in all areas, including economic reforms, what political structures should be established, and Russia's interests in the international arena. This period saw the triumph of the 'Atlanticist' school of thought. Represented primarily by Andrei Kozyrev and some of his younger advisers in the Foreign Ministry, it was backed in the Cabinet by powerful personalities such as Yegor Gaydar (until his removal), and enjoyed the overall support of Boris Yeltsin. Differing scarcely from the foreign policy practised under Mikhail Gorbachev and Eduard

Shevardnadze between 1987 and 1991, it concentrated on relations with the West. A key element was pragmatism: economic interests were no longer served by military confrontation. Paul Goble views this shift as Russia confronting its greatest challenge, namely 'the shift from mission to interests', from a vision that is 'grand, systematic and redolent of being the proper task of a great power and thus starkly in contrast to the grubby and petty questions of interest' (Goble, 1994, p. 43). The result was an increasing Soviet disengagement from the Third World that, by late 1991, had resulted in a virtual renunciation of earlier Soviet commitments to radical client states and movements - as in Afghanistan, Cuba, and Cambodia - and a substantial reduction in overall Soviet involvement in the developing world. The aim became adhesion to the Western club, 'a specialised civilised club' - characterised by the G7 meeting, adhering to the principles of the UN Charter, the Helsinki declarations (CSCE Charter), and the Paris Charter on human rights. As Kozyrev summarised: 'The most important function of Russian foreign policy is to create an international environment/relations that will enable Russia to become a 'democratic, market oriented, civilized nation' (Mesbahi, 1993, p. 182).

Arms control and foreign aid were the linchpin of relations with the West. On both accounts, Russia became disillusioned. The former was more a function of the process itself, the latter more directly a result of unfulfilled Western promises (and exaggerated Russian expectations) (Light, 1994, p. 68).

Arms control negotiations proved enormously complex since, once the USSR had disintegrated, agreements had to suit not just Russia, but also the other states that they would affect. When the then US President George Bush and the Russian President Boris Yeltsin announced in June 1992 START II proposals, they could only come into effect once reductions agreed in START I had been completed; Ukraine was then reluctant to ratify START I without security guarantees from the West and Russia.[1] START II was signed in January 1993. Dividing the force and weapons levels agreed in the treaty on Conventional Forces in Europe (CFE) negotiated by the USSR was equally complex, and the costs of dismantlement were also prohibitive. By the end of 1992 the closest the West came to cooperation was an extension of membership to all the former Soviet states of the NACC (North Atlantic Co-operation Council).[2] The 'Partnership for Peace' proposals began only in 1994, and in December of that year Russia declined to join. Concerning economic aid, Russia, after all, seemed to have travelled furthest down the road of economic reform; nevertheless, pledges were frequently made at times of domestic crises, and far more aid was promised than delivered - even if this was in part due to Yeltsin's failure to implement agreed-on policies.

By the close of 1992, this disappointment was reflected in a growing divergence of Russian and Western foreign policies in the 'far abroad', Kozyrev reminding the West of Russia's 'special interests, different from Western interests and at times even competing'. One example were conflicting attitudes over Serbia and Bosnia/Herzegovina, and US and Russian interests with regard to potential arms sales. Yeltsin and the Russian government were under increasing attacks between the summer of 1992 and early 1993 from parliament under Ruslan Khasbulatov and from the State Security Council under Iurii Skokov. The growing consensus was borne out in 1993 by the adoption, after months of strenuous debate, of the Russian foreign policy concept in the spring of 1993 and the Russian military doctrine in the autumn of 1993. The final submission of the draft to Parliament in March 1993 was symbolically accompanied by a change in the structure of foreign policy formation, with responsibilities handed over from the Russian Ministry of Foreign Affairs to Parliament. Parliament threatened to strip the ministry of responsibility for relations with the 'near abroad' by creating a separate ministry for CIS affairs (Kanet, 1993, p. 12). Khasbulatov, Skokov and Alexander Rutskoy, together with influential groups such as the Civic Union and the army, and eventually Boris Yeltsin, coalesced their thoughts into the 'Neo-Eurasianist' school of thought.

The main thrust of this new direction was that Russian interests extended beyond the West; the priority was closest to home. In the 'far abroad', Russia needed to build relations with major global and regional states, in particular with Germany, Turkey, Iran, China and Japan (Arbatov, 1993, p. 29). Next came relations with the United States of America. In Europe, Russia would not wish to join Western institutions, but is keen to prevent East/Central Europe from doing so. Thereafter came global security interests, perceived as Russia's position as a permanent member of the UN Security Council, its role in international organisations, Russia's status as inheritor of the Soviet nuclear legacy, its commitments under arms control treaties, and Moscow's obligations to participate in peace-keeping operations according to UN resolutions (Arbatov, 1993, p. 31). However, under the new consensus, it was Russia's relations with the 'near abroad' that were given top priority.

The reasons behind this reversion in policy are evident from the above. Twenty-five million ethnic Russians live in these neighbouring states, and as such are a powerful political force to be reckoned with in policy formation. The bordering states are in upheaval, and, self-perceived as the 'continuer state', Russia feels legitimised to intervene. It is also eager for other nations not to intervene in its place. In December 1992 Marshal Evgenii Shaposhnikov, former commander-in-chief of the CIS Joint Armed Forces, said that 'Turkey, Iran and especially the U.S. are among those most actively poised to act' (Kanet, 1993, p. 7). The view has become widespread among Russian political elites - even those around Yeltsin and Kozyrev - that the bloodshed in 'lands which simply cannot qualify as "foreign territories" must be halted, even if that means direct use of Russian military force' (Kanet, 1993, p. 7).

This consensus is based on two major premises: that, as a 'great power', Russia deserves a special status; and that Russia fails to accept the full logical implications of a recognition of the new borders (e.g. non-intervention). The 'great power' status of Russia is a particularly sensitive part of the nation's redefinition. 'No idea is more central in Russian history than that Russia cannot be measured in the same way as other states, that Russia has a special mission in the world and a new word by which to describe it' (Goble, 1994, p. 42). Yeltsin, commemorating Victory Day and the departure of foreign troops from

Berlin stated: 'Russia won the war, hence it deserves a special status in Europe and elsewhere.' In his arguments for Russia becoming 'the eighth member of the G-7 forum', he stated that as 'Russia is a big country, a superpower', it has the moral right to take part in the tackling of international issues (Lepingwell, 1994, p. 6). Samuel P. Huntington suggests that the 'clash of civilisations will dominate global politics', and Russia, strategically situated between Europe and Asia and embodying this duality within its own borders, is as such the 'globally most important torn country' (Goble, 1994, p. 43).

The difficulty experienced in recognising borders is now a persistent leitmotif in Russian foreign policy thinking. Although the successor states declared independence, Russia will not accept present demarcations. After all, Russia has no historical precedent as a nation-state, the multilateral federation having been invented in 1922. The process of disentanglement is further exacerbated by the fact that the landmass is contiguous. In an interview in July 1994, Foreign Minister Kozyrev stated that in 'a sense there is some coincidence (between the interests in Russia today and the interests of the Soviet Union) owing to the simple fact that we do not have borders other than the former Soviet borders. This is due to the simple fact that those borders that are now emerging - which you could call the borders between the newly created independent states - were never defined as interstate borders. They are administrative lines between republics in an overcentralised country. It would cost billions and billions of dollars to delimit and demarcate those borders according to international law' (Raphael, Rosett and Crow, 1994, p. 38).

Section III: Russia's actions in the near abroad

To assess the impact of this shift, the form adopted by Russian foreign policy in the 'near abroad' needs to be analysed. Three types of intervention have occurred to date: bilateral, CIS, and international. Equally, if not more, significant are ways in which intervention has not occurred.

The most significant example of bilateral intervention is Moldova. When the USSR disintegrated, the area east of the Dniester river ('Transdnestria'), dominated by ethnic Russians, declared itself independent, fearing that Romanian-speaking Moldova intended to unite with Romania. Fighting broke out between the central Moldovan authorities and separatist forces. After several weeks the foreign ministers of Moldova, Romania, Russia and Ukraine managed to negotiate a ceasefire, in April 1992, but it soon broke down. When the fighting resumed Russian arms were used by the Transdnestrians and soldiers from the 14th Russian army stationed in that area were accused of fighting with them. In June 1992 another ceasefire was negotiated. Although 10 members of the CIS agreed to deploy a joint peace-keeping force in Moldova, the troops which eventually arrived were Russian rather than CIS forces. They managed to keep a fragile peace and a political solution to the dispute looked more likely following the defeat of the nationalist parties in the March 1994 elections. While at times the local military leaders seemed to be acting independently of Yeltsin, it now appears likely that Moldova will be forced to allow permanent bases to the Russian military as part of the solution to the Transdniestrian problem.

Russian troops, together with Georgian and South Ossetian troops, were also keeping the peace in South Ossetia, an autonomous area within Georgia, where conflict smouldered for two years when the Georgian Government ended South Ossetia's autonomy and South Ossetians opted for independence from Georgia and unification with North Ossetia (an Autonomous Republic within the Russian Federation). Here, however, there seemed to have been little effort to find a political solution to the conflict.

Russian policy in Abkhazia, the second ethnic conflict that rent Georgia, was more ambiguous than in South Ossetia. Kozyrev stated that 'we have no alternative to engagement in Abkhazia. And Georgia and Abkhazia have no alternatives to it themselves. That is why they are asking us to intervene' (Raphael, Rosett and Crow, 1994, p. 39).

Throughout 1992 and 1993 Georgia accused Russian troops of participating in the conflict in support of Abkhazia. Russia has shown a revived political will to reassert itself since the entry of Georgian forces into Abkhazia in August 1992. The Russian Army gave covert help to the Abkhazh, while Defence Minister General Pavel Grachev openly talked of the need for Russia to re-establish its presence on the Black Sea (Abkhazia has a long Black-Sea coastline with at least one good port). Under threat of economic sanctions from Russia, a ceasefire was finally negotiated in July 1993, under the terms of which the Georgian leader, Eduard Shevardnadze agreed to withdraw his troops from the area and both sides agreed to withdraw heavy weaponry.

The second form of intervention has been with the assistance of CIS forces. The CIS has been the principal means of restoring Russian influence in Central Asia. In May 1992, at the Bishkek summit of the CIS, four of the five states, together with Russia and Armenia, signed the CIS security treaty. Turkmenistan did not sign, but made a separate bilateral agreement with Russia. While the Central Asian states have their own armies, they are reliant on Russian officers to run their militaries and the Russian army for protection of the CIS border with the outside world. Particularly incisive was the case of Tajikistan, where the Russian army is guarding the Afghan-Tajik border. After some hesitation, the Russian army appeared to support the Tajik popular front, a communist-dominated group. In July 1993, an attack by Tajik rebels on a Russian post on the Tajik-Afghan frontier led to a major reinforcement of the Russian border troops. While Moscow liberals warned that Russia was in danger of being drawn into another 'quagmire' comparable to the war in Afghanistan, Russian soldiers and diplomats proclaimed that the Tajik border was Russia's border. The main justification for continuing Russian military presence in Central Asia have been Russian fears of 'Islamic fundamentalism' spreading from Iran and Afghanistan via Central Asia to the Muslim peoples of the Russian North Caucusus and the Volga regions.

The third form of intervention is in collaboration with outside states. For example, Russia has been involved with the CSCE in the conflict between Armenia and Azerbaijan over the issue of Nagorno-Karabakh, where Moscow was keen to facilitate a ceasefire.

In other cases Russia has not intervened. Moscow in 1994 did not use the Crimea or debt as a means to undermine the Ukraine; after all, re-absorbing Ukraine is likely to be a high priority of any neo-imperialist dreams. Nevertheless, relations with this nuclear power have been clouded by disputes over the division of the Soviet armed forces, particularly over nuclear weapons and over the Black Sea fleet. The problem of the Crimea is still more serious. Following the serious decline of the Ukrainian economy, the Russian majority in the Crimea now appears to favour independence from the Ukraine, or even union with Russia. The Russian government has so far maintained its respect for Ukraine's territorial integrity.

Kazakhstan also occupies a place of priority on the Russian agenda. It is an area of vital Russian interest for ethnic, economic and security reasons. Some speculate that the North may secede and integrate into the Russian Federation. Russia and Kazakhstan have common security concerns, of which the greatest are the fear of China and the spread of nationalism and Muslim fundamentalism. The destabilisation of Kazakhstan might invite China's expansion and precipitate a conflict between Russia and China, in circumstances most unfavourable for Moscow.

Moreover, Moscow usually accepts that the Baltic Republics are independent in a way that Kazakhstan, for example, is not. Russia reluctantly agreed to withdraw its troops from all these states and seems intent on using economic and diplomatic pressure. Lithuania has secured the withdrawal of Russian forces based there, but the question of access for the Russian army to Kaliningrad is still unresolved. Russian generals have linked the withdrawal of Russian forces from Estonia and Latvia to the rights of Russians, and especially ex-servicemen, living there.

Conclusion

Since 1993 Yeltsin and Kozyrev have mounted a campaign to gain world recognition for Russia's special role in conflict-resolution. It is also taking a much more assertive position over the issue of minority rights and in many Republics the situation has still to be played out.

On the one hand, foreign observers and policy-makers should not be alarmed by this assertion of an independent stance. It is not simply the response by an enfeebled Russian President to an internal political threat, but rather to a deeper process of redefinition and 'rebirth' as Russia discovers its own national interests, dignity, and independent role in regional and global affairs. Moreover, the West itself did not intervene. It has not offered explicit security guarantees against future Russian expansionism. Nor did the West respond to Russian suggestions for UN assistance and auspices in fulfilling peace-keeping missions in the FSU.

On the other hand, Russia persists in failing to come to terms with the inviolability of borders and intervenes in what it continues to regard as domestic affairs. Events have shown that this intervention was not always solicited, and has also often exacerbated rather than reduced conflict. An essential principle of international peace-keeping operations is the neutrality of the peace-keepers. Russian peace-keepers in the conflicts in the FSU, by contrast, were frequently accused of 'taking sides' and the distinction between armed intervention and sending in forces to keep warring sides apart sometimes seemed blurred. Such policies have immediate reverberations for domestic politics: the national-democratic camp is able to feed its extreme-right nationalist dogma into this increased interventionism. Consequently, what was initially perceived as being in Russia's interests has not materialised as such.

Internal political and economic trends speak of conflicting tendencies for future intervention. Politically, a more interventionist policy is likely.

The May 1993 Referendum called for a much more assertive foreign policy in protecting Russian minorities and in forcing Ukraine, Belarus and Kazakhstan to turn over their nuclear weapons. The Liberal Democratic Party in the December 1993 elections raised understandable fears, in Russia's neighbours and the West, of the danger of an aggressive Russian imperialism. While support for Zhirinvosky may well have now peaked, the December 1993 elections showed the continuing strength of nationalist and Communist feelings among the voters. Yeltsin's New Year Message of January 1994 declared that the former republics had learned that they needed to live together, while even Vladimir Shumeiko, a leading member of the radical 'Russia's Choice' bloc, called in April 1994 for a new Union. However, economic frailty may hinder implementation of these political goals. Not least, it is unclear whether the Army will have sufficient resources for simultaneous operations in Tajikistan, Georgia, Moldova, and, potentially, Nagorno-Karabakh.

Russia will continue to exert an indispensable role in the region. As the dominant economic and political regional force, it is difficult to see how Russia's influence is likely to diminish in the short- to medium-term. New alliances offering security guarantees are likely to emerge. Discussions have already taken place concerning the establishment of a common security system for Eastern Europe that would include the former western republics of the USSR. It is clear that increasing multilateral intervention should be encouraged - on the basis of the UN, CSCE, or CIS.

History looms: the region has been part of Russia for most of the time since it was conquered in the eighteenth century. It has attained independence since then only for short periods, when Russia has been weakened. A well-organised provocation might make it impossible for Yeltsin or a future, more imperially-minded, leader to avoid pressure to send in Russian forces again. Nevertheless, in the words of Peter Duncan, 'it is essential to recognize Russia's desire to be treated with respect, as a great power with its own interests and the capacity to contribute to the world community' (Duncan, 1994, p. 10).

Notes

1. START II pledged that by the year 2003 Russia and the USA would cut their nuclear arsenals to 3,000 - 3,500 warheads each, a reduction of two-thirds of their current level; both sides agreed to eliminate all

multiple warheads, while Russia undertook to get rid of all its heavy land-based intercontinental missiles and the USA to reduce the number of nuclear warheads on submarines to 1,750, a reduction of 50%.

2. This was initially established to allay the security fears of central European and Balkan states.

Bibliography

Adams, J. S. (1994), 'Who Will Make Russia's Foreign Policy in 1994?', *RFE/RL Research Report*, 11 February

Arbatov, A. G. (1993), 'Russian Foreign Policy Priorities for the 1990s', in Johnson, T. P. and Miller, S. E. (eds), *Russian Security After the Cold War, Seven Views from Moscow*, CSIA Studies in International Security No.3, Brassey's

Blackwill, R. D. Blackwill and Karaganov, S. A. (eds), (1994), *Damage Limitation or Crisis? Russia and the Outside World*, Brassey's, Cambridge

Crow, S., (1993), 'Russia Asserts Its Strategic Agenda', *RFE/RL Research Report*, Vol.2, No.50, 17 December

Dawisha, K. and Parrott, B. (1994), *Russia and the New States of Eurasia: The Politics of Upheaval*, Cambridge University Press

de Nevers, R. (1994), 'Russia's Strategic Renovation', *Adelphi Paper*, No. 289

Duncan, P. J. S. (1994), 'Russian Neo-Imperialism: Fact or Fiction?', Submission to the House of Commons Defence Committee, 12 May

Duncan, P. J. S. (1993), 'Russia's Relations with the Newly-Independent Republics of Central Asia', *The Oxford International Review* 5.1

Foye, S. (1993), 'End of CIS Command Heralds New Russian Defence Policy?', *RFE/RL Research Report* 2.27

Goble, P. A. (1994), 'Russia as a Eurasian Power: Moscow and the Post-Soviet Successor States', in Sestanovich, S. (ed.), *Rethinking Russia's National Interests*, Vol. XVI.1, Center for Strategic and International Studies, Washington D.C.

Hauner, M. (1992), *What is Asia to Us? Russia's Asian Heartland Yesterday and Today*, Routledge, London

Hauner, M. (1989), 'Central Asian Geopolitics in the Last Hundred Years: A Critical Survey from Gorchakov to Gorbachev', *Central Asian Survey* 8.1

Huntington, S. P. (1993), 'The Clash of Civilizations?', *Foreign Affairs,* Summer

Kanet, R. E. (1993), 'Coping with Conflict: The Role of the Russian Federation, Program in Arms Control, Disarmament, and International Security', *ACDIS Occasional Paper,* University of Illinois, October

Karp, R. C. (ed.) (1993), *Central and Eastern Europe: The Challenge of Transition,* Oxford University Press, Oxford

Lepingwell, J. W. R. (1994), 'The Soviet Legacy and Russian Foreign Policy', *RFE/RL Research Report* 3.23

Lepingwell, J. W. R., Rahr, A., Teague, E. and Tolz, V. (1994), 'Russia: A Troubled Future', *RFE/RL Research Report* 3.24

Light, M. (1994), 'International Relations of Russia and the Commonwealth of Independent States', in *Eastern Europe and the Commonwealth of Independent States 1994,* 2nd edn., Europa Publications, London

Mesbahi, M. (1993), 'Russian foreign policy and security in Central Asia and the Caucusus', *Central Asian Survey* 12.2

Rahr, A. (1992), '"Atlanticists" versus "Eurasians" in Russian Foreign Policy', *RFE/RL Research Report* 1.22

Rahr, A. (1993), 'The First Year of Russian Independence', *RFE/RL Research Report* 2.1

Rahr, A. (1994), 'Russia's Future: With or without Yeltsin', *RFE/RL Research Report* 3.17

Raphael, T., Rosett, C. and Crow, S. (1994), 'An Interview with Russian Foreign Minister Andrei Kozyrev', *RFE/RL Research Report* 3.28

Simes, D. (1994), 'The Return of Russian History', *Foreign Affairs* 73.1

Shlapentokh, D. (1994), 'The End of the Russian State and its Geopolitical Implications', *The Round Table* 330

Slater, W. (1994), 'The Diminishing Center of Russian Parliamentary Politics', *RFE/RL Research Report* 3.7

White, S., Gill, G. and Slider, D. (1993), *The Politics of Transition: Shaping a Post-Soviet Future,* Cambridge University Press

4 The problems of Russian security in Central Asia: late Cold War experiences in the post-Cold War world

CHRISTOPHER WYATT

Introduction

My aim here is to draw several parallels between the late Cold War experience of the USSR and the post-Cold War experience of Russia. Both states have much in common. The Soviet Union was disturbed by the destabilising influences of a resurgence of both Islamic self-realisation and Islamic militancy within Central Asia and, although the Soviet Union is no more, Russia still has foreign policy interests in the region. These are threefold: the first of these is to protect the lives and property of the ethnic Russians still living in Central Asia. The second is to protect the economic investment Russia has in the region, especially concerning oil and minerals. The final foreign policy consideration is the prevention of the spread of both Islamic self-realisation and Islamic militancy into those parts of the Russia which are Muslim. If these semi-autonomous republics, such as Tatarstan, Bashkiria, or Daghistan, break away from the Federation, there will be a strong case for regions such as Yakutia to secede. This would mean the loss of great natural resources to Moscow. Consequently, for the implementation of these foreign policy aims, a two-tier strategy has evolved. The first tier consists of the frontline states of Tajikistan, Uzbekistan, and Turkmenistan. The second tier is the construction of a democratic, secular bulwark in the shape of Kazakhstan.

The Afghanistan experience contained a lesson that the Soviet Union did not learn. As Islamic awareness spreads, attempts to meet it with conventional force will not succeed. The reason for this is that the peoples of Afghanistan and Central Asia, living in a post-Cold War and a post-colonial present, will not be separated from their cultural heritage. Over the last 70 years Islam has been ever present, yet hidden, in Soviet Central Asia. It is unsurprising that it has exhibited itself more visibly after such a long period of repression. The failure of exactly this type of repression in Afghanistan contributed greatly to Soviet difficulties in the latter days of the USSR. With the collapse of the Soviet Union, a new relationship with the states of Central Asia was called for. The fall of the Najibullah Government in Afghanistan only made the need for such a new relationship even more pressing.

I shall first discuss the problem of the Soviet Military intervention in Afghanistan, arguing that the rationale for such intervention was primarily defensive, rather than an attempt to seize a 'warm-water' port in the Persian Gulf. The Soviet Government clearly did not wish to have a series of Islamic states on their Southern border, and when the Taraki administration seemed on the verge of collapse intervention became necessary to prevent Afghanistan coming under the influence of Iranian, and other, anti-Soviet forces. Such a policy was also mirrored in Soviet Central Asia, where attempts were made to discourage Islamic teaching and religious practices. However, Soviet military and political failings in Afghanistan, followed by withdrawal, meant that Central Asia could not be governed as it had been before. With the decline of Soviet influence in the region, the possibility of an active, 'forward', defence disappeared. This was frustrating for an army which was trained for offensive actions.

Once the states of Central Asia became independent it became necessary for them to rely upon Russian military and economic assistance. Russia, a new state, was pushed back from its former Soviet frontier to the Russo-Kazak border. Yet it still had to be involved in Central Asia, to protect its people and interests abroad and to defend - through forward means - the territorial integrity of the Federation. There is, however, one major difference between the old involvement in Afghanistan and the new one in Central Asia. Where the Soviet Union could leave Afghanistan relatively quickly, the Russians cannot do the same in Central Asia. There are 25 million Russians outside the Federation and it will not be able to leave their own people behind. An evacuation of all the Russians in Central Asia would be an immense task and it could not be done particularly rapidly, if at all. Such a difficult position for Russia, as well as the states of Central Asia, will have to be dealt with using some sensitivity and responsibility.

The Afghanistan experience

Analysis of Soviet aims concerning their involvement in Afghanistan and Central Asia falls into two schools. The first of these is the 'opportunistic' view, which argues that Soviet aims in the region were responses against 'targets of opportunity'. The second school is the 'defensive' view. This holds that the USSR was 'a frail, slightly paranoid, and extremely cautious power'. The defensive school argues that Soviet aims in Afghanistan were motivated by the perceived threat posed by Islam to the Muslim population of the USSR. The Soviet need to intervene in Afghanistan was compounded by the Iranian Revolution. Soviet fears were also exacerbated by the demographic increase in the Muslim populations of Central Asia, compared with those of the rest of the country (Atkin, 1989, Forward).

   For the Soviet invasion of Afghanistan, this chapter will argue that the defensive theory better suits the facts available than does the opportunistic school. With a rising Islamic population in Central Asia, it became crucial to prevent Muslim influences coming into the USSR. In Afghanistan, the Communist Government of Taraki became weakened by a loss of public support. It seems that the Government might have fallen then, but the Soviet Union sent in advisors to assist Taraki to control the countryside and cities. It appears that the Soviet Union would have been content with such a move, until three events occurred which dangerously threatened the stability of the situation. These were the riots at the ethnic Iranian Afghan city of Herat, the Iranian Revolution, and the Afghan intra-Khalq coup which brought Hafizullah Amin to power. The rise of Iranian religious fervour in 1978 and 1979 had spread to Herat. The local population protested against the Communist Government and the presence of Soviet advisors. Instability had, therefore, spread in 1979 to engulf Iran, then in the throes of its Islamic Revolution, and to those ethnic Iranian areas inside Afghanistan. Protest in Herat also gained influence due to the religious standing of that city. These protests quickly spread throughout the countryside, leaving Amin holding tenuous control of the cities. This same control was also in danger of collapsing as Amin continued to carry out repressive policies, which were resented by the people. It was in this atmosphere that Amin requested more Soviet troops to be sent to protect his Government. At the same time it was decided to replace Amin as head of the Communist People's Democratic Party of Afghanistan (PDPA) Government. For some time the Soviets had become disillusioned with the Khalq faction of the Afghan Communist Party and had decided to replace them with the Parcham faction. Both Babrak Karmal and Dr Najibullah were members of this faction. Hafizullah Amin was removed when an attempted coup failed and Soviet airborne commandos were brought in to remove him on the night of 27 December 1979. Despite stiff resistance from the crack Afghan 4th Armoured Corps, the Soviet commandos fought through to Amin's headquarters, where a KGB team battled it out with Afghan bodyguards. Eventually Amin was cornered and died in the gun battle. While this was happening, Russian tanks were crossing the Amu Darya and the invasion proper began. The Parcham leader, Babrak Karmal, was brought in to head the new Government of the PDPA (Arney, 1990, pp. 97-114).

With this action, the USSR had invaded Afghanistan and installed a quiescent client regime. Soviet measures similar to those taken in Central Asia were taken in Afghanistan to try to stamp out the influence of Islam. A. Rasul Amin provides an insight into this process. Afghan history was 'reconsidered', along with politics, religion, sociology, and culture, in the light of Marxist-Leninist philosophy. The main purpose of this was to gain 'converts to communism' and to provide 'disinformation about the war'. Within the Afghan state, Soviet aims were centred around providing: 'increased fragmentation, atomization, alienation, and ultimate social disintegration under centralized Soviet domination.': in other words, a policy of *divide et impera*. This quality of Soviet control exhibited itself in the establishment of closer ties with groups such as Uzbeks and Tajiks, who were ethnically akin to their neighbours in Soviet Central Asia. After the invasion, the threat to the Afghan regime was externalised and was labelled 'imperialist aggressors of the West'. The USSR, in contrast, was referred to as 'our old faithful friend', a term qualified with such epithets as 'generous', 'valiant', and 'fraternal'. In order to justify their actions the Soviets and Parchami faction labelled Hafizullah Amin as a CIA agent, at the same time taking credit for saving the Afghan nation from the enemies of socialism. This message was disseminated in every manner possible. With the past rewritten, measures were employed to increase literacy among the young. This would drive a wedge between them and their illiterate kinsmen and provide a youth imbued with a Soviet view of the world (Amin, 1987, pp. 301-6).

Similar measures were taken to reduce the role and power of Islam in the lives of the Afghan people. Islam, in whatever form practised, was a factor which united the Afghan people against the new PDPA regime. The Afghan Communists had launched 'a virulent campaign against religion' which 'denounced' and 'mocked' Islam as 'outmoded superstition' and which sought to replace it with 'scientific Marxism'. In the campaign religious leaders were 'arrested, imprisoned, tortured, and killed', 'Village mosques were defiled', and 'Korans destroyed'. This turned these devout Muslims against the Khalqi regime and sought to blame the worst excesses of the campaign on Hafizullah Amin. The newly-installed

Parchami Government now adopted a more subtle approach. This was to harness Islam as a means of controlling the country, a method which was practised in Soviet Central Asia. The Soviet model for this stressed a 'Godless Islam' which emphasised passivity and cooperation with the Soviet Government. Under the Parchami regime Babrak Karmal instituted a Department of Islamic Affairs which was placed under the control of the Khad secret police. This was then tied to the Muslim Board of Central Asia and Kazakhstan in Tashkent, which was headed by Siyanuddin Babakhanov. Karmal then proclaimed that:

'It is the sacred obligation of every Muslim Afghan to support the government.... misguided elements hired by bloodthirsty American imperialism exploit Islam against Islamic principles.... these murderers and terrorists are ignorant of God's commandments.... [The Mujahideen] are not Muslim and every true Muslim must strongly condemn them.'

At the same time the Government seized full control of the finances for mosques, thus 'destroying the autonomy of mullahs and religious leaders'. This 'made them totally dependent on the regime, subject to direct control and manipulation'. The Parchami leaders, Karmal and Najibullah, were also regularly photographed in mosques in order to counter their reputations as Godless atheists (Amin, 1987, pp. 307-10).

The Parchami regime also undertook other measures to ensure their control of the country. They seized the previously free press, ensuring that they were 'totally controlled' by the state. This control and censorship extended into the realm of film-making and the regime embarked upon the 'production of a number of documentary films relating to the revolutionary transformation in Afghanistan'. The Government also began to control education, turning Afghan schools into 'agencies of Sovietisation'. School textbooks were also Sovietised, all of them containing the same preface:

'Dear Children:
Your revolutionary regime has firmly resolved to bring deeprooted change in the infrastructure of your society. The education and training of the younger generation is the first goal of your democratic regime whose Party leadership has already laid the foundation of a new progressive education system that will help to train the "new man".'

In 1985 teachers of all subjects were 'duty-bound to lecture classes about Afghan-Soviet friendship, the Soviet system, and the "fruitful endeavour" of the PDPA'. In order to press the message during the students' free time, student organisations were established. At the age of ten, students joined the Pioneers and, at fifteen, the Democratic Youth Organisation of Afghanistan. In the universities new subjects were introduced which would further Sovietise Afghan youth: Historical Materialism, The Revolutionary History of Workers, The History of Russia, The New History of Afghanistan, Dialectical Materialism, Scientific Sociology, and The History of World Literature. This latter course covered the writings of Marx, Lenin, and Fidel Castro. Moreover, 'the Faculty of Theology was eliminated' (Amin, 1987, pp. 311-21).

The Parchami Government also established its control over the Afghan people in other ways. It was just as necessary to reach out to the old as well as to the young, so new literacy campaigns were established to re-educate adults. In the drive to re-educate, adults were 'subjected to systematic propagandising manipulation and Marxist instruction in structured classes'. When adults did learn to read, the only 'materials available to them are [were] totally-controlled Marxist propaganda'. In addition, Afghans were sent to the USSR for indoctrination on exchanges, to go to school, or for holidays. The inhabitants of Soviet Central Asia, such as Uzbeks, were also encouraged to keep their 'brothers in Northern Afghanistan informed about the greatest material and cultural achievements of the Central Asian peoples under Communism'. They were also exhorted to 'extend help to our backward brothers on the other side of the Oxus to enrich and develop their primitive literature and culture'. Finally, Afghans were kept in check by the secret police, which had 'formed extensive networks of spies and informers' (Amin, 1987, pp. 322-30).

The measures that were employed by the Parchami Government were based upon practices which had been implemented in Soviet Central Asia. In 1927 Stalin was displeased with the progress in Sovietising Central Asia. In order to speed this process up a programme was devised which bears an amazing likeness to the measures taken in Afghanistan. The first measure was to induct natives into new agitation and propaganda, or 'agitprop', cadres to spread Soviet doctrine. The second was to publish anti-religious propaganda in native languages, so as to give the people another vehicle to understand Soviet thinking. Third, new material was to be written. This was to be based in terms and discussing situations which were familiar to the people. The fourth measure was to teach people the role of religion within the phenomenon of class exploitation in Marxist terms. Fifth, the schools and the Komsomol, the Soviet youth organisation, were to teach atheism. The same function would have been carried out by the Democratic Youth Organisation of Afghanistan in the 1980s. Finally journals on anti-religious themes were to be distributed to the people of Central Asia. All these measures were carried out in Afghanistan under the PDPA regime (Keller, 1992, p. 40).

The Parchami Government also had the benefit of subsequent Soviet experience in the control of the Muslim populations. The evolution of a Soviet strategy for dealing with Islam was a slow one but, by the time of the Soviet invasion of Afghanistan, it had become apparent that Islam would not disappear overnight and that a scientific 'Godless' state-controlled Islamic structure would be a suitable temporary substitute, until such time as religion withered away as the notion of 'God' was replaced with Soviet Socialist Materialism. This vehicle for Sovietisation was also a key feature of the Parchami regime after the Khalqi excesses of 1978 and 1979. The control of Soviet Central Asia was made easier under these conditions. Soviet authority found a willing supporter in the person of Babakhanov, who lead the Muslim Spiritual

Board of Central Asia and Kazakhstan, which was seen as a 'force for reform'. Shirin Akiner sees Babakhanov as a 'compliant figure, a product par excellence of the "years of stagnation"'. (Akiner, 1993, pp. 22 and 23).

Such state control of religion was extensive, as Murial Atkin points out with regard to Tajikistan. Here, 'an estimated two thousand Muslim Mullahs enjoy state authorisation and function in officially sanctioned Islamic establishments'. Moreover, mosques, madrassas, and saints' tombs were preserved by the Soviet authorities and converted to 'tourist attractions, museums, or non-religious teaching centers'. What becomes most apparent from this is the way in which Islam was used in order to both legitimise the regime in power and Sovietise the country:

> 'The leaders of official Islam try to demonstrate that the irreligion is a harmonious component of Soviet life.... Given that many citizens continue to identify with Islam, the leadership prefers an interpretation of the religious teaching that accepts socialism and harmonizes with it.'

What the Soviet authorities disliked was the influence of Sufism, as those who preached it wandered throughout the countryside and were hard to keep under any form of control. In addition, the mystical element of Sufism, which makes it unique, was a factor which rendered the dissemination of Soviet official Islam more difficult (Atkin, 1989, pp. 16-24).

Another problem for the Soviet authorities was that of Islamic revivalism, which began to grow in Central Asia. This became especially strong in Uzbekistan and Tajikistan. In Uzbekistan, 'Communist Party countermeasures.... against revivalist groups were unsuccessful'. Soviet authorities became increasingly concerned, especially once it became apparent that this phenomenon was connected with events in Afghanistan: 'Since 1981 the volume of material in the Soviet Central Asian news media that has been devoted to the "Islamic problem" has grown enormously, strongly suggesting a stimulus provided by occurrences in Afghanistan and Iran.' The change and development of Soviet counter-measures against the problem of Islamic revivalism is clearly demonstrated by Alexandre Bennigsen:

'The character of anti-islamic literature has undergone a noticeable change since 1980. Before the Soviet invasion of Afghanistan, these publications stressed the anti-scientific nature of all religions (including, of course, Islam), the "archaic" nature of Muslim customs, and the contradictions between socialist and religious morals. Today these publications insist on the need to reorganize atheistic propaganda and education of the youth (the majority of anti-islamic publications are devoted to this particular topic) and on the absolute incompatibility of [unofficial] Islam and Marxism-Leninism.'

Other measures were also taken to prevent the spread of an Islamic creed which went against the official teachings of the Muslim Spiritual Board of Central Asia and Kazakhstan. The Komsomol central and district committees began to hold seminars on 'atheistic propaganda and atheistic education'. In addition, a new anti-Islamic institution was formed in Tashkent, termed the House of Scientific Atheism. Yet even the shortcomings of this organisation became clear. T.K. Dzhavliyev, head of the Surhan Darya district branch of the republican House of Scientific Atheism of the Uzbek SSR, stated that, 'There can be no harmless religious beliefs'. The threat of Islamic revivalism as a political movement was acknowledged to be an extremely dangerous one (Bennigsen, 1984, pp. 28-44).

The Islamic resurgence so feared by Dzhavliyev and so many others was to be further exacerbated by the failure of the Soviet forward policy in Afghanistan. The lack of success of Soviet military and political activities rendered any forward defence untenable. The chief failings of Soviet policy in Afghanistan fell into two main categories. These were the failure to win the war on the ground against the Mujahideen and the inability to win the 'hearts and minds' of the Afghan people.

The Soviet failure to win the war against the Mujahideen groups had its basis in their military doctrine. This was geared around having to fight in Europe. The work of former Soviet General Victor Suvorov is illuminating in this regard (Suvorov, 1982[1]). Soviet military thinking was directed against a confrontation in Europe, which the Red Army was expected to win by repeating the successes of the 'Great Patriotic War'. The influence of this war was the one dominating factor which led to a war machine that was both inflexible and had not learned from the advances in military strategy, tactics and thinking which had taken place since 1945. Edward Girardet encapsulates the issue well: 'It [the Soviet Army] proved to be a heavy, lumbering machine better suited to fighting in the lowlands of Europe than against a basically peasant population in the mountains and deserts of Afghanistan' (Girardet, 1985, pp. 30 and 31).

Western commentators are unanimous in the verdict that the Soviet Union was fighting the war in the wrong way. David Isby writes:

'Motorized rifle divisions are not the type of forces that gain victory in counter-insurgency warfare. In the words of Douglas Blaufarb and George Tanham, two veteran U.S. experts in the field, "the first principle of successful counter-guerrilla tactics is to take the guerrilla as the model and fight him in his own style.... This principle means the broad deployment of forces in small units relying largely on weapons they can carry".' (Isby, 1989, p. 59)

Oliver Roy stated that: 'The Soviet Army adopted conventional tactics, which in 1984 were hardly adaptable to the reality of guerrilla warfare'(Roy, 1989, p. 48). Anthony Arnold came to the same conclusion: 'So far it appears that the Soviet high command has not learned how to cope with classic guerrilla tactics.' (Arnold, 1985, pp. 98 and 99).

Consequently, the Soviet Army became aware that its approach was not working and decided to change its tactics. This involved the use of helicopter-borne troops in small groups. These soldiers were, according to Mujahideen sources, 'extremely brave' and were feared by the guerillas. The lesson was gradually being learned, but was not being applied in the most useful of ways. Command and control were not as coordinated as they should have been and officers on the ground were not able to take the initiative (Girardet, 1985, p. 41).

The Soviet Army was also beset by other problems, most notably the terrain upon which they were required to fight. Even equipped with maps, the Soviet troops did not know the ground anything like as well as the men who farmed the land and fought in the Mujahideen. It was, therefore, easy for them to ambush Soviet patrols and cut them off from their main lines of communication and supply. The Soviet Army also had logistical difficulties. In order to keep the troops fully supplied with food and ammunition, convoys had to be despatched through the narrow mountain passes. These were extremely vulnerable and many such convoys were attacked with serious losses:

'The Soviets still do not have full control of the supply routes. In spite of the fact that the Kabul/Sher Khan highway was patrolled and protected by the Soviets themselves. Within only two months, March and April 1981, the Mujahideen destroyed 80 tanks and 120 armoured vehicles on this strategic and most important supply route.'

What became clear was that the Soviet troops were not able to control the countryside (Safi, 1986, p. 110).

The Soviet Army also had to contend with the problem of Mujahideen cross-border attacks. Due to the repression of the PDPA regime many Afghans fled across the border to either Pakistan or to Iran. They then organised and armed themselves, with outside assistance from Wahabi Saudi Arabia, the Pakistani Military Intelligence Branch, The Iranian Revolutionary Government, the Americans, and the Chinese. In addition many foreign Muslim subjects went to join the Mujahideen, from countries like Egypt and Algeria. This money, arms, and organisation allowed the different Mujahideen groups to formulate an effective resistance to the occupation of their country. They then crossed the border, attacked the Soviet and Afghan troops, and returned. The Soviet troops were limited in the fact that they could not cross into Pakistan or Iran. Consequently the Mujahideen could only be engaged in Afghanistan and, even then, on territory which they knew better than the Russians. They, therefore, held the initiative (Girardet, 1985, pp. 37 and 39).

Attempts by the Soviets to deal with this problem with aerial interdiction also failed. The Afghanistan experience was to demonstrate brutally the limitations of aircraft in counter-insurgency warfare. Once the Mujahideen were armed with Stinger portable, disposable, surface-to-air missiles, they were able to keep the Soviet air forces at bay by forcing them to fly high. This greatly reduced accuracy when bombing targets and other interdictive measures. Moreover, the mountainous terrain of the Hindu Kush further restricted Soviet aerial efficacy (Safi, 1986, p. 109; Girardet, 1985, pp. 42 and 43).

One of the major problems faced by the Soviet forces was the unreliability of their own Central Asian troops. In February 1980 Central Asian units were being removed and replaced with Slav ones. Taras Kuzio reports on this matter and his findings deserve to be cited at length:

Central Asians have proved to be reluctant to fight in Afghanistan. The use of Central Asian troops was a failure, and by March 1980 most were either sent home or not used for combat purposes. Two Soviet deserters remembered when they were sent to Afghanistan in 1980, that there were 106 Tajiks in their unit: "They all refused to fight and they were sent home. A lot of Tajiks, Uzbeks and Turkmen were sent back. A few were shot on the spot but most were returned to the Soviet Union". An ethnic affinity with the Afghans, and common religion and dislike of Russians are given as reasons for refusing to fight and on some occasions defect to the guerrillas. A German journalist who travelled illegally inside Afghanistan in 1985 met a Tajik deserter fighting with the guerrillas. He complained of poor treatment inflicted upon Central Asians by Russian officers, who believed they sympathised with the Afghans. The Tajik said that the

[Central Asian] soldiers are "generally not inclined to fight".' (Kuzio, 1987, p. 113)

The same tensions were observed by a Soviet Estonian soldier who was serving in Afghanistan. He mentions Kazak dislike and resentment at Soviet exploitation of that country. Later in the same interview he characterises the resentment and anger of Central Asians in general as a 'blind rage' (Philips, 1986, p. 113). Soviet uncertainty regarding the loyalty and reliability of their own Central Asian troops also spread to the Afghan Army. These men were thought of as suspect. The Estonian soldier referred to them as 'old men and half-wits' (Philips, 1986, p. 106). The problem for Soviet troops was that Central Asian soldiers were suspect, Afghan soldiers even more so and, consequently, Slav soldiers were the only ones trusted to campaign in Afghanistan reliably. For the Afghan people the presence of the Slav invader must have brought back fears of the old Russian imperialism returning to Afghanistan under the guise of Sovietisation. If the Soviets were to win the war in Afghanistan, they would have to do so spectacularly and very rapidly. A protracted war would allow time for resentments to grow and for the people of Afghanistan and Soviet Central Asia to actively oppose Sovietisation. Losing such a protracted war in Afghanistan would have the same effect as losing the Russo-Japanese War in 1905 - it was a spur to Islamic resurgence in the region (Bennigsen, 1980, p. 47).

The failure of the USSR to win the information war was crucial. The attempts to win the population over by propaganda failed because it encroached upon their cultural and religious beliefs. The Red Army could not win the war in the passes. Yet the chief Soviet error lay in the direct alienation of the Afghan people. The Soviet Army was disliked by the Afghans, something the Estonian soldier freely admitted. Edward Girardet mentions 'barely disguised hatred' in connection with the same thing. He also states that:

'Afghan soldiers and civil servants who deserted from the government ranks have frequently spoken of Russian, as opposed to Central

Asian, disrespect and contempt towards them. The Russians, they say, have also adopted brusque, unfriendly and even racist attitudes.' (Philips, 1986, p. 104; Girardet, 1985, pp. 45-7)

The means the Soviet troops employed to fight the Mujahideen also alienated the people. Their use of chemical weapons against the guerillas provoked international outrage. Girardet recounts instances of the use of blistering agents and chemical irritants. The use of butterfly mines and booby-traps, such as dolls, toys, or cigarette packets, also alienated the Afghans. These were intended to maim, rather than kill, on the basis that it would be more difficult for the Mujahideen to travel with wounded men, women, and children. The Afghans did not understand the nature of the 'total war', in which innocent people suffer. Afghan farmers who saw their children maimed by these devices were likely to join the Mujahideen (Arnold, 1985, p. 99; Girardet, 1985, pp. 33 and 213). The violence perpetrated against the Afghans by the Soviets on the ground also inspired Afghan men to join the Mujahideen. The Estonian soldier stated that orders were given to troops to massacre inhabitants of villages. They were not allowed to take these orders with them, but were still under an obligation to obey them:

'The tactics used in the event of punitive operations were basically the same. When we entered a village, we had to shoot down all the people who were the slightest bit suspicious-looking. Generally speaking, all the men who were capable of combat were under suspicion.' (Philips, 1986, p. 110)

Naturally, there were many massacres of the type described, such as at Logar on 13 September 1982 (Gall, 1989, p. 2).

All such activities alienated the Afghan people who responded with resistance, both active and passive. The passive resistance included activities such as the shopkeepers' strike of February 1980 in Kabul and Herat. During the war this spread to Kandahar and other major towns (Khalilzad, 1980, p. 30). The physical resistance put up by the

Mujahideen eventually proved to be too much for the Soviet Army to endure. The war was not being won in Afghanistan and the Soviet public began to lose sympathy with its continued prosecution. The last Soviet troops left Afghanistan in February 1989, after the peace accords of the preceding year. The ignominious retreat of the Soviet Army was seen by Central Asians as proof that they could aspire to lead themselves. It would also be instrumental in the rise of the Muslim revivalist movement.

The decline of Soviet power in Central Asia

The invasion of Afghanistan was a point of no return for the Soviet Union. Once they had intervened it would become increasingly difficult for them to extricate themselves from the morass they had created. The Soviet Union had intervened reluctantly in Afghanistan, but their withdrawal would herald a period where the military deficiencies of the Red Army would become apparent to all. These weaknesses also extended into the political sphere. Once the peoples of Central Asia saw their Soviet overlords leave Afghanistan the opportunity for protest against the centre became a reality. The only outlet for tensions and protest lay in Islam. There was a dramatic rise in those practising Islam in Central Asia in the 1980s, despite the efforts of the state to dissuade people from doing so. After the withdrawal from Afghanistan Soviet defensive strategy became more defensive. This stance became dangerous, especially in the light of *glasnost* and *perestroika*. The peoples of Central Asia were beginning to see Islam as a vital part of their development, for example to be an Uzbek was also to be a Muslim (Broxup, 1987, p. 283). In this atmosphere, the Soviet Union could not survive as the centre was challenged on the periphery by new allegiances. The USSR became involved in Afghanistan in order to protect Soviet gains in that country. Taraki had pleaded throughout early 1979 for Soviet assistance in the form of troops, planes and tanks (Kornienko, 1994, p. 4). Later, Amin was also to request Soviet assistance in the same way (Kornienko, 1994, p. 5). What is apparent is that the Soviet Politburo was staunchly against any intervention at all. In the course of a telephone conversation between Taraki and Kosygin on 18 March 1979, Taraki repeatedly requests Soviet military assistance. Kosygin clearly did not wish to involve the Soviet Army in Afghanistan and refused to even consider Taraki's request that they could enter the country disguised as PDPA Government troops.[2] Two days later Kosygin carried the same line, stating that: 'Our common enemies are waiting eagerly for the moment when Soviet troops will appear on the territory of Afghanistan. It will give them a pretext to bring in hostile armed units to your country.'[3] On the same day Brezhnev argued the same case: 'We have considered this question [of sending Soviet troops to Afghanistan] very carefully and have come to the conclusion that it should not be done.'[4]

However, events changed with the coup of Hafizullah Amin and the unwillingness of Congress to ratify the SALT II treaty. Relations with the Americans were already at a low ebb and something had to be done in order to protect the new PDPA regime at Kabul (Kornienko, 1994, p. 8). By 6 December, the Politburo was openly discussing the possibility of sending a special detachment to Afghanistan.[5] Within three weeks the Red Army was crossing the Amu Darya River into Afghanistan. The intention was always to withdraw Soviet troops from Afghanistan as soon as the PDPA Government was able to stand up on its own:

'Three successive Afghan Governments pressed us to give assistance in defending that country from invasion from outside by forces of counter-revolution ... I [Brezhnev], wish to state this very definitely: we will be ready to commence withdrawing our troops as soon as all forms of outside interference directed against the government and people of Afghanistan fully cease.'[6]

The 'forces of counter-revolution' were the Islamic resistance movements to the Soviet invasion of Afghanistan that were trained by, and which operated from, Pakistan and Iran. The purpose of the invasion was to ensure the survival of the PDPA regime against Islamic forces. The Soviet contingent was to be there for only a short time. This explains why it was always subordinate to Turkestan Military District (*Independent*, 14 February 1989, p. 12; Girardet, 1985, p. 30). Once the PDPA regime was able to stand on its own the Soviet troops left. When the Soviet troops arrived in Afghanistan, the Khalq wing of the PDPA held a weak control over the country. When they left the Parchami Government of Dr. Najibullah was much more durable, as demonstrated by events at Jalalabad in 1989 (O'Ballance, 1993, pp. 199-202).

The Soviet withdrawal led to an awakening of both national and religious self-realisation among the peoples of Central Asia. T.H. Rigby states: 'Two recent developments in this area are clearly worrying Moscow. One is the rise of ethnic nationalism, which these people share with those in other non-Russian areas. ... The second is a certain resurgence of Islamic belief and practice.'(Rigby, 1990, p. 78) The two areas are clearly intertwined in Central Asia and in the Russian Federation, such as Daghistan and Tatarstan. Soviet power, in dealing with this twin threat, began to suffer from an inability to control the situation. Yuri Andropov, while head of the KGB, stated that Soviet control of the mountainous areas of the Caucasus 'did not exist at all' (Spolnikov, 1994, p. 109). How much more so would it not exist in the mountains of Tajikistan on the Afghan border? In such an atmosphere it is only natural that Islamisation and increased ethnic awareness will spread. Such a spread was greatly facilitated by Afghan Mujahideen activity in Central Asia. In 1984, 'Hezb-e-islami have claimed a membership of 3,000 inside Central Asia, and the distribution of leaflets in Tajikistan and Uzbekistan' (Kuzio, 1987, p. 113).

The traditionally tight control of Soviet Central Asia was significantly loosened with the advent of *perestroika*. As Victor Spolnikov put it, 'Islamic fundamentalism in Central Asia came to life with the disintegration of the unitary state system of the Soviet Union' (Spolnikov, 1994, pp. 108-11). This process of disintegration began with Gorbachev's reforms. Once the peoples of Central Asia had more freedom to express themselves, they had more latitude to find their identity after decades of Sovietisation. In such an atmosphere the demise of the Soviet Union would only be a matter of time.

The twin factors of Islam and national identity are 'inextricably mixed' in Central Asia as religion was seen 'as being part of national life'. Many Muslim practices were still observed in the Soviet Union, such as the Ramadan fast and religious marriage and burial. Even some members of the Komsomol acted in this fashion (Broxup, 1987, pp. 283-4). The foundations for Islamic and national self-awareness was already in place as Sovietisation never succeeded in stamping Islam out altogether. The problems this posed for the Soviet authorities is well encapsulated by the First Secretary of the Communist Party of Tajikistan, Makhkamov, in 1986:

'A part of the population, especially in rural areas, unquestioningly follows the prescriptions of Shariah. ... As a consequence the leaders of various sectarian trends have become more active. ... The level of religiosity of the population of our republic has noticeably increased. Numerous facts show that the anti-social activity of Muslim clerics is growing and that the education of children in Islamic dogma is increasing. Production and distribution of ideologically dangerous literature is growing. Also, more religious video films which are brought from abroad are being shown. The most reactionary members of the clergy are trying to revitalise nationalistic survivals and give new life to nefarious rites and customs. We are especially worried by the fact that a certain portion of our youth is attracted to religion.' (Broxup, 1987, pp. 287 and 288)

The authorities were also concerned to prevent the spread of Sufism over which the institution of Soviet Official Islam had no control. Surveys in Central Asia taken between 1973 and 1986 demonstrated a dramatic rise in those professing to be Muslim believers. It is clear that 'since the war in Afghanistan there has been a real and extraordinarily powerful religious revival'. This revival has become more politicised as it has evolved, especially in the light of Soviet attempts to check its spread in favour of its own official system. As Broxup states, such actions 'will only exacerbate the already existing xenophobia and stimulate a nationalism in which Islam will play a dominant role' (Broxup, 1987, pp. 288-92).

Independence and instability

The demise of the USSR was inevitable once these nationalist and religious tensions became the basis upon which new states could be formed. The old Soviet boundaries formed the new frontiers of the new states. These new states inherited several problems, which were the legacy of the Soviet system. Apart from economic, cultural, and political problems, large minorities were to be found in every Central Asian state (Akiner, 1993, Appendix 2, pp. 72 and 73). This has become a factor for tension between the Central Asian states themselves and between them and Russia. Russia as a power has shown itself to be deeply concerned about the rights, livelihoods, and security of Russians living in Central Asia.[7]

As the dominant power in the region, Russia has taken upon itself the mantle of the former Soviet Union. Many of its policy aims are similar to those of the old USSR, while some are new to it. Russia has three basic policy aims in the area. The first of these is to protect Russian national interests. This consists of protecting its economic interests and ensuring the security of the ethnic Russia Diaspora in Central Asia. Its second aim is to prevent the spread of Islamisation in Central Asia, which is seen as a factor for destabilisation. This comes as a particularly worrying development for Moscow as it regards the Southern borders as, in effect, its own. Russia relies upon the Central Asian states to keep the peace on the Southern tier of the former Soviet Union. Radical Islamic movements, trends, and resistance will disrupt the regimes trying to maintain control and stability in Central Asia, most notably Uzbekistan and Tajikistan. The final aim is to prevent national and religious self-awareness and activity spreading into the Russian Federation. One fundamental Russia aim that has been consistent from the time of the breakup of the Soviet Union has been the maintenance of the territorial integrity of the Federation (*Izvestia*, 4 August 1993, p. 4 in *The Current Digest of the Post-Soviet Press*, XLV.31, pp. 7 and 8)).

This situation has led to the emergence of a two-tiered 'buffer state' strategy. The two tiers are both differently defensive. The front tier is offensively defensive - an active, forward defence. The second tier is a passive bulwark - a defensive, relatively stable, and cooperative regime. The frontline states of the first tier are Uzbekistan and Tajikistan. Turkmenistan is relatively stable and seems unlikely to become too heavily involved (*Nezavisimaya Gazeta*, 21 January 1993, p. 5 in *The Current Digest of the Post-Soviet Press*, XLV.3, pp. 9-12).

Uzbekistan and Tajikistan have the problem of Islamic resurgence within their own borders. The more stable Kazakhstan forms the defensively defensive bulwark between the Southern Central Asian states and Russia's Southern border.

The Tajikistan situation is the most unstable in Central Asia. Russia's main aim here is to check the spread of Islamic 'oppositionists', as the Russian press calls the forces of the Islamic Revival Party, the Islamic Renaissance Party, and the Mujahideen elements supporting them (*Rossliskiye Vesti*, 20 July 1993, p. 1 in *The Current Digest of the Post-Soviet Press*, XLV.29, p. 12). These 'oppositionists' seek to turn Tajikistan into an Islamic state, something which was attempted, and which failed in October 1992 (Rubin, 1993-1994, p. 80). In this aim the Tajik resistance to the Government at Dushanbe is supported by the Afghan Hezb-islami Mujahideen faction led by Gulbuddin Hekmatyar (Rubin, 1993-1994, pp. 82 and 83). It is believed that this is one of the only Mujahideen faction backing the 'oppositionists' and that Jamiat-islami and General Dostam's Uzbek militia remain neutral and aloof from the fighting (*Sevodnya*, 13 August 1993, p. 1 in *The Current Digest of the Post-Soviet Press*, XLV.32, pp. 15 and 16).

The Russian Diplomatic Service has entered into several agreements in an attempt to limit the spread of the 'oppositionist' movement. An agreement has been signed with Tajikistan on 25 May 1993, where Russia has undertaken to assist in the defence of that country. Russian President Boris Yeltsin has stated that he sees Tajikistan's Southern border as Russia's own and will strive to defend it (*Izvestia*, 19 February 1993, p. 4 in *The Current Digest of the Post-Soviet Press*, XLV.7, p. 20; *Nezavisimaya Gazeta*, 16 July 1993, pp. 1 and 3 in same volume. 28, pp. 10 and 11; *Nezavisimaya Gazeta*, 28 May 1993, p. 1 in same volume.21, pp. 16 and 17). The second agreement has been made with the Afghan Government of President Burhanuddin Rabbani in which that Government has undertaken not to become involved in the destabilisation of Tajikistan (*Pravda*, 20 July 1993, p. 2 in *The Current Digest of the Post-Soviet Press*, XLV.29, pp. 14 and 15). This has lent credibility to claims that Jamiat-islami has refrained from involving itself in the turmoil of Tajikistan. Gulbuddin Hekmatyar's Hezb-i-islami, however, does not view itself bound by agreements made by the central Government with whom it is fighting in Afghanistan.

The 'oppositionist' forces in Tajikistan are also helped by the prevailing infrastructure of the country. Tajikistan is a poor country, as economic indicators demonstrate (*Central Asia Survey*, February 1994, 1.1, pp. 33-5; Cevikoz, 1994, p. 48; Rubin, 1993-1994, p. 73). Poverty is almost always a key factor where discontent against the central Government becomes open rebellion. Much of the 'oppositionist' movement is centred upon the predominantly agricultural regions of Gorno-Badakhstan, Garm, Kulyab, and Kurgan Tyube. The main industrial regions are further to the North (*Economist*, 1 August 1992, p. 55). Moreover, many of the inhabitants of these regions are also different from other Tajiks, claiming different lineages and practising different forms of Islam, for example (Rubin, 1993-1994, p. 74). All these factors demonstrate that the 'oppositionist' groups are formed in similar circumstances to those from which the Afghan Mujahideen evolved.

The Russian response has been to use force in support of the Tajik Government. In large measure this has been unsuccessful. Artillery and air strikes have been of limited success in the mountainous territory in which the 'oppositionists' move (*Izvestia*, 31 July 1993, pp. 1 and 2 in *The Current Digest of the Post-Soviet Press*, XLV.31, p. 8). Another problem is their physical location, which is hard to determine. Troops garrisoning the outposts along the 1,400 mile long Afghan-Tajik border are always uncertain whether they will be attacked from the front by Afghan Mujahideen or from the rear by Tajik 'oppositionists' (*Sevodnya*, 23 July 1993, p. 2 in *The Current Digest of the Post-Soviet Press*, XLV.29, p. 14). One such outpost, Number 12, was surrounded and attacked from both these directions in July 1993 (*Izvestia*, 17 July, 1993, pp. 1 and 8 in *The Current Digest of the Post-Soviet Press*, XLV.29, p. 10). Only the timely arrival of reinforcements from the Russian 201st Motor Rifle Division, stationed in Tajikistan, prevented the garrison from being wiped out (*The Current Digest of the Post-Soviet Press*, XLV.29, p. 11). The Russian forces in Tajikistan also have many of the same difficulties endured in Afghanistan. Motor Rifle Infantry are not the best troops to employ in mountainous territory. The Russian Army has still not adapted itself for warfare in these conditions.[8] Moreover, the same cross-border complications apply in Tajikistan that had done so in Afghanistan. Where Mujahideen operated from Pakistan and Iran into Afghanistan during the war there, the 'oppositionists' operate from bases in Afghanistan into Tajikistan. Their men are trained and equipped in Afghanistan and can always retreat there if harried by Russian troops (*Nezavisimaya Gazeta*, 29 July 1993, pp. 1 and 3 in *The Current Digest of the Post-Soviet Press*, XLV.30, p. 11). Russia's credentials as a peace-making power are also compromised by its shelling of Tajik refugee settlements and bases inside Afghanistan, even though there has been no agreement to do this with the Kabul Government (Rubin, 1993-1994, p. 67).

Russian attempts to broaden the shoulders upon which the Tajikistan burden is to be spread have also been unsuccessful. Turkmenistan has refused to become involved, President Saparmurad Niyazov arguing that the situation will not change with 200 more Turkoman troops in Tajikistan. Moreover, he feels that such involvement would sour his relations with Kabul (*Sevodnya*, 6 August 1993, in *The Current Digest of the Post-Soviet Press*, XLV.31, p. 9).   Kazakhstan and Kirghizstan have both pledged to send troops, but as yet they have not been forthcoming (*Pravda*, 20 July 1993, p. 2 in *The Current Digest of the Post-Soviet Press*, XLV.29, p. 15).   Of the regional powers, only Uzbekistan has sent troops.

There are two reasons for this. First, to protect Uzbek nationals in Tajikistan, which form 23.5% of the population there, and second, to prevent the spread of trouble into the Ferghana Valley, towards part of which Tajikistan has a claim (Rubin, 1993-1994, p. 75; *Izvestia*, 6 August 1993, p. 2 in *The Current Digest of the Post-Soviet Press*, XLV.31, p. 10; *The Economist*, 31 October 1992, pp. 76 and 77). Russian attempts to involve the United Nations and the OSCE (the Organisation for Security and Cooperation in Europe) in a peace-making role have not borne fruit (*Izvestia*, 4 August 1993, p. 4 in *The Current Digest of the Post-Soviet Press*, XLV.31, p. 8).   The situation in Tajikistan is a delicate one which cannot be solved with the use of force. Attempts to do so will remain unsuccessful, while the 'oppositionists' and the Mujahideen continue to possess the initiative (*Nezavisimaya Gazeta*, 20 July 1993, p. 1 in *The Current Digest of the Post-Soviet Press*, XLV.29, p. 13; *Sevodnya*, 23 July 1993, p. 2 in same volume and number, p. 14).   Engagement of these forces in Tajikistan will, more often than not, be on their terms as they will decide when to attack.

The other key front line state is Uzbekistan. Russia views the cooperation and stability of Islam Karimov's regime as the cornerstone of its policy in Central Asia (*Moskovskiye Novosti*, 24 January 1993, p. A12 in *The Current Digest of the Post-Soviet Press*, XLV.3, p. 12). Although Karimov's regime is stable at the moment, it is also comparatively repressive. The regime still attempts to employ a version of the old Soviet official Islam. However, many Uzbeks are turning away from this in favour of different, unofficial, Islamic teaching. As Uzbekistan has become independent, many Uzbeks have begun to ask themselves what it means to be an Uzbek. One of the key factors in this self-identification is to be a Muslim. Naturally, many Uzbeks turn away from official Islam towards other forms of Islam (Critchlow, 1994, p.

233-47; Fierman, 1994, p. 242; Abduvakhitov, 1993, pp. 90-7; Ibrahim, 1993, pp. 17-27). There has, consequently, been something of an Islamic revival in Uzbekistan. Karimov's response has been to try to repress its development, but there are still signs that it continues to grow (*Izvestia*, 20 January 1993, p. 1 in *The Current Digest of the Post-Soviet Press*, XLV.3, p. 24; *Izvestia*, 28 January 1993, p. 1 in same volume.4, p. 31). As this movement spreads, the long-term security of the Karimov regime can be called into question. The spread of Tajik 'oppositionist' activity into the Ferghana Valley is a factor that may ignite another Tajikistan situation inside Uzbekistan (*The Economist*, 30 January 1993). Instability, therefore, might spread throughout the first tier of Russian defence, threatening to undermine its security. The only part of this tier which looks stable is Turkmenistan, where proceeds from natural gas may enrich the population, giving them a stake in the security of the country and making them less inclined to rebel against the Turkoman Government (*Nezavisimaya Gazeta*, 21 January 1993 in *The Current Digest of the Post-Soviet Press*, XLV.3, pp. 9-12).

The second tier of Russia's defence concerns Kazakhstan. The rule of President Nursultan Nazarbayev is a relatively stable one. The role of Islam in Kazak life is not as great as it is in Tajikistan or Uzbekistan. Moreover, Kazakhstan's reserves of oil and natural gas promise future wealth, which may aid stability (Hiro, 1994, pp. 14 and 15). The chief factor for change lies with the large Russian community in Kazakhstan. This community, in the Soviet period, outnumbered the Kazaks in their own country, but more recently many have left and returned to Russia (Olcott, 1987, Appendix I).

However, there is still a very large ethnic Russian minority in Kazakhstan. The majority of the Russians live in the North and many wish for the Northern Kazak oblasts to be incorporated into Russia proper (Jackson, 1994, pp. 1-4). This is also, to some extent, echoed by public opinion within Russia. Alexander Solzhenitsyn has stated that he would like to see the Northern oblasts belong to Russia (*Newsweek*, 6 June 1994, p. 11). More extremely, Vladimir Zhirinovsky, who was born in Alma Ata, wishes for the whole country to be taken over (*Time*,

27 December 1993, pp. 16-18). At the moment, the second tier under Nazarbayev looks secure and stable, but if the movement for the secession of Northern Kazakhstan to Russia gathers momentum it will become much less so. This, in itself, might not alter its stability, but it could leave a smaller Kazakhstan that feels embittered and considers itself robbed of territory, industry, and natural resources.

The security of Russia's two tiered defence in Central Asia is questionable in the long term yet, for the time being, it seems stable enough. However, what the Russian Government does fear is,

'an Islamic state within the borders of the former Soviet Union. It fears that militant Islam will spread through Central Asia, and end up in the Urals where the Muslim autonomous region of Tatarstan is struggling for independence.' (*The Economist*, 31 October 1992, p. 77)

This fear is well founded. Melvin Goodman sees Brezhnev's rationale for the invasion of Afghanistan as being to 'prevent the uniting of the diverse peoples of Central Asia against the Russian heartland' (Goodman, 1994, p. 87). In such a confrontation Russian Muslims would play a part. The seeds of radicalism are there. At a Constituent Congress of the Islamic Renaissance Party of the Muslims of the Soviet Union in Astrakhan in June 1990, 60 of the 140 delegates came from Daghistan (Makhanov, 1994, p. 201).

The Chechen Republic declared its independence from Moscow in 1991, leading to violent conflict with Russia, a conflict in which Islam clearly played a part: '400 clergymen from the Muslim region rallied in Grosny and swore on the Koran to wage a holy war if Russia sent in troops' (*Independent*, 3 August 1994, p. 8). Certainly, the Islamic Renaissance Party (IRP) and others are strong within the Russian Federation:

'By the time of the August 1991 Soviet coup and counter-coup, the IRP claimed about 30,000 members, and presumably far more sympathisers, in three general areas: Central Asia, where it was strongest in Tajikistan and the Ferghana Valley of Uzbekistan; the Caucasus, where it was strongest in the Chechen-Ingush ASSR of Russia: and Russia and Siberia, where most of its followers were Tatars though living in Moscow and elsewhere as well as Tatarstan. (Dunn, 1993, p. 36; Menon and Barkey, 1992-1993, p. 74; Rubin, 1993-1994, p. 87; *Telegraph*, 23 March 1992)

There is undoubtedly a strong secessionist movement in Siberia and the Far East which, if successful, will deprive Moscow of many of its natural resources and its Pacific coastline. Secessionism could easily spread throughout Russia, radically altering its cartographical position (*The Economist*, 11 September 1993, p. 46; 30 January 1993, p. 41; 5 September 1992, pp. 41 and 42; 14 March 1992, pp. 61 and 62).

The figures given by the Islamic Foundation demonstrate the strength of the Islamic population in areas wishing to secede from the Russian Federation. Tatarstan has a Muslim population of 5.2 million out of a total population of 6.1 million. In Bashkiria 82.5% of the population are Muslims. In Daghistan this figure is 85% and in Checheno-Ingushetia it is 90% (Khan, 1993, pp. 9 and 10).[9] With such large Muslim populations the secessionist elements of all these regions, among them the Islamic Renaissance Party, have an ample base from which to recruit new members and consolidate their strength.

Conclusion

What has become clear is that many of the lessons of the Afghan experience have not been learned by the Russian Army in Tajikistan. Military operations are still conducted in the same way they were in Afghanistan, with motorised infantry. The Russian Army also has to operate within certain political parameters that did not apply in Afghanistan. Moreover, they are still a long way from winning the hearts and minds of the people of Tajikistan. The two tiered system of the defence of Russian interests in Central Asia is also weak and unstable in the long term. The long-term stability of the Karimov regime in Uzbekistan is open to question, and many Russian commentators feel that it is only a matter of time before the Russian public tires of the fighting in Tajikistan (for example, *Nezavisimaya Gazeta*, 20 July 1993, p. 1 in *The Current Digest of the Post-Soviet Press*, XLV.29, p. 13). The position of Kazakhstan as a buffer is weakened by a Russian chauvinism which threatens to divide the country. The Russian aim has been to prevent the spread of movements like the Islamic Renaissance Party into the Russian Federation. It is, however, already there. It seems unlikely that Russia will be able to show the Muslim regions the benefits of remaining within the Federation. What does seem likely is that these regions will eventually secede, which will, in turn, prompt others to go the same way. The collapse of empire breeds instability as the periphery distances itself from the centre. The 'domino effect' of the loss of influence in Afghanistan, Central Asia, and, later, in parts of the Russian Federation is an inevitable part of this process.

Notes

1. Suvorov, Victor (1982), *Inside the Soviet Army*, Hamish Hamilton, London. A typical statement is that the helicopter was viewed by the Soviet military as a flying tank, rather than as a tool for aerial interdiction or offence in its own right.
2. Record of the telephone conversation between A.N. Kosygin and N.M. Taraki, 18 March 1979 in *Journal of South Asian and Middle Eastern Studies* (hereafter *J.S.A.M.E.S.*), XVII, Number 2, Winter 1994, pp. 20 to 25. All the documents printed in this issue are covered by a letter establishing their authenticity.
3. Record of the Conversation between Kosygin, Gromyko, Ustinov, Ponomariev, with Taraki, 20 March 1979 in Moscow in *J.S.A.M.E.S.*, XVII, Number 2, pp. 26 to 36.
4. Memorandum of the Conversation between Brezhnev and Taraki 20 March 1979 in Moscow in *J.S.A.M.E.S.*, XVII, Number 2,

pp. 37 to 42.

5. Abstract from the Minutes N 176 of the Politburo of the CPSU's Central Committee, to Brezhnev, Andropov, Gromyko, Suslov and Ustinov, 6 December 1979. *J.S.A.M.E.S.*, XVII, Number 2, p. 59.

6. From Leonid Brezhnev's Speech before the Voters of the Baumansky Constituency in Moscow, 22 February 1980, cited in *The Truth About Afghanistan: Documents, Facts, Eyewitness Reports* (Novosti Press Agency Publishing House, Moscow, 1980) p. 15.

7. For example, see *Rossiiskiye Vesti*, 18 March 1993, p. 2 and *Izvestia*, 17 March 1993, p. 1, both in *The Current Digest of the Post-Soviet Press*, XLV, Number 12, pp. 20 and 21. See also William D. Jackson, 'Imperial Temptations: Ethnics Abroad' in *Orbis*, 38, Number 1, Winter 1994, pp. 1 to 17.

8. For example, see *Sevodnya*, 16 July 1993, p. 1 in *The Current Digest of the Post-Soviet Press*, XLV, Number 28, p. 11: 'It is also known that successful operations against a well-organised enemy employing guerrilla warfare methods require at least a tenfold superiority in men and weapons.'

9. Muhammad Iqbal Khan (1993), *Muslims of Central Asia and Russia*, The Islamic Foundation, pp. 9 and 10. While reading these statistics, it has to be borne in mind that these figures refer to all Muslims, practising and non-practising, in the regions concerned.

Bibliography

Abduvakhitov, A. (1993), 'Islamic Revivalism in Uzbekistan' in Eickelman (ed.), *Russia's Muslim Frontiers*, Indiana University Press

Akiner, S. (1993), *Central Asia: New Arc of Crisis*, Whitehall Paper Number 17, R.U.S.I., London

Amin, A. R. (1987), 'The Sovietization of Afghanistan', in Klass, 1987

Arney, G. (1990), *Afghanistan*, Mandarin, London

Arnold, A. (1985), *Afghanistan: The Soviet Invasion in Perspective*, Hoover Institution Press, Stanford University, California

Atkin, M. (1989), *The Subtlest Battle. Islam in Soviet Tajikistan*, Foreign Policy Research Institute, Philadelphia

Bennigsen, A. (1980), 'Soviet Muslims and the World of Islam', *Problems of Communism*, 29.2

Bennigsen, A. (1984), 'Mullahs, Mujahidin and Soviet Muslims', *Problems of Communism*, 33.6

Broxup, M. (1987), 'Islam in Central Asia Since Gorbachev', *Asian Affairs*, 74

Cevikoz, U. (1994), 'A Brief Account of the Economic Situation in the Former Soviet Republics of Central Asia', *Central Asian Survey*, 13.1

Critchlow, J. (1994), 'Nationalism and Islamic Resurgence in Uzbekistan', in Malik, 1994

Dunn, M. C. (1993), 'Central Asian Islam: Fundamentalist Threat or Communist Bogeyman?', *Middle East Policy*, ll.1

Fierman, W. (1994), 'Policy Toward Islam in Uzbekistan in the Gorbachev Era', *Nationalities Papers*, 22.1

Gall, S. (1988), *Afghanistan. Travels with the Mujahideen*, New English Library (first published as *Afghanistan: Agony of a Nation* in 1988)

Girardet, E. R. (1985), *Afghanistan: The Soviet War*, Croom Helm, London

Goodman, M. (1994), 'Perestroika: Its Impact on the Central Asian Republics and their Future Relations with Moscow', in Malik 1994

Hiro, D. (1994), 'Facing Two Ways', *The Middle East*, May

Ibrahim, D. (1993), *The Islamization of Central Asia: A Case Study of Uzbekistan*, The Islamic Foundation

Isby, D. C. (1989), *War in a Distant Country -Afghanistan. Invasion and Resistance*, Arms and Armour Press, London, 1989

Jackson, W. D. (1994), 'Imperial Temptations: Ethnics Abroad', *Orbis*, 38.1

Keller, S. (1992), 'Islam in Soviet Central Asia, 1917-1930: Soviet Policy and The Struggle for Control', *Central Asian Survey*, 11.1

Khalilzad, Z. (1980), 'Soviet Occupied Afghanistan', *Problems of Communism*, 29.6

Khan, M. I. (1993), *Muslims of Central Asia and Russia*, The Islamic Foundation

Klass, R. (ed.) (1987), *Afghanistan. The Great Game Revisited*, Freedom House Press, New York

Kornienko, G. M. (1994), 'The Afghan Endeavour: Perplexities of the Military Incursion and Withdrawal', *Journal of South Asian and Middle Eastern Studies*, XVII. 2

Kuzio, T. (1987), 'Opposition in the U.S.S.R. to the Occupation of Afghanistan', *Central Asian Survey*, 6.1

Makhanov, M. (1994), 'Islam and the Political Development of Tajikistan after 1985', in Malik 1994

Malik, H. (ed) (1994), *Central Asia: Its Strategic Importance and Future Prospects*, Macmillan, London

Menon, R. and Barkey, H. J. (1992-1993), 'The Transformation of Central Asia: Implications for Regional and International Security', *Survival*, 34.4

O'Ballance, E. (1993), *Afghan Wars 1839-1992*, Brassey's, London

Olcott, M. B. (1987), *The Kazaks*, Hoover Institution Press, Stanford University

Philips, P. (1986), 'A Soviet Estonian Soldier in Afghanistan', *Central Asian Survey*, 5.1

Roy, O. (1989), 'Afghanistan: War as a Factor of Entry into Politics', *Central Asian Survey*, 8.4

Rigby, T. H. (1990), 'The Afghan Conflict and Soviet Domestic Politics', in Saikal and Maley, 1990

Safi, N. (1986), 'Soviet Military Tactics in Afghanistan', *Central Asian Survey*, 5.2

Saikal, A. and Maley, W. (eds) (1990), *The Soviet Withdrawal From Afghanistan*, Cambridge University Press, Cambridge

Spolnikov, V. (1994), 'Impact of Afghanistan's War on the Former Soviet Republics of Central Asia', in Malik, 1994

Suvorov, V. (1982), *Inside the Soviet Army*, Hamish Hamilton, London

5   Nationalism and inter-ethnic conflict: the case of Armenia and Azerbaijan

EIREN MOBEKK

Introduction

I shall attempt to analyse the conflict between Armenia and Azerbaijan over Nagorno-Karabakh in relation to contrasting theories of nationalism, by examining the utility of some key approaches to the study of nationalism as a means of explaining the relationship between nationalism and inter-ethnic violence. This will form a background to a new interpretation of this relationship.

First, it may be useful to give an outline of each of these theories and then a brief history of each country involved in this conflict, in order to set the scene for current events. Next, there will be an overview of the situation since 1988, when the present conflict began with an uprising in Nagorno-Karabakh. It would, of course, be possible to give much more detail on both the historical and present situations, but these summaries have necessarily to be brief and so I have included only the main events.

Following this overview of the historical background and contemporary conflict, each theory will be compared with the empirical evidence of this case study. As we shall see, weaknesses in all of these theories will suggest that an alternative view of nationalism may be proposed. I shall suggest that nationalism can be seen as a 'revolutionary', rather than 'reactionary', characteristic of international politics and that theoretical approaches designed to analyse revolution may be applied to both this case study and to nationalism in general. It is, however, important to stress that this study does not suggest that all nationalist movements need be revolutionary and that the historical characteristics of individual cases must be understood.

Nationalism

Nationalism is an ambiguous concept, which has been explained and defined in several ways, as have the important concepts related to it, such as nation, national identity and national consciousness. There are many theories about nationalism, of which some do, to some extent, support each other, whereas others are rivals in the explanation of the phenomenon.

It can be argued that there is a general agreement, at least among the leading scholars of the subject, that nationalism - as known today - is a modern phenomenon arising after the French Revolution. This can, however, be strongly disputed on historical grounds. It is also viewed as a European 'invention' that has been exported to the rest of the world with different degrees of success.

There is, however, disagreement over whether it is possible to trace the origins of nationalism and nations back to early ethnic cleavages and historic divisions, as Smith (1986) argues, or if it is purely due to recent social and economic changes, as Gellner (1983) holds. The matter is further complicated by disagreement over the concepts of nation and state. Smith (1976) argues that a nation can exist without a state, and a state cannot exist without a prior existence of a nation (Smith, 1971, p. 169). Whereas other political scientists argue the view that a 'state need not be a nation, a nation must be a state' (Snyder, 1977, p. 32). This, it can be said, is an argument about what came first, the state which created the nation, or the nation which became a state. Definitions vary as to whether the emphasis is put mainly on the ethnic/cultural aspects, or political ones. Kellas defines a nation as, 'a group of people who feel themselves to be a community bound together by ties of history, culture and common ancestry' (Kellas, 1991, p. 2). Whereas Alter defines a nation as, 'a politically mobilised people' (Alter, 1989, p. 11).

Nationality and national identity are also concepts that defy exact definition. They can be used in the concrete sense, as people bound together by language and connected with the concept of a state. They can also be used in the abstract sense, as a sentiment, a feeling bonding a people together (Snyder, 1977, p. 72).There is also a conflict between those scholars that argue, that 'national consciousness' developed before nationalism, which then became a means with which to reach the aim of a nation-state, and those that hold that 'national consciousness' is a construct of nationalism itself.

Many alternative theories of nationalism have been proposed. To begin, I shall outline a few which will not be employed here to provide a context to the following discussion. Kedourie strongly criticised the doctrine of nationalism and viewed nationalism as based on linguistic and cognitive factors. He argued that there has never 'naturally' been any nations: they were created by and induced in, people (Kedourie, 1986, p. 120). In Kedourie's view, topographical or linguistic 'natural frontiers' also do not exist (Kedourie, 1986, p. 125). Smith criticised Kedourie because he overlooked the advantages of nationalist revivals and that legitimising new regimes through nationalism can have a positive, as well as a negative, effect (Smith, 1971, p. 23). Kedourie's theory can be argued to be based on too few variables and that a variable like 'will' is very difficult to operationalise, making it difficult to use.

Kellas' (1991) theory of nationalism encompassed a wide range of variables as explanatory factors of nationalism. These include sociobiology, psychology, sociology, anthropology and economy. In this interpretation, ethnocentrism is viewed as genetically determined behaviour which in turn can explain and provide conditions for xenophobia, nepotism, slavery and genocide (Kellas, 1991, p. 161).

Kellas connects this to economic factors, a combination which tends to make his theory somewhat difficult to apply.

Coakley (1992) forms a theory of nationalism by collating several alternatives to form a new approach. He argues that there are so many similarities between them that this is possible (Coakley, 1992, p. 13), but there are also features unique to all of the theories, and by 'lumping' them together, it can be argued that he erases the basis of the individual theories, and the reasons why they were developed.

This brings us to the four theories of nationalism that will form the basis of a later discussion of whether it is possible to use them in an explanation of the nationalistic conflict between Armenia and Azerbaijan over Nagorno-Karabakh. The first theory is by H. Kohn who defines nationalism as; 'a state of mind, permeating the large majority of a people and claiming to permeate all its members; it recognizes the nation-state as the ideal form of political organization and the nationality as the source of all creative cultural energy and economic well-being' (Kohn, 1948, p. 15). He argues that nationalism is an 'act' of consciousness, a frame of mind, that it is; 'formed by the decision to form a nationality' (Kohn, 1948, p. 5). Nationalism is not to Kohn a natural phenomenon inherit in human beings, but it is viewed as a product of social and intellectual factors at a specific stage in history. Kohn holds that nationalities cannot be identified with clans, or tribes, but they are a product of historical development. Nationality is a historical and political concept that has changed its meaning during time (Kohn, 1948, p. 13). Kohn divides between two different kinds of nationalism; a Western and an Eastern type. In the West, argues Kohn, a new class emerged and became powerful. It was in these societies that nationalism found expression in political and economic changes. Where this new class did not develop a powerful basis, in the East, however, nationalism found its expression through culture (Kohn, 1948, p. 4). He emphasises that nationalism in the West was a means by which to build a political entity and to manipulate the present, without too much 'sentimental regard' for the past. The Eastern type, however, was based on myths of an ideal 'homeland', a nationalism closely linked with the past, and was not so easily able to manipulate the present. Kohn argues that it was due to the 'backward' state of the political and social development, that nationalism outside the Western world became expressed through culture and history (Kohn, 1948, p. 329).

The question is whether Kohn's division of nationalism can be applied to the resurgence of nationalism in the contemporary world. Can the Eastern type of nationalism help to explain certain factors in the outbursts of nationalism in the ex-communist states? Can the strong ethnic cleavages, with strong emphases on culture and history, be explained by the 'backwardness' of political and social development in the countries involved? These questions will be addressed at a later stage.

The second theory is that of E. Gellner. This theory argues that nationalism was a product of modern developments. Nationalism is seen as a theory of political legitimacy, and it can only exist where the existence of a state is taken for granted (Gellner, 1983, p. 4). The theory stresses the importance of material and socio-economic conditions for the rise of nationalism, and also political and social upheaval and change. The roots of nationalism are seen to be embedded in the distinctive structural requirements of the industrialised society (Gellner, 1983, p. 35). The theory sees nationalism as emerging when the agrarian society transformed into an industrialised one. To function as an industrialised community, homogeneity was needed, which was gained through a common educational system. The plurality of languages and ethnic groups had to be moulded into homogeneity due to industrialisation. This was achieved through education, which trained people for life in the industrial society. The educational system provided everyone with a common culture. Nationalism then, according to Gellner, becomes the result of a new form of social organisation based on education (Gellner, 1983, p. 48). Nationalism, Gellner argues, was not invented by the intellectual elite and forced upon the political system, but it was due to the stage of development and industrialisation of society, hence its successes.

The theory states that nationalism does not have roots in human psyche (Gellner, 1983, p. 34). It is viewed as a socio-economic phenomenon. According to the theory, industrialisation gives a mobile and cultural homogenetic society, which demands equality. In the beginning of industrialisation, however, there was bound to be inequality, which led to a portion of the people feeling devastated. This latent political tension becomes imminent if that group can find symbols that can separate them from the ruling class (Gellner, 1983, p. 75). This is to argue that the symbols are not inherent, but invented and 'discovered', after the crisis, as a way of making life better for the 'out-group' against the ruling 'in-group'. It can be argued, however, that the causal link might be turned the other way around. That is to say that, due to pre-existing differences, inequality is intensified, and this becomes clearer due to industrialisation. This is, however, what Gellner calls the 'early stage'. In the next stage, it is only a 'genuine prior barrier to mobility and equality which will engender a new frontier' (Gellner, 1983, p. 75).

Gellner went on to argue that in 'earlier times' people were not conscious of their culture, it was like 'the air they breathed'. When mobility and communication on a larger scale developed, however, it became the essence of social life, and the culture in which one was taught to communicate became the core of one's identity (Gellner, 1983, p. 61).

Gellner's theory focuses on the emergence of nationalism in the era of industrialisation. Can it, however, be used to explain post-industrial nationalism? The theory emphasises socio-economic reasons for nationalism, and de-emphasises the ethnic and cultural aspects. Can this way of viewing nationalism shed any light on contemporary conflict in post-industrialised countries?

The third theory of nationalism to be considered is A. Smith's. Contrary to Gellner (1983), Smith's book *The Ethnic Origins of Nations* (1986), considers ethnicity as a forerunner for nationalism. The roots of nationalism are viewed to be ethnic bonds and identities, which developed into ties and identities with the nation through nationalism. In this theory, the emphasis is not completely on the modern aspect and development of nationalism, but it is traced back to ethnicity as well. The change from ethnicity to nationalism is, in Smith's view, due to (among other things) the decline of religion. Smith claims that secular nationalism took over where religion lost ground. The growth of the bureaucratic state, with its centralised and industrialised structures, was also (according to his interpretation) necessary for ethnicity to become politically mobilised. Although Smith argues that nationalism has roots in ethnicity, he also states that, as a basis for national identity, both common ancestry and common language are insufficient. What is crucial in defining national identity is political action (Smith, 1971, p. 20). According to Smith it is the political community, no matter how artificially organised, that produces belief in common ethnicity. It can be argued, however, that ethnic identity comes first in the causal chain and, based on that, coherent political action can be taken, which in turn reinforces the feeling of ethnicity.

Smith's theory, then, claims that the thoughts and feelings leading people into national consciousness are not completely new or modern. Myths, languages, history etc. are as much a part of nationalism as modern communication and education. He also argues that it is possible to have a nation without a state, or both together, but one cannot have a state without the existence of a prior nation, which in his opinion is based on the ethnic group (Smith, 1971, p. 169). Smith does, however, tie nationalism closely together with self-government as his definition of nationalism shows: 'an ideological movement for the attainment and maintenance of self-government and independence on behalf of a group, some of whose members conceive it to constitute an actual or potential "nation" like others' (Smith, 1971, p. 171).

Smith argues, in *Nationalism in the Twentieth Century*, that there are two reasons for the present resurgence of nationalism. The first is 'the existence of a strong ethnic tradition and deep popular sentiments on which nationalists can draw'. The second is 'the operations of the bureaucratic cycle, which throw up two kinds of nationalism, a state oriented a romantic ethnic nationalism' (Smith, 1979, p. 182). This will later on be used to see if it indeed can explain the specific outburst of nationalism between the states of Armenia and Azerbaijan.

The fourth theory is that proposed by B. Anderson. Anderson sees nationalism and nationality as cultural artifacts. Nation is defined as 'an imagined political community - and imagined as both inherently limited and sovereign' (Anderson, 1983, p. 6). Anderson tries with this theory to explain how people came to imagine themselves as part of a nation. The theory states that nationalism is time specific, that is to say, it could only arise historically when three fundamental conceptions lost ground (Anderson, 1983, p. 36). The three conceptions were, first, the idea that script-language gave access to the 'truth', known only to a few. Second, that society was - and should be - ruled by monarchs ruling by 'divine' right. Third, that 'the conception of temporality in which cosmology and history were indistinguishable origins of the world and man identical' (Anderson, 1983, p. 36). When these conceptions 'withered away' people searched for a new way of linking and bonding. In Anderson's view 'print-capitalism' made it possible for a large number of people to think about and consider it. Print-languages laid the basis for national consciousness in three specific ways. They created a field where common exchange and communication now was possible on a much larger scale. The connection a people got through print, Anderson argues, was the beginning of the formation of 'imagined communities'. Print-capitalism also gave a new fixture to language, which, according to Anderson, helped to build an image of antiquity, which is central to the subjective idea of the nation. Print-capitalism also created languages of power (Anderson, 1983, p. 44).

Print-capitalism, in this theory, becomes the principal precondition for nationalism. It spreads the idea of nation and gives growth to national consciousness. This can be argued to explain why nationalism has emerged in different types of societies. People recognised each other as belonging to the same large group, although they would never meet face to face, because they were bound by language. This is how, in Anderson's view, a people imagine a nation and linguistic nationalism is established. Other processes are also need for nationalism to develop, that is 'modern' processes such as scientific discoveries, which break down 'old ways' of viewing the world.

Anderson also argues that when religion declines, nationalism has an appeal due to the same type of feelings it can invoke. He stresses, however, that it is 'short-sighted to think of imagined communities of nations as simply growing out of and replacing religious communities' (Anderson, 1983, p. 22). According to Anderson, then, popular linguistic nationalism was developed first and then - in the middle of the nineteenth century - 'official' nationalism developed. This was a response by 'powerful' groups, who felt threatened by the arising of linguistic nationalism, and the exclusion from it, and from popular imagined communities (Anderson, 1983, p. 109). For Anderson, all communities are 'imagined' except for small, face-to-face, groups, but consciousness and bonds are real, even if they are 'imagined'.

This theory also focuses on the roots of nationalism, and is held by its supporters to explain (to some extent) the development of nationalism. Can it, however, explain the growth of nationalism today?

As mentioned before, these four theories will later be used to see if they can explain the conflict of nationalism between Armenia and Azerbaijan over Nagorno-Karabakh. The theories chosen are the main theories currently employed to analyse nationalism. Gellner's theory is primarily 'modern' and based on industrialisation, and excludes ethnic origins. Smith's point of departure, however, is ethnic 'roots' and groups. Anderson's 'imagined communities' incorporate both, but at the same time views the phenomenon differently. Lastly, Kohn's classic division between Eastern and Western nationalism portrays yet again another way of dealing with the complexities of nationalism. To some extent, all of these theories (as most other theories of nationalism) include similarities, but they are each different in their basis.

The background

To provide a background to the example which I wish to examine as a case study, first it may be useful to give a brief overview of the history of Armenia and Azerbaijan. I shall highlight the most important events in the development of the respective states and nations involved in the post-Cold War dispute. There is, however, slightly less information about Azerbaijan, due to the fact that scholars have written substantially less about its history, at least in the European languages, than about Armenian history.

Armenia

The earliest mention of the Armenians is by Hecataeus in 550 BC (Der Nersessian, 1969, p. 20,) and Armenia has a long, violent and turbulent history of foreign domination and rule. Assyrians, Persians, Romans and Turkic peoples have fought over Armenia through the centuries. To the Assyrians, for example, Armenia was known as Urartu, that is, 'the land around Ararat'.

Armenia converted to Christianity in AD 301, making it the oldest Christian state in the world. It is usually argued that Armenian Christianity developed independently (Walker, 1991, p. 15) and the Church has been vital for the preservation of the sense of Armenian identity through centuries of foreign dominance and oppression. It became a vehicle for identifying 'us' from 'them', and a strong unifying factor (Myklebost, 1989, p. 37).

The Armenian alphabet, which is very distinctive, was invented in the early fifth century. This allowed for the Bible, and other important texts to be translated into Armenian. This both reinforced the sense of national unity and strengthened the Church. In AD 387, however, the Romans and Persians divided Armenia between them, a decision which would set a recurring pattern for the future.

During the ninth century, Armenia experienced a degree of autonomy under its own monarchy; however, in 1045 it was annexed by the Byzantine Empire. Shortly thereafter, in 1064, it was overrun by Seljuk Turks. A great proportion of the Armenian population fled to Cilicia, where they founded a new kingdom, which lasted from 1080 until 1375, when it was destroyed by the Egyptian Mamluks. This kingdom was, and is, also referred to as 'Little Armenia'.

The Ottoman Turks were the next conquerors, who, by the sixteenth century, had occupied all of Armenia. Under Ottoman rule the Armenians were organised in semi-autonomous 'millet'. The Armenians were useful for the empire as administrators, bankers and the like, and the area was known as the 'loyal millet'. In 1828, however, Russia took over Persia's part of Armenia, and opposition against Ottoman rule spread, as the 'Armenian province' was created. This led the Turks to doubt the loyalty of the Armenians. After the Russo-Turkish war in 1877-78, hopes of an independent Armenia grew, but came to nothing.

The Turks stationed armed Kurds at the border with Persia, as 'border-guards' - however, the Armenians in the same area were not allowed to bear arms and violence and harassment occurred. As a reaction against this, Armenian revolutionary movements were formed: the Armenakans in 1885, the Hunchaks in 1887 and the Dashnaks in 1890. Their activities led to Turkish action against Armenia, infamously the massacres of 300,000 Armenians in Turkish Armenia during the years of 1894-96 (Walker, 1991, p. 24), a source of much subsequent dispute.

Despite the Russian conquest of Transcaucasia, attitudes remained much the same. In 1903, the Armenian Church property was nationalised, and during the revolution in 1905 Russian authorities initiated a slaughter of Armenians. These killings, according to Myklebost (1989, p. 139), left a legacy of hatred between the Armenians and the Azeris. Some Armenians, especially the Dashnaks, had worked together with the Young Turks to bring about the revolution in 1908, but the Young Turks, however, soon came to view the Armenians as a threat to the state. In 1909, there was a massacre of 30,000 Armenians (Walker, 1991, p. 25).

When the First World War broke out, many Armenians enrolled in the Ottoman Army. However, they were soon viewed as a dangerous 'fifth column', which would support Russia and the Western Alliance. They were, therefore, disarmed and forced into labour battalions. In April 1915 Armenian intellectuals in Istanbul were massacred by the authorities (Walker, 1991, p. 27). Then, what has been called 'deportations' began. These started in April, and by September all Armenians in Turkey had been driven from their homes, the men killed and the women and children being taken towards the deserts of Syria. Few survived the death marches, and 1.5 million died as a result of the genocide. The Turkish authorities argued in their defence that the Armenians had staged a revolt and this had to be quelled.

On the 28 May 1918, an independent state of Armenia was proclaimed. It was in a hopeless position, however, due to the large number of refugees from Turkey, famine and an enormous economic crisis. Pressure from Turkey was severe, and 15-30,000 Armenians were killed in Baku in the same period by the Azeris, who had joined forces with the Turks. Armenia managed to hold on to its independence for two years, but then resigned and looked towards Russia, which was seen by it as a preferable ruler to Turkey.

Azerbaijan

The Azeris are probably descendants of the indigenous inhabitants of the area, but were influenced both linguistically and culturally by Turkish settlers. Azerbaijan also has a long and violent history of foreign domination and rule. In the fourth century BC an independent state was established in the region. The Persians took control over the area in the third century AD, and it was part of their empire until the Muslims conquered it in the seventh century. From the eleventh century, assimilation of the conqueror and the conquered was marked (Anon, 1992, p. 450).

The Azeris have, then, been Muslims for centuries, and according to Bennigsen (1967, p. 5) possessed an 'ancient' civilisation. According to Bennigsen (1967, p. 5), the unity among Arab-Iranian-Turkish culture, to which the Azeris belonged, was confined to a small intellectual elite, which was above linguistic and other differences.

In the sixteenth century Azerbaijan was again dominated by Persia, although the Ottoman Turks also intruded into the area. From 1735, however, for a short period, local Khanates had a degree of independence from both Ottomans and Persians. Russia was, however, advancing through the Caucasus, and by 1805 several of the Khanates were Russian protectorates. In 1828 Azerbaijan was, due to the Russo-Persian conflict, divided between the two.

After the Russian Revolution, Azerbaijan also established an independent state, which lasted for two years due to the fact that Allied and Central power troops were stationed there. When they withdrew Azerbaijan was invaded by the Red Army in April 1920, and the 'Soviet Republic of Azerbaijan' was established.

The present situation

This brings us to the events of the present conflict, which began in 1988 and is still continuing.

The conflict is based on the fact that Nagorno-Karabakh is an oblast ruled by Azerbaijan, but has a majority of Armenians comprising about 75% of the total population. The oblast (NKAO) was 'given' to be ruled by the Azeris, by Stalin, in 1921. At that time, the area had a majority of 94% Armenians. Karabakh is divided from Armenia by a small stretch of land: the Lachin corridor. Karabakh has had the status of an 'autonomous' oblast since 1921, but it was still ruled by the Azeris. The Armenians in the area have felt disadvantaged due, according to them, lack of education in their own language, repression of their culture and Church, and socio-economic deprivation. According to Walker, attempts were made consistently to destroy their cultural identity (Walker, 1991, p. 2).

With Gorbachev's reform-programme, the Armenians of Nagorno-Karabakh saw the opportunity to secede from Azerbaijan. So, on 20 February, the provincial council of the region gathered in Stepanakert, and made a resolution to leave Azerbaijan and to join Armenia (Saroyan, 1990, p. 14). This was greeted with joy in Yerevan, the capital of Armenia (especially due to the negative attitude adopted by Azerbaijan) and there were strikes both in Armenia and Karabakh.

Gorbachev asked for a month of quiet without disruption, to try to find a solution.   At the end of February - between the 27th and the 29th - however, the Sumgaim tragedy occurred and Baku turned into a scene of massacres of Armenians.   This was allegedly started due to a radio report stating that two Azeri youths had been killed in Armenia.   The official figure of deaths is 32 (Walker, 1991, p. 124), but estimates vary widely depending on sources.

Karabakh then asked to be attached directly to the Russian Federation, but to no avail.   The atmosphere grew more tense during March, especially in Yerevan, when it seemed that nothing would be done.   The strikes and the unrest continued.   In June there were demonstrations in Baku, and on the 13th Azerbaijan rejected the decision of the 20 February.   As a response, Armenia unanimously voted on the 15 June for Karabakh to become a part of Armenia.   However, consent was required by Azerbaijan, due to the Soviet legal system, and the vote was rejected two days later.   During the end of 1988, Armenians living in Azerbaijan started crossing the border, and the Azeris were fleeing in the opposite direction.   The refugee situation started to become a problem.   In January 1989, Karabakh achieved a special status, and was to be administered directly from Moscow.   Throughout 1989, unrest continued in Armenia and Karabakh.   Following a general strike in Azerbaijan in May, an economic and energy blockade was imposed against Armenia (Anon, 1992, p. 445).   The special status for Karabakh ended in November, although no solution was found, and Azerbaijan was again given control of the oblast.   Armenia then declared the region to be a part of the 'Armenian Republic'; this, however, was declared unconstitutional by the Supreme Soviet in January 1990.   The flow of refugees in both directions now continued at a higher rate.   Clashes between the two groups occurred more and more frequently, and became more violent as there was, and is, no shortage of weapons.

In September 1991, Armenia held a referendum on independence. 99.3% of the population voted in favour of secession from the former Soviet Union.   In Azerbaijan, independence was declared the 30 August, but it was not put into effect until the 18 October.

During 1991 there was much inter-ethnic violence, rumours of deportations, and allegations that Soviet troops were cooperating with the Azeris. However, a peace treaty was signed on the 23 September. The agreement gave greater autonomy for the Armenians in Karabakh, in exchange for Armenia not claiming any part of the region (Anon, 1992, p. 452). Clashes, however, were reported immediately after the agreement was signed, and demonstrations against it were held. A serious setback came when an aircraft carrying Azeri negotiators crashed, killing all on board. The Azeris accused the Armenians of shooting the plane down. By the end of 1991, the conflict had escalated, and Stepanakert had been bombarded. Throughout 1992 the conflict escalated even further, and in June the President of Azerbaijan, Mulitabov, lost the elections, due to the fact that the Azeris were losing the war with Armenia. Elcibey won with the promise of 'in Nagornyj Karabakh rasch aufzuraumen' (Manutscharjan, 1992, p. 963). After he was elected Azerbaijan moved into Karabakh, and took several Armenian villages. Since then, a near-continuous heavy battle has been on the agenda. There have been accusations, from both sides, that other states have intervened in the conflict.

The Armenians fear that Karabakh will be emptied of Armenians due to the refugees and casualties. They do not want another situation similar to Nakhichevan, which in 1921 had an Armenian population of 45-50%, but today is reduced to about 2%.

The situation in Armenia today is harsh, due to the blockade imposed by Azerbaijan. The situation in Azerbaijan is also bleak due to the number of refugees, which creates enormous problems. Both countries are now practically ethnically homogenous, due to the fact that minorities have fled to their respective countries. There have been suggestions of how to solve the conflict; however, no solutions enabling peace to return have yet been able to satisfy the warring parties.

Competing theories of nationalism

If the conflict between Armenia and Azerbaijan over Nagorno-Karabakh is viewed with Kohn's theory of nationalism in mind, several features become apparent. In applying his definition of nationalism - where a 'state of mind' and the aim to form a 'nation-state' are central - contrasts with the present case are clear. Nagorno-Karabakh with its movement for rejoining Armenia, did recognise the nation-state as 'the ideal form'. Their economic well-being was seen to be enhanced by joining Armenia, and it would reinforce their cultural identity, of which it was felt they had been deprived when ruled by Azerbaijan (Fuller, 1993, p. 89). There was a majority feeling that they were being deprived of their rights, both economically and culturally, as a fairly homogenous group - sharply differentiated from its rulers - which wanted another type of political organisation.

For the Azeris, however, the situation was somewhat different. Their resurgence of nationalism came as a reaction to the claims of Nagorno-Karabakh and Armenia. When Armenia claimed that Karabakh should be reunited with it - due to history, ethnicity and other reasons - huge demonstrations broke out in Azerbaijan as a reaction towards this (Anon, 1992, p. 451). It was a joint feeling of the deprivation of territory belonging to 'us' against an illegitimate and aggressive 'outsider'. These feelings escalated when the conflict started to become violent, so it can, therefore, be argued that it was the group's reaction against aggression which originally led to the growth of nationalism in the conflict with the Azeris. It was protection of an already existing nation-state which flared into the growth of nationalism in Azerbaijan.

Ethnic cleavages, history and culture play a major part in the conflict, and such aspects have also been given as reasons for the demands of Karabakh. It would, therefore, seem reasonable to see Kohn's 'Eastern' type of nationalism as able to be used to explain this case. The Eastern type relies on the fact that a strong class which became powerful, did not emerge. In both societies, however, it can be argued that such a strong class did exist. In Armenia a strong intellectual elite, as well as a middle-class, can be held to have existed from the time of the Ottoman Empire. The nationalism in Armenia today, however, seems to be what could be termed the 'ethnic' kind. Nagorno-Karabakh is referred to in historical terms as part of 'Greater Armenia' and, of course, the cultural homogeneity with the population of the area is emphasised. However, the more a conflict of nationalism escalates, it seems that the original reasons for the conflict become blurred, and emphasis is put on the others that are more clearly visible and which can easily arouse a sense of unity and common hatred. That is to say, even if a conflict seems to be 'ethnic' now, it did not necessarily begin as one. The sense of distrust and hatred is kept alive, and events such as the 'bloodbaths' between the Armenians and the Azeris from 1905 to 1920, are being used as a tool to strengthen nationalistic feelings.

In Azerbaijan, it can be argued, that the 'powerful class' was not so strong, or so developed, as in Armenia. Especially since (prior to the independent Azeri state in 1918-20) there had been no history of independent Azeri state-building, a contrast with Armenia (Saroyan, 1990, p. 16). The conflict from the Azeri side has obviously also shown itself in ethnic cleavages, but in 1988 the demonstrations continued in Baku, against the government. These were due to dissatisfaction with the economy and dissatisfaction with the general circumstances of the people. It was, however, when the conflict started to produce casualties that it became 'ethnic'.

Kohn also stresses, that it is 'backwardness' that makes nationalism find expression through culture and history. It seems to some extent, however, somewhat overstated to claim that all former Soviet states were 'backward' due to the system of their society.

Kohn's division between Eastern and Western nationalism, then, does not seem fully to encompass the resurgence of nationalism in this particular conflict. It can be argued that, to some extent, the Eastern type fits part of the pattern, but not completely. The conflict appears as a strong ethnic cleavage, and this may be so, but it is difficult to argue that it is due to 'backwardness' or a weak 'power class'. What might be a more appropriate term is 'ethnic nationalism', where history and culture are fundamentals, but where, according to Snyder 'it appears spontaneously when an institutional vacuum occurs' (Snyder, 1993, p. 12). However, it is also clear that the intensity of ethnicity grew stronger as the conflict grew longer. As Snyder puts it: 'War made the state, and state made war and together they made nationalism' (Snyder, 1993, p. 13). This can be seen clearly in Azerbaijan, when the demand for better economic policies became tied in with the fact that they were losing the war in Nagorno-Karabakh (in 1992). A new government was demanded to improve the fiscal policy, so the war against Armenia could be won.

What is important to keep in mind is that there are three actors in the conflict, not only two, and that it was Karabakh which started the war by choosing to join Armenia. Nationalism in this area can be argued to be more a reaction against economic deprivation and human-rights violations (Fuller, 1993, p. 89), than 'age-old' animosities. Kohn's theory, then, might help us to classify nationalisms to some extent but in this case it does not seem to explain its resurgence, or why it appeared in the shape and form that it did.

Gellner's theory emphasises the 'modern' aspects of nationalism, and so may be supposed to help to explain the present conflict. Gellner emphasises socio-economic reasons for the rise of nationalism. In the initial stages of the crisis in Nagorno-Karabakh, it does seem that socio-economic factors, among other things, played a major role. That is to say, the Armenian population was extremely dissatisfied with the standard of living, and generally the socio-economic conditions. Azerbaijan was lagging behind Armenia in that sector, and the Armenians in Karabakh compared themselves with them (Yamskov, 1991, p. 640). There was a belief in Karabakh that this difference was due to deliberate policies from the government in Azerbaijan, since it controls the economy of the oblast. The government felt, however, that this area was faring better than the others and funds were directed from Karabakh to poorer areas (Yamskov, 1991, p. 640). This, it can be argued, was one of the reasons why a brighter future became part of the Armenian agenda: after re-unification general living conditions would rise and welfare would be better. In the case of Nagorno-Karabakh, then, it can be argued that these were socio-economic reasons for the rise of nationalism.

It remains somewhat doubtful, however, if this can be argued for Armenia as well. This is due to the fact that it is costly to support an irredentist movement. According to Horowitz (1991, p. 15), irredentism includes an, 'ideology of common fate, that hardly lends itself to abrupt termination'. This means that even if Armenia wanted to withdraw, due to the high cost of the conflict, it would be close to impossible for it to do so. It, then, becomes somewhat difficult to argue that Armenia's nationalism is based on socio-economic reasons for wanting to unify with the area. On the contrary, supporting the movement in Nagorno-Karabakh became a socio-economic catastrophe of vast dimensions, which it is too late to withdraw from.

To Azerbaijan it seems that, even if the Karabakh is an area with higher levels of economic development than the rest of the country, its importance lies more in the fact that its loss means the loss of territorial control than in any socio-economic factors. It is more of a reaction against losing part of the 'nation-state' and the claimed violation of national sovereignty than because of socio-economic loss.

Gellner also states, however, that political and social upheaval is a pre-condition for nationalism. In this case upheaval was, of course, evident: with the disintegration of the Soviet Union, both states were in a state of social and political upheaval and change. This, can be argued, to have played a part in destabilising the relationship between the states, and the minorities living within them.

Gellner's theory does not acknowledge nationalism as having roots in human psychology. The ethnic-historic lines that can be drawn, however, cannot be disregarded. Especially since much of the cleavage is widened by the fact that the Azeris are viewed as Turks by the Armenians. This evokes a lot of painful memories from the Ottoman Empire, not least the genocide in 1915, where 1.5 million Armenians perished. This is crystallised by the fact that the Azeris themselves did not think of themselves as 'Azeri' before 1917. They usually described themselves as 'Turk' and their language as Turki (Bennigsen, 1969,

p. 27). So, when Gellner argues that in 'earlier times' people were not conscious of their culture, it can be argued to some extent that this is true for the Azeris. However, one can make a clear distinction between being aware of one's culture and having a 'national consciousness'. A 'national consciousness' might not have existed as such, but the awareness of religion, tradition, culture and language were present.

The Armenians have long been conscious of their shared culture. Their continuous religious, historic and ethnic existence cannot be denied. This is not to argue, however, as Suny points out (1993, p. 4), that all Armenians were always in agreement about these issues, and that they all perceived the 'Armenianness' the same way. There were divisions among them, as among most people. They were, and are, a group based on the perception of, and identification with, a common culture, history, religion and language.

To some extent, then, Gellner's theory can be argued to shed some light on the emergence of 'new' nationalism. This is only in the sense that 'new' nationalisms can contain socio-economic factors, and that social, political upheaval and change also is a condition under which nationalism may be said to flourish. However, one cannot explain deep-seated ethnic bonds only as 'invented symbols' developed after the conflict has arisen. Ethnic ties and relations seem to have to be included, to some degree, in an explanation of a conflict that is experiencing so much inter-ethnic rivalry, and which has a history of the same type of conflict. That is not to argue that the 'ancient hatred' thesis is correct, but using only a few variables - all based on socio-economic factors and development - is, in this case, too narrow an approach.

Part of Smith's theory will now be used to see if it can explain the contemporary nationalism of the case. Smith includes ethnicity when explaining nationalism, and the change from ethnicity to nationalism is, in his view, due to (among other things) what he claims is a decline of religion. For the Armenians, however, the Church has for centuries been the main source of identification. It created a unifying feeling, due to the fact that it was as a 'Christian people' surrounded by 'Muslims' that the Armenians survived, and that Armenia was the first Christian state in the world. Religion was, and is, a strong factor in Armenian identity. One reason for this may be that, after the loss of the Cilician kingdom in AD 1375, the Armenians possessed no state of their own, and the Church became their means of identification. As Jones states: 'Religion became central to the preservation of Armenian identity' (Ramet, 1989, p. 173). Some early revolutionary parties, however - for instance the Hunchaks in 1887, which was socialist - did denounce religion and remain strongly nationalistic, but it had several problems, however, including the fact that Armenians often remained convinced that socialism was alien to them. The Armenians were, even then, nationalist, not socialist (Suny, 1993, p. 74). The bond between the Church and the people was never severed and, as Scarfe has put it 'nationalism became a natural dimension of Church activity' (Ramet, 1989, p. 180). Nationalism arose around and within the Church itself.

It is, therefore, somewhat difficult to hold that nationalism in Armenia is in part due to a 'decline in religion'. On the contrary, the Armenian Church seems to share many anti-Turkish feelings widespread among the population. In the case of the Armenians, then, Smith's view cannot be valid, since religion and nationalism are so intertwined.

In Azerbaijan, the identification with religion differs somewhat according to belief. In Azerbaijan, there is a majority of Shi'a Muslims (about 70-75%) and a minority (25-30%) are Sunni Muslims. However, according to Bennigsen, the confusion between religion and nationality is strong for both groups (Bennigsen, 1985, p. 143). Traditionally, the Armenians have been viewed as rivals to the Azeris, however, not only due to religion. Moreover, the difference in socio-economic status and the fact that the Armenians were more educated has been a stronger reason for the cleavage than 'Muslim' against 'Christian'. Islam did give the Azeris a sense of unity, but it is doubtful, however, whether it is a strong part of contemporary nationalism. According to an Azeri journalist the Azeris had a 'weak sense of solidarity in the past and minded our own business. The developments (in NKAO, Armenia and Azerbaijan) have helped to unite us. A national feeling and a state of awareness have emerged in the community for the first time' (Saroyan,

1990, p. 18).

It can be argued, then, that with reference to Azerbaijan, Smith's view can to some extent fit. However, it might not be so much the decline of religion, but more that the two exist side by side, in a separate way. That is to say, that nationalism did not arise due to some form of secularisation, but more as a reaction to it. In Azerbaijan, Islam had not given the strong sense of identity and unity that the Church had provided in Armenia.

Smith also argues that there are two reasons for the resurgence of nationalism, one which is the existence of ethnic traditions and sentiments which nationalists can 'use'. Initially, ethnicity was not much cited as a reason for their actions by the Armenians in Nagorno-Karabakh. Instead, socio-economic and cultural deprivation were held as reasons for the wish to secede. As mentioned before, it was when the conflict grew deeper, on both sides, that it established itself as an 'ethnic' conflict. Strong sentiments about ethnic issues do exist, however, and they are being mercilessly used by nationalists to deepen the conflict. It can be argued, however, if it can be held to be a reason for the resurgence of nationalism or if, in this case, it is more appropriate to use it as a condition for, or as an extra factor which reinforces, the already existing cleavage and nationalisms.

The second reason Smith argues is, the existence of the bureaucratic cycle, which can produce two types of nationalisms: a state-oriented, and a 'romantic ethnic', nationalism. This can to some extent be compared with Kohn's division of Western and Eastern nationalism. Nagorno-Karabakh, however, can be argued to experience both simultaneously. That is to say, when their decision to join Armenia was blocked, they opted for secession and the creation of their own state. It became a state-oriented nationalism. It also became to some extent ethnic, in the sense of emphasis on history, culture and language. Part of Smith's theory, then, can to some extent help to explain the resurgence - or, perhaps rather, the fact - of existing ethnicity being a significant factor in nationalism as a political ideology.

Anderson's theory of nationalism does also include ethnic roots, but is mostly based on linguistic measures, print-capitalism and 'modern' processes. If one accepts Anderson's definition of nations as 'imagined communities', then the nations in this case have already been imagined, and the patterns and solidarities are already there, so it does not assist in furthering the explanation of nationalism in contemporary society. Even if the societies of Armenians and Azeris are 'imagined', the emergence of nationalism due to the creation of those communities (it can be argued) is now non-existent, because the creation of them has already happened. This argument, it may be noted, can be applied to print-capitalism as well. It was developed at the same time as the first emergence of nationalism and can hardly be said to have any direct influence on the resurgence of contemporary nationalism. The Armenians in Nagorno-Karabakh had been deprived of their right to have education in their own language. This is due to a law which states that the majority's language shall be the educational one, so only rarely were they taught in Armenian. There were also other attempts to destroy their cultural identity (Walker, 1991, p. 2). Statistics show that in 1980 there were 112 schools in Nagorno-Karabakh that taught in Armenian, whereas 31 in Azeri and only 5 in Russian (Moll-zade, 1992, p. 25). It can be argued, then, if one holds the view that they have been deprived in this way, that due to the wider communications possible with Armenia after the disintegration of the Soviet Union, the Armenians of Nagorno-Karabakh 'rediscovered' the community of language. 'Print-capitalism' might, then, have helped to reinforce the structure of a 'imagined community' at that point.

Print-languages were, in both Armenia and Azerbaijan, a force in developing a sense of unity and cultural identity but, due to illiteracy, this could not possibly become a force in the majority of the population until later. For the Armenians in Karabakh, language is a feature which clearly distinguishes 'us' from 'them'. However, it is difficult to argue that language, as such, plays a part in the resurgence of nationalism in the area today.

Anderson and Smith included the same view of religion and its impact on nationalism, in their theories. As already discussed, this is not viable.

Religion has not been completely replaced by secular ideologies, or nationalism. On the contrary, it seems to exist in Armenia intertwined with nationalism, and is a part of it. It can be argued, then, that while Anderson's theory might help to explain the development of nationalism in other cases, it does not seem to be very useful in explaining the violent resurgence of nationalism in this specific area.

Conclusion

In looking at the conflict between Armenia and Azerbaijan it is important to keep in mind that it erupted in Nagorno-Karabakh. It started as a secessionist movement, however, with the aim of joining Armenia. This then developed to an irredentist movement in Armenia, aiming to retrieve the 'ethnically kindred people and their territory across borders' (Chazan, 1919, p. 10). It is always rare for a state to follow the path of irredentism, due to the costs it incurs, but it is especially surprising, since it was possible for Armenia to support the secessionist movement without such a serious financial commitment. If a state supports a secessionist movement, it is also able to withdraw whenever the costs are deemed to be too high, but if the state is irredentist, however, it cannot easily terminate the relationship.

The conflict has passed through different phases, and it can be argued that it has consisted of different types of nationalism depending on the phase and actor examined. When the conflict started it was mainly a conflict between the local Armenian population of Nagorno-Karabakh and the government of Azerbaijan, and the emphasis was mainly socio-economic. That is to say, the Armenians demanded an improvement of their socio-economic situation, because it was felt that the government was treating them unfairly. The economy, it was argued, could be improved if it was not hindered by the Azeri government, and the general living conditions and standards could reach a much higher level. Comparisons were made with Armenia, where conditions were in fact far better. Thus, the reasoning was that by joining Armenia this would lead to socio-economic improvement, although the argument also included cultural conflict with the government. This was also seen in terms of destruction: Armenians were culturally deprived, it was said, and wanted the right to live as Armenians and not have their culture eradicated.

At the start, then, the focus of the Armenians in Nagorno-Karabakh, was on human-rights violations and socio-economic factors. As the conflict grew, however, these arguments seem to have been lost in the 'ethnicity' of it all, and focus was turned to the 'obvious' ethnic cleavages.

Rather than working from established theories when explaining this first phase of nationalism among the local Armenians in Nagorno-Karabakh, it might be useful to apply a new approach: Davis's 'J-curve'. This might to some extent shed light on the arising of nationalism in this area. Davis's J-curve is usually applied to revolutions and states that a revolution, or a revolt, will not simply occur because people are oppressed and deprived of the most fundamental things. Rather, it will occur when the population have been given some freedom and prosperity, but realise that even greater prosperity and freedom can be achieved. In this view, initial gains form a foundation for future rebellion.

In this case, then, it can be noted that, although the Armenians knew that they were disadvantaged during the years of Azeri rule, they did not revolt. When Gorbachev introduced '*perestroika*' and '*glasnost*', however, the situation began to improve. Communications across the border with Armenia became easier, and with it came the realisation that the people with whom they identified themselves linguistically, historically and culturally had superior socio-economic circumstances. So, by comparison, their own situation seemed even worse than before. Due to this, then, a 'revolt' was started, and the conflict between the government and the minority arose. This is not to argue that nationalism emerged due to the 'fall of communism' as such, but more due to state disintegration, and the security, economic and infrastructural problems that emerged from it. Nationalism was then reinforced by the pre-existing ethnic differences, and used as a means to reach the desired end.

So, it can be argued that the emergence of nationalism in Nagorno-Karabakh can be compared with a revolution. It has many points of resemblance to situations usually considered to be 'revolutionary'. Revolution is the creation of something new, it is a desire for progress and a better, and more just, future (Dunn, 1979, p. 5). This is exactly what the Armenians in Nagorno-Karabakh demanded at the beginning of the conflict: they wanted equality and a better living standard. Revolutions may arise when 'material civilization is felt to be lacking, and it is known that it is possible to be achieved, but that their leaders are failing to bring it to them' (Dunn, 1971, p. 23). This was a feeling prevalent in Karabakh, specially since the government reallocated funds, which should have gone to the oblast, to other poorer parts of the country, because (in the government's view) Karabakh was a 'rich' area.

Dunn (1971, p. 15) argues that when a group succeeds in arousing the majority of the population who are already discontented with the prevailing order, then a sense of justification of the destruction of the existing order can be infused in them, making it easier to revolt. The Armenians in Karabakh had been discontented with the situation during the Soviet period; however, it was only when disintegration began, and it became possible to vent one's dissatisfaction, that the population came together under the leadership of an elite group. This justified the 'revolt' on the grounds of persecution, cultural deprivation and socio-economic stagnation.

Dunn (1971, p. 254), also argues that the most fertile situation for revolutionaries is temporary enemy occupation. Many political revolutions that have had massive popular mobilisation have been wars of national liberation. This, it can be argued, is exactly what is happening in Karabakh. The Armenians in the area feel that it should belong to Armenia, because of history, ethnic and linguistic reasons. It can be argued that they feel that their territory has been 'occupied' by a foreign force, and that they are fighting for their 'national liberation'.

Revolution also includes violent and rapid political and social change. The situation in Karabakh, however, exhibits aspects of this: the situation is violent, but it was not violent from the start. It began as a non-violent conflict between the Armenians in Karabakh and the government of Azerbaijan. The situation cannot be said to be rapidly changing, it began in 1988 and is still in existence today. It has, however, led to some political and social change, in the sense that there is a political vacuum due to the war.

Although it cannot be stated that the nationalism in this area is 'a revolution' as such, it does seem to have several points of resemblance to revolutions, so as to make applying the theory of revolution one way of viewing the conflict, in search of a better understanding and explanation of it.

The second phase came when Armenia became involved and actively supported the movement in Karabakh. Armenian nationalism cannot be explained by referring to a desire of achieving a better socio-economic structure. On the contrary, by supporting and following an irredentist ideology, the structures of society and economic wealth might dissolve. The reference to territory then became the focal point for Armenia.

Nagorno-Karabakh has, according to Walker (1991, p. 73), been Armenian since at least the second century BC, and part of the Armenian kingdom until its fall. It was inhabited by Armenians since that time, and Armenians argue that Karabakh joined Azerbaijan only in 1923. Moll-zade (1992, p. 35), however, points out that it had been a Muslim Khanate since the eighteenth century. In his opinion, then, it is a mistake to claim that Karabakh is 'Armenian' on territorial-historical grounds. Both sides in the conflict take episodes of history to support their own view and then conveniently leave out the rest. In fact, Nagorno-Karabakh, like the whole of Transcaucasus, has been ruled by different peoples, and it was part of the old Armenian kingdom until the eleventh century, when it received a sort of independence. In the seventeenth century it became part of the Ottoman Empire, and in the eighteenth century it became a Muslim Khanate. Then, in 1805, Russian troops invaded the area (Halbach, 1988, p. 518). So, when the historical background of the territory is considered, one may note that it has been ruled both by Armenians and Turkic peoples. But territory, it can be argued, was an important aspect of the rise of nationalism, and it was also easier to mobilise nationalism due to the emphasis on territory and 'Greater-Armenia'.

If one agrees with Posen that 'an offensive advantage exists, when hard-to-defend pockets of co-nationals reside in territories dominated by another national group' (Snyder, 1993, p. 19), then it can be argued that due to the structure of the situation, an offensive nationalism was aroused so as to mobilise the people and support the cause. The rise of this nationalism stems from the fact that, due to the disintegration of the Soviet Union, the borders became insecure and the governments too weak to protect them. The minorities demanded their own states or, as Karabakh, fusion with a neighbouring state. The disintegration destabilised the area in such a way that nationalism occurred.

This does not mean that the conflict was 'lying in wait' ready to explode and that it was communism which kept it contained, but it was as a result of the disintegration of the Soviet Union that nationalism emerged as a reaction.

Azerbaijan's initial stages of nationalism can be also argued to be a reaction, first towards the secessionist movement in Nagorno-Karabakh, and then to irredentist moves from Armenia. This was, as mentioned before, once again closely linked to territory, but in the case of Azerbaijan it might be seen as even more so than in that of Armenia. This is due to the fact that Azeri nationalism is based on the protection of the nation-state. It can be said to be a nationalism brought on by threats to sovereignty and to the entity which has existed since 1923. To Azerbaijan, then, it is a question of national security and of being able to protect its borders. When a state which is in this situation cannot show its population that it is able to do that, it will lose confidence. This happened in relation to Mulitabov, who was rejected for a man deemed more capable of securing the nation-state.

As the conflict grew more intense, however, it is possible to distinguish a third phase. This is when ethnicity became all-important, and it seemed (through the media) that there was no other reason for the conflict than an 'ancient hatred' and the ethno-religious cleavages. So, ethnicity in this conflict does play a part in nationalism, but it does not, however, seem to play a part in the rise of nationalism as such. Instead, it deepens the conflict and makes nationalism grow: the hatred between the peoples widens due to its existence. Hamburg argues that when a conflict cannot be solved at an early point, bitterness grows and a part of the population makes hate and violence an organisational principle of their existence. When that happens the actor can 'invent' historical and cultural myths to reinforce the self-confidence in their group, and ethno-centrism appears (Hamburg, 1993, p. 117). It seems that this is part of what has happened in this conflict, and it cannot be denied that ethnic differences and memories of past massacres and cruelty are very much present, both in the Armenian and Azeri populations. However, they have also lived in peace. The different cultures, languages and religions of these peoples do create two distinct groups, which makes identification of 'us' and 'them' easy, but it seems fair to argue that these differences were deliberately used after nationalism and the conflict had broken out. So, when the Sumgaim tragedy happened, it reinforced an already existing hatred of Turks and reinforced memories of similar situations. It can be argued, however, that it was not so much a question of recalling memories, but more a question of them having been brought back through the use of the media for propaganda. It cannot be argued that there exists an inherent ethnic hatred for another group, rather this has been taught through various forms of media, education and communication.

The ethnicity question and its impact on nationalism cannot be ignored. It is an important part of nationalism, but to hold it as the sole reason for the eruption of contemporary nationalism is not viable. At least in this case, it might serve as a tool for nationalists to further their cause.

It has been argued, here, that the conflict cannot be seen as simply the result of one type of nationalism. It includes at least three phases in which different types of nationalism can be detected. The nationalisms among the participants in the conflict vary in background, reason and rise.

The usefulness of explaining the eruption of nationalism in the Caucasus with reference to any of the theories of nationalism can be noted to be somewhat limited. Kohn's divisions become more of a classification than an attempt of explanation, and in this case do not seem to classify very clearly. They can, however, be said to be somewhat useful in the interpretation of the ethnic aspect of this conflict.

Gellner's theory seems to be able to explain the nationalism seen in Nagorno-Karabakh to some extent, but seems to be at more of a loss when it comes to Armenia and Azerbaijan. It is useful due to the emphasis it puts on socio-economic factors, but it can be argued to be somewhat narrow since it excludes ethnic ties and bonds.

Smith's theory, when it comes to the part of religion, is not very useful at all. As shown before, in none of these areas has religion been replaced by nationalism, nor has nationalism grown due to a decline of religion. Smith's emphasis on the importance of ethnic roots, however, and his suggestion of the ways in which they are used by nationalists, can be seen to apply in this conflict.

Anderson's theory, it can be argued, can only assist us in a very indirect way in explaining part of the pattern of the conflict. The theory seems best suited for explaining the initial development of nationalism rather than its contemporary rise.

Nationalism, in a conflict such as this, is plainly difficult to explain. There are many factors that need to be taken into consideration and evaluated. It can be argued that one cannot put forward one theory for contemporary nationalism, which will be suitable for all existing cases, but that nationalism may be area- and time-specific, although this does not mean that generalisations are necessarily impossible.

Ethnic cleavages in this area do exist but it is after nationalism has already emerged that these become mobilised as a force in the population. It seems, however, that it is possible to argue that due to system-disintegration, resulting insecurity, failure to meet socio-economic threats and weakness in infrastructure, nationalism can result. The ethnicity surrounding it serves to reinforce the conflict and it can eventually seem as if it was the reason why the conflict erupted in the first place.

Solutions to this conflict do not seem to be immediately at hand. One suggestion has been to make Nagorno-Karabakh an area with independence and sovereignty, as are the Aaland-islands. This was suggested by Eide at a Conference for Human Rights in Oslo in 1991; however, this proposal does not seem to have been greatly discussed. The UN has not done much apart from 'urging' the warring factions to stop hostilities and withdraw their forces. The Security Council has adopted resolutions which include 'expressing its grave concern at the human suffering the conflict has caused' and 'calls on all parties to refrain from all violations of international humanitarian law', but this has not led to any solution of the conflict, and the battlefields seemed worse than ever after it. The OSCE Minsk Group has not been able to suggest any viable solutions either, and when the conflict/war escalated further in 1993 the reaction was a statement issued by the Group that included the observation 'the escalation was extremely alarming' and that 'the Group strongly condemns the attacks on the civilian population', and that they 'urge the parties to stop fighting'. To end the conflict, however, there must be more done than 'urging' and 'expressing concern'. Although there have been negotiations, the populations seem to be on militantly opposite sides and a quick solution seems unlikely.

Bibliography

Aalerud, M. (1992), 'Transkaukasus fra sovjetisk overkjoring til nasjonalistisk rakjoring', *Internatsjonal Politikk* 1.2

Alter, P. (1989), *Nationalism*, Routledge, London

Anderson, B. (1983), *Imagined communities*, Verso, London

Anon (1992), *Eastern Europe and the commonwealth of independent states*, Europa Publications, London

Barth, B. (1969), *Ethnic groups and boundaries*, Universitetsforlaget, Oslo

Bennigsen, A. (1967), *Islam in the Soviet Union*, Pall Mall Press, London

Bennigsen, A. (1984), 'Mullahs, Mujahidin, and Soviet Muslims', *Problems of Communism* 33

Bennigsen, A. and Wimbush, S. (1985), *Muslims of the Soviet Empire*, Hurst, London

Brogen, P. (1992), *World conflicts. Why and where they are happening*, Bloomsbury Publishing, London

Bremmer, I and Taras, R. (1993), *Nations and politics in the Soviet successor states*, Cambridge University Press, Cambridge

Chazan, N. (1991), *Irredentism and international politics*, Lynne Rienner Publishers, Boulder

Coakley, J. (1992), *The social origins of nationalist movements*, Sage, London

Dawydow, J. and Trenin, D. (1993), 'Ethnische Konflikte auf dem Gebiet der ehemaligen Sowjetunion', *Europa Archiv*, Folge 7

Der Nersessian (1969), *The Armenians*, Thames and Hudson, London

Dalhoff-Nielsen, P. (1992), *Krudtonnen Kaukasus*, Denmark

Dragadze, T. (1989), 'The Armenian-Azerbaijani conflict; structure and sentiment', *Third World Quarterly* 11.1

Dunn, J. (1972), *Modern revolutions*, Cambridge University Press, Cambridge

Fraser, N. *et al.* (1990), 'A conflict analysis of the Armenian-Azerbaijani dispute', *Journal of Conflict Resolution* 34.4

Fuller, E. (1992), 'The Transcaucasus Republics', *RFE/RL Research Report* 1.7

Fuller, E. (1993), 'Mediators for Transcaucasus' conflicts', *The World Today* 49.5

Gellner, E. (1990), *Nations and nationalism*, Blackwell, Oxford

Gotz, R. and Halbach, U. (1992), 'Die Nachfolgestaaten der USSR', *OstEuropa* 42.11

Govorukhin, S. (1990), 'A rehearsal?', *Moscow New Weekly* 7

Halbach, U. (1988), 'ie Armenier in der Sowjetunion', *Europa Archiv*, Folge 43

Hamburg, D. (1993), 'Ethnische Konflikte', *Europa Archiv*, Folge 4

Iskandaryan, A. (1993), 'More stimuli for war than peace', *New Times International* 18

Kamenk, A. (1976), *Nationalism*, Arnold Publishers, London

Kedourie, E. (1986), *Nationalism*, Hutchinson, London

Kellas, J. (1991), *The politics of nationalism and ethnicity*, Macmillan, London

Kohn, H. (1948), *The idea of nationalism*, Macmillan, New York

Mackenzie, K. (1992), 'Azerbaijan and the neighbours', *The World Today* 48.1

Manutscharjan, A. (1992), 'Nagornyj Karabach im Kampf um das Selbstimmungsrecht', *OstEuropa* 42.11

Moll-zade, D. (1992), *The conflict between Armenia and Azerbaijan over Nagorno-Karabagh*, Norwegian Institute of Human Rights, Oslo

Morgenthau, H. (1918), *The tragedy of Armenia*, Spottiswoode and Ballantyne, London

Myklebost, H. (1989), 'Armenia and the Armenians', *Norsk geografisk Tidskrift*, vol. 43

Myklebost, H. (1992), 'Armenere fra genocid til glasnost', *Nordisk Ostforum* 6.1

Neumann, I. (1993), 'The Caucasus between Russia, Turkey and Iran', *Norwegian Institute of International Affairs* 495, June

Ra'anan, (1991), *State and nation in multi-ethnic societies*, Manchester University Press, Manchester

Ramet, P.(1989), *Religion and nationalism in Soviet and East-European politics*, Duke University Press, London

Sakwa, R. (1990), *Gorbachev and his reforms 1985-90*, Cambridge University Press, Cambridge

Saroyan, M. (1990), 'The "Karabagh Syndrome" and Azerbaijani politics', *Problems of Communism* 39

Simmonds, G. (1977), *Nationalism in the USSR and Eastern Europe*, University of Detroit Press, Detroit

Smith, A. (1971), *Theories of nationalism*, Duckworth, London

Smith, A. (1979), *Nationalism in the twentieth century*, Robertson, Oxford

Smith, A. (1985), 'Ethnie and nation in the modern world', *Millennium* 14.2

Smith, A. (1991), *The ethnic origins of nations*, Blackwell, Oxford

Smith, G. (1990), *The nationalities question in the Soviet Union*, Longman, London

Snyder, J. (1990), 'Nationalism and the crisis of the post-Soviet state', *Survival* 35.1

Snyder, L. (1977), *The meaning of nationalism*, Greenwood Press, Westport

Suny, R. (1993), *Looking toward Ararat*, Indiana University Press, Cincinnati

Waage, P. (1993), *Jeg, vi og de andre*, Cappelen, Oslo

Walker, C. (1991), *Armenia and Karabavh*, Minority Rights Publications, London

Walker, C and Lang, D. (1991), *Armenia*, A Minority Rights Group Report, March

Yamskov, A. (1991), 'Ethnic conflict in the Transcausasus', *Theory and Society* 20.5

DOCUMENTS

CSCE-Minsk Group Press Release, CSCE Secretariat, Prague, 13 April,1994.
CSCE-Documents, Helsinki Monitor, Vol.3, No.2, 1992.
UN-Security Council, S/RES/ 874, 14 October, 1993.
UN-Press Release, SC/5677, 29 July, 1993.
UN-Press Release, SC/5744, 12 November, 1993.
UN-Security Council, S/RES/884, 12 November, 1993.

6 Between Europe and Asia: security dimensions of Turkey's role in the Middle East

RAMAZAN GÖZEN

Introduction

This chapter seeks to show that Turkey is a reliable ally for the Western states and a solid pillar of NATO. Its importance in this respect, is as a 'stabiliser' in the Gulf and Arab world, rather than in the security of Europe, itself.

There is no country that bridges the two continents of Europe and Asia other than Turkey. The Bosphorus Bridge and Fatih Sultan Mehmet Bridge in Istanbul symbolise the fact that Turkish territory is the shortest route to the Middle East from Europe. Maybe because of this geopolitical position, Turkey has a number of peculiarities which cannot be found elsewhere.

Although Turkey is a Middle Eastern country, it has been undergoing a transformation towards Westernisation in the last two centuries. How successful this process has been is beyond the scope of this chapter, but it is certainly true that this process is yet to be completed, as can be seen in every aspect of Turkey, from its domestic culture to its foreign policy orientation. It is also possible to see a number of contrasts in Turkish politics and society that are a result of this mixture of Western and Eastern values.

Turkish territory is made up of Anatolia in Asia and the Thrace in Europe. Istanbul - the biggest city of Turkey - is situated at the junction of those two zones. Despite a mostly Muslim population (albeit with substantial non-Muslim minorities), Turkey is ruled by secular and Western-oriented democratic principles, along with liberal market-economic policies. Although it has a long Islamic history, the Turkish state manifests this objective of Westernisation in manyof its aspects.

Despite this, Turkey has not been excluded from the recently growing Islamic fundamentalist challenge to Western values. Thus, Turkey has been facing an identity crisis, trying to choose between the Western and Islamic ways of life. As a result, it is difficult to put Turkey into any of the stereotypical classifications of world societies: such as Western, Asian or Middle Eastern.

Geography makes it inevitable that Turkey plays a crucial role in the security of both Europe and Asia, and history links it with the Middle East and Central Asia. The first aspect of Turkey's security role is, therefore, its own contribution to the security of the surrounding region. In this role, Turkey had strategic and political significance and acted as a bastion of the regional security during the Cold War. Turkey's two strategic straits were a crucial sea barrier to the Soviet Union's control of the Mediterranean, while the Anatolian peninsula obstructed potential Soviet expansion to the South. Economically, the capitalist economy linked Turkey to the West and Turkey's pro-Western political orientation was in contrast to most neighbouring states. Being dependent on the importation of industrialised goods from the West, the Turkish economy still cannot manage without the West: nor can it sustain its imports without exporting to the West. With such an economy, Turkey is tied to the Western world in the post-Cold War period. This dependency means that Turkey continues to be a stronghold of Western secular values in the Middle East, and its interests lie firmly with those of the West.

Turkey's role in NATO

Turkey's principal significance in security terms stems, therefore, from its orientation towards the West. It is the only 'Islamic' and Middle Eastern country in the NATO Alliance, acting as an extension of the Western world into a troubled region. Although Turkey might be useful to the Western Allies for security in the Balkan region and in the Mediterranean, it has been a far more important actor in the Middle East, with a strategic location that was the principal attraction to the allies for its admission to the NATO Alliance in 1952.[1] In this respect, the Korean War - which had provided an important stimulus for transforming the North Atlantic Treaty into the North Atlantic Treaty Organisation (NATO)[2] - was a turning point for Turkey's acceptance to the Alliance (Whetten, 1984, esp. p. 251; Harris, 1972, pp. 39-42 and 50; McGhee, 1990, pp. 77-90). The Korean War indicated that the Cold War, which had centred on Europe, was spreading to other regions and so, potentially, to the Middle East (McGhee, 1990, pp. 83-84; Whetten, 1984, p. 251).

The two recent international crises in the Gulf and in the former Yugoslavia vindicate the value of this view. Unlike Turkey's active role in the Gulf crisis and the War (1990-91), it has not been permitted to take the same responsibility in the war in the former Yugoslavia. The reasons given for Turkey's lack of a military role in the former Yugoslavia are that it could not be a neutral actor, due to the legacy of Ottoman rule. This is surprising, because of Turkey's role in the Gulf War, as the Ottomans were also present in both Iraq and Kuwait until the First World War. This fact did not prevent Turkey's closure of the Turkish-Iraqi oil pipelines and the use of the Incirlik air base by US forces against Iraq.

So, Turkey's role in supporting the West in the Middle East has been diverse: strategic, military, diplomatic and political. As a major regional actor, Turkey's stance in any problems in the Middle East may change their outcomes, making it of importance to securing this vital region. This role is amply illustrated by the latest example of Turkey's military support for the Western world, in the 1991 Gulf War, which will form the subject for more detailed evaluation here, although there were, of course, earlier examples of Turkish pro-Western activity. It tried to draw the most important regional actors into the Baghdad Pact (1955-58), attempting to involve Iraq, Iran, Lebanon, Jordan and others. However, it was not successful in this mission, and this failure led to the deterioration of Turkey's relations with those countries. As a result of Turkey's abortive attempts to increase security in the region, these countries became closer to the Soviet camp, and although the results of the ensuing conflicts with Syria and Egypt might have been favourable to the West, Turkey's pro-Western policies seemed likely to alienate it from other regional actors. Unsurprisingly, in the 1960s and 1970s, Turkey came to be hesitant in its pro-Western stance in the Middle East. So much so, that its cautious policy towards the conflicts and wars in the region has been described as 'neutrality'.

In the Gulf crisis of 1990-91, Turkey abandoned this policy and opted for the Gulf Coalition. Turkey was facing a 'security dilemma' in choosing between the Western world and Iraq: the implications of Turkey's NATO membership clashing with the benefits of its relations with Iraq. This was made a more acute security dilemma because Turkish-Iraqi relations had been so deep as to be 'security interdependence'.

Turkish-Iraqi relations:'security interdependence'

Among its neighbours, Iraq was the country with which Turkey had had least problems since the early days of the Turkish and Iraqi republics. This was mainly due to common interests that led to them becoming interdependent. Their interdependence was based on three important elements which concern their security: beneficial economic relations between the two countries, the Kurdish problem, and the Water Problem.

Above all else, it is geography which has been the most important factor in the enhancement of this interdependence between modern

Turkey and modern Iraq. Since their independence (after the collapse of the Ottoman Empire), the interactions between the two countries have been based on factors other than religion and imperialism. Despite their independence from the Ottoman Empire, they remained dependent on each other.

The Western-oriented principles of Turkish foreign policy may also have been a factor in Turkey's indifference to the Middle East at least until the mid-1960s. Although Iraq's socialist Ba'ath party may, further, have encouraged a pro-Soviet and ultra-nationalistic foreign policy, geography and related factors have been influential - if not determinative - on their foreign policies. Among other issues, the construction of the twin oil pipelines, the cross-border rivers and the ethnic minorities in both countries have further drawn the two countries towards one another in such a way that these have become continuing sources of cooperation between them.

During the early years of their independence, neither Turkey nor Iraq could act freely, because of, on the one hand, Iraq's occupation under the British Mandate (which lasted until official independence in 1932) and, on the other hand, Turkey's occupation. However, the interests of Turkey and Iraq soon converged within a series of bilateral and multilateral co-operative schemes: originally, the Saadabad Pact (1937).[3] After the Second World War, the two countries became members of the Baghdad Pact (1954-58). The overthrow by General Abdul Kerim Kassem of the Hashemite Kingdom in 1958, and Iraq's ensuing withdrawal from the Baghdad Pact, did not end cooperation between Turkey and Iraq. For instance, after the military coup in Iraq in 1958, a Turkish delegation attended the anniversary of the revolution in Baghdad (Vali, 1971, p. 301). Nor did the military coup in Turkey in 1960 interrupt Turkey's relations with Iraq. Although there were incidents on the Turkish-Iraqi border during the military regimes in Iraq and Turkey, in 1960 and in 1962, with Iraqi aircraft bombing Turkish border villages, Turkish governments did not break their relations with Iraq.

Not until a decade after the end of the Baghdad Pact did there emerge a new form of cooperation between the two countries: the construction of the oil pipelines gave this Turkish-Iraqi cooperation a new momentum, and resulted in the linkage of Turkey and Iraq by growing economic interaction.

The Turkish-Iraqi oil pipelines

The oil pipelines are an important asset, not only for the Turkish economy, but also for relations with Iraq. The construction of the oil pipelines between Turkey and Iraq is not only a result of the geographic advantages, but also a by-product of Turkey's dependence on oil imports. From the early 1970s, Turkey faced the growing burden of their oil crisis which was, in turn, highly influential in Turkish foreign policy. So strong an influence was this, that much of Turkey's re-orientation towards the Middle East can be explained by the search for cheap oil from the region. First, this involved securing a reliable flow of oil from the region. Second, aware of the increasing wealth and lucrative markets of the oil-producing countries, Turkey reinforced its efforts to pay for the oil bill with exports to oil-exporting partners (Mango, 1989, pp. 19-25). Since then, the 'search for oil' has been one of the main objectives of Turkey's external economic policy and a primary motive for deepening economic relations with its neighbours. This has inevitably influenced Turkish foreign policy behaviour. Turkey's neutrality in the 1973 Arab-Israeli war had saved it from the Arab retaliatory embargo that had been imposed on those countries that gave support to Israel.

However, this does not mean that Turkey did not face economic problems caused by increasing oil prices. Following the quadrupling of oil prices during the Arab-Israeli war, Turkey suffered the burden of an increasing oil bill, which had risen from $274 million in 1973 to $804 million in 1974, to $1121 billion in 1977 and to $2610 billion in 1980.[4] This increase amounted to some 20% of Turkey's overall import bill (*OECD Economic Surveys: Turkey*, November 1989, pp. 12-13). The oil problem became more dramatic particularly when the country faced an acute shortage of foreign currency, which exacerbated the economic and social pains of the whole country by the late 1970s. In response to these troubles, Turkish governments had to reduce the amount of the country's oil imports from 11,658 million tonnes in 1977 to 8,173 million tonnes in 1979 (*Journal of Turkish Oil Affairs* - see Note 4 - Table 49 p. 139), and so experience a painful shortage of oil. The fact that Turkey was dependent on the import of oil continued into the 1980s, its import amounting to an average of around 90% of its oil requirements. In 1989, 18.6 million tonnes of the total 20,762 million consumed oil were imported with a cost of $2,464 billion (*Cumhuriyet*, 21 August 1990, Table; *Journal of Turkish Oil Affairs*, p. 139).

It is clear, in retrospect, that Turkey's difficult circumstances propelled it towards two alternatives. The first possibility was to strengthen its position in the Middle East oil-producing countries to ensure continuous, and possibly cheaper, oil flows. The second alternative was to expand oil explorations in new areas.

A clear case of the second alternative can be seen in the Turkish attempt to explore new oil fields, including those in the Aegean Sea, after the 1973-74 oil crisis.[5] Such attempts heightened the disputes between Turkey and Greece and, in the following years, became a recurring source of contention between the two countries. The latest case of such crisis - which erupted in 1987 - reflected Turkey's continuing attempts to find oil in the Aegean Sea. This obviously has serious security implications as both Greece and Turkey are in NATO.

The most noticeable dimension of the first alternative, on the other hand, was the construction, at Turkey's request, of the first oil pipeline between Kirkuk in Iraq and Yumurtalik in Turkey. The first oil pipeline, 986 kilometres long, was completed in 1977 to pump initially 0.8 million barrels per day, or some 35 million tonnes per year.[6] The capacity of Iraqi oil exports through Turkey was further boosted to 1.5 million barrels per day, or some 70.9 million tonnes per year, when the 890 kilometre-long second pipeline was completed in June 1987.[7] Furthermore, the construction of a third pipeline between the two countries was being considered just before the Iraqi invasion of Kuwait.[8] As a result, Turkey had come to import a large amount of its oil requirements from Iraq. In 1989, the Iraqi share of Turkey's total oil imports amounted to an overwhelming majority of 63.8%. And in 1990, Turkey had planned to import some 8.5 million tonnes from Iraq of its total planned imports of 19.1 tonnes, with 3 million tonnes of expected domestic production.[9]

Thus, the oil pipelines were important assets for Turkey (Tashan, 1987, p. 36). Their importance stemmed from their economic, financial, strategic and even political advantages for Turkey.

The oil pipelines were a source of oil for the Turkish economy, but Iraq was placed in an advantageous position due to the oil pipelines being able to supply around 60% of Turkey's oil needs. Iraq was Turkey's closest oil supplier, which thus reduced the costs of transportation of oil. Indeed, Turkey's oil pipeline network was so constructed as to enable oil to be imported through it to be pumped to refineries around the region, and to Kirikkale refinery, in central Turkey.[10]

Moreover, Turkey used to receive concessional oil from Iraq, as a repayment of Iraq's $2 billion debt to Turkey. Iraq's debt had been reduced to $700 million by the repayments in oil. Furthermore, Turkey used to receive some $3,000 million annually as pipeline fees from Iraq. In addition to the pipeline fees, Turkey gained revenues from the port services provided to ships in connection with the transportation of oil, and other goods, to and from Iraq, via Turkish ports.

Another economic and financial advantage of the oil pipelines was their contribution to the economic activity in the region. The operation of the oil pipelines and other economic interactions with Iraq had been helpful in creating jobs for Turkish people in various fields.

Finally, there were strategic and political advantages for Turkey's relations with Iraq. The oil pipelines were helping Turkey to secure improved access to the Iraqi market in other areas. The growth in Turkish-Iraq trade relations can be partly attributed to Turkey's permission for the construction of the oil pipelines, and to Turkey's provision of an outlet for Iraq's export of oil to third countries viaTurkey.

The Turkish-Iraqi economic relations

Turkish-Iraqi economic and trade relations were based on the 1965 Turkey-Iraq Commercial Agreement (Mudurlugu, 1987). In the period from 1965 to 1974, the volume of trade increased, greatly in percentage but only slightly in value, from $16.3 million in 1965 to $43.4 million in 1973. Turkey's imports from Iraq amounted to $33.3 million (Mudurlugu, 1989, p. 27). In 1974, however, there was a very sharp increase in the trade volume, of some $357 million, in which Turkey's imports from Iraq was recorded at $327 million. Coinciding with the construction of the oil pipeline between Turkey and Iraq, Turkey started to import more oil from Iraq, rising to $694 million in 1977. In contrast, Turkey's exports to Iraq during the 1970s remained low, the highest being $113 million in 1979 (Mudurlugu, 1989; Devlet Istatistik Enstitusu, 1991, pp. IV.31).

A striking improvement in Turkish-Iraqi economic and trade relations was seen after the start of the operation of the oil pipelines in 1977. In 1980, the volume of trade rose to $1.372 billion, in which Turkey's exports did not change much in comparison to the previous years. However, by 1984 the trade gap between Turkey and Iraq was almost closed as Turkish exports to this country increased to $934.3 million (Mudurlugu, 1989; Devlet Istatistik Enstitusu, 1991, pp. IV.31-4; *OECD Economic Surveys 1986/1987: Turkey*, June 1987, p. 22). As a result, Iraq became one of Turkey's biggest trade partners during this decade, once climbing to the top of Turkey's annual imports, and becoming the second in Turkey's annual exports. In total, between 1982-1986, Iraq had always been within the top five of Turkey's trading partners (*OECD Economic Surveys, 1986/1987: Turkey*, June 1987, Table 9 p. 22; Irbec, 1990, p. 71) and within the top three in the Middle Eastern region.[11] Iraq's place in Turkey's exports spectrum moved from 4.6% in 1980 to its highest level of 13.1% in 1984, becoming the second only after ex-West Germany. Although Turkey's export to Iraq declined to 8.4% later in 1988, Turkey's imports of oil from Iraq stayed increasingly high, at an average 10-15% throughout the 1980s (Irbec,

1990, Tables 22 and 23 pp. 67-8; Devlet Istatistik Enstitusu, 1991). Turkey's payments for its high level of oil imports from Iraq were almost balanced by Turkey's revenues from its exports to that country. This advantage can be seen in the fact that Turkey began to extend credits to Iraq in the 1980s. From the early 1980s onwards, as the Iraqi regime had faced repayment difficulties, Turkey extended export credits to Iraq that once climbed to $2.5 billion. Repayment of these credits was covered by protocols between the two countries concluded during the Iran-Iraq War.[12] So, Turkish-Iraqi trade relations produced 'balanced benefits', based on Turkish imports of Iraqi oil and Turkish exports to Iraq.

In addition to Turkey's gradual penetration into the Iraqi market, Turkish-Iraqi economic relations widened to embrace other fields, including the export of Turkish workers, the activities of the Turkish construction firms, transportation, transit trade, tourism (Irbec, 1990; Manisali, 1987, p. 100. On the spill-over of Turkey's economic relations with the Middle East in general, see also Demirer, 1985; Yalcintas, 1986; Guven, 1990).

The place gained by Turkish construction firms in Iraq constituted the second most important benefit after oil. In the field of construction activities, out of a total $18.9 billion worth of contracts gained by Turkish firms in the whole Middle East between 1974 and March 1990, Iraq's share was 12%, or some $2.5 billion. However, in this sector, Iraq was not the leading partner: Libya and Saudi Arabia dominated it with their respective shares of 46.7%, or some $9.4 billion, and 27.8%, or $4.9 billion (Turkish Constructors Association, 1990, Tables 1, 2 and 3 pp. 18-19; Irbec, 1990, Tables 33, 34 and 36 pp. 91 and 95; *Newspot*, 24 May 1990 and 17 June 1991; Ayanoglu, 1990, pp. 13-14 and 16; Kalaycioglu, 1988, p. 92). An additional advantage generated by the construction firms was the promotion of Turkish exports to these construction sites and increasing transfers of foreign exchange to Turkey.[13]

Iraq's relative weakness in comparison to Turkey's other trade partners was also visible in other sectors of Turkey-Middle East economic relations. On Turkey's export of workers to the Middle East, which increased from 434 in 1967 to 451,419 in 1988, Iraq's share showed a decreasing trend from 1981 to 1988, whereas the share of Saudi Arabia demonstrated an accelerating trend in the same period, becoming the biggest market for Turkish workers in the Middle East.[14] Thus, by 1988 the number of the Turkish workers who worked in Iraq was 38,388, or 8.5% of the total Turkish workers in the Middle East, in comparison with 188,672, or 41.8%, in Libya and 220,764, or 48.9%, in Saudi Arabia. The number in Kuwait was a mere 1,350.

In the field of Turkish joint-ventures, Saudi Arabia and Kuwait dominated the Middle Eastern share mostly in the form of banking services, industrial and agricultural joint ventures.[15] Especially after 1987, Arab capital in Turkey increased significantly from TL56,268 million (approximately $82.5 thousand) in 1986, invested in 168 firms, to TL121,715 million (approximately $141.4 thousand) in 1988, invested in 384 firms: an 100% increase in two years (Irbec, 1990, p. 127). The striking point here is that Iraqi joint ventures with Turkish firms have remained relatively trivial in comparison with the increase in Kuwaiti and Saudi Arabian investment in Turkey throughout the 1980s. Within the context of the 1985 Agreement between Turkey and Kuwait,[16] Kuwait's investment in Turkey was showing an increasing trend.[17]

As for foreign aid from the Middle Eastern countries to Turkey, Iraq did not feature in this because it was, itself, seeking credits (even from Turkey) to finance its war with Iran. But Turkey did have access to several Middle Eastern financial sources, both bilateral and multilateral aid, such as the funds of the Gulf states and the Saudi-controlled Islamic Development Bank. It is the case that whereas Turkey was extending foreign aid to Iraq, the Kuwaiti Central Bank extended loans to the Turkish company TUPRAS (Turkish Petroleum and Refineries Co.) for Turkey's oil imports several times in the 1980s (*Ankara Home Service*, 2100 GMT, 9 August 1985, *Summary of World Broadcast*, Middle East/W 1335, A1/7, 23 August 1985). In addition, Turkey drew capital from the funds created primarily by the oil-rich Arab Gulf states. Between 1979 and 1989, Turkey received a total loan of $1.459,63 billion from various Middle Eastern funds.[18]

Finally, there has been a substantial increase in the amount spent by, and the number of, tourists coming from the Middle Eastern countries. Once again they were dominated by those tourists coming from Saudi Arabia, Iran, Kuwait, and other Gulf countries (Irbec, 1990, pp. 135 and 141).

The examination of Iraq's place in Turkey's foreign economic relations encourages the conclusion that Iraq's importance had been significant in two branches: foreign trade and oil, along with substantial involvement by Turkish construction firms in Iraq. In comparison, in other fields, the Gulf countries (and especially Saudi Arabia) have occupied the preponderant place in Turkey's foreign economic relations within the Middle East.

In evaluating Middle Eastern security and Turkey's 'dilemma', Iraq's importance to Turkey in the fields of oil, trade and construction should not be overlooked. Aware of these benefits in its relations with Iraq, Turkey had remained 'neutral' when Iraq attacked Iran in 1980. Nor did it feel that it enjoyed the luxury to oppose the Iraqi regime for its Ba'athist ideology. Rather, Turkey was opportunistic in securing economic advantages from both Iraq and Iran, under the so-called 'neutral' foreign policy. Turkey's maintenance of its economic and trade relations during the Iran-Iraq war showed the importance of maintaining this cooperation despite the latter's aggressive foreign policy actions.[19]

The economic interconnectedness between Turkey and Iraq also affected other aspects of Turkey's Middle East policy. Turkish governments in the 1980s had aimed to create an economic zone between Turkey and the Middle East as a whole, to improve regional economic cooperation by exchanging economic resources: Middle Eastern oil and petro-dollars for Turkish exports and other services and commodities.[20] The idea was to develop an area dominated by these economic, rather than military, interactions, hopefully leading to a Middle East free of wars. Therefore, Turkey's political-economic involvement in the Middle East also had a security dimension beyond the narrow confines of Iraq.

The same logic could, however, be applied to Turkey's relations with Iraq. It is, after all, one of the most critical states in the 'local security complex', of which Turkey is a part. From the Turkish perspective, security was to be built not upon military deterrence or the 'balance of power', but on boosting mutual interests. So, ending cooperation would mean relinquishing this opportunity. The most notable problem facing this approach is the Kurdish separatist movement.

The Kurdish Problem and security interdependence within the local security complex

A central aspect of 'security interdependence' between Turkey and Iraq has been the Kurdish Problem.[21] It constitutes part of the 'security complex' for four Middle Eastern countries: Turkey, Iraq, Iran, and Syria.[22] The heart of the problem lies in the fact that the creation of a Kurdish state in the region would be detrimental to the territorial integrity of these four countries: a potential Kurdish state would 'slice-off' the areas in which the Kurdish population lives. Such a possibility could lead not only to increasing instability in the Middle East as a whole, but also to the fragmentation of the Kurdish-populated countries. It might, therefore, lead to regional instability indirectly, as these states disintegrated.

Two interrelated aspects of the Kurdish Problem can be identified, as far as Turkey is concerned: the 'domestic' and 'external' dimensions. With the greatest Kurdish population,[23] Turkey has faced growing Kurdish separatism since the late 1880s. There has long been a Kurdish separatist movement that has been struggling to create an independent Kurdish identity and state within Turkish territory. This struggle has had to be directed against the established authorities - first, the Ottoman Empire and, then, the Republic of Turkey. Despite the Turkish aim to create an unitary nation-state since the formation of the Turkish Republic in 1923, this has not been successful. It has faced a conglomerate of socio-economic, political, ideological and strategic problems among which are those of accommodating the Kurds living within the country. Despite the variety of the factors involved, the source of the 'Kurdish Problem' lies mainly in the fact that Turkey has failed to integrate the Kurds into the mainstream of the Turkish state and society. Although that does not mean that the Kurds have been ostracised from participation in the Turkish state, the Kurds - especially in south-eastern Anatolia - were not able to achieve the living-standards obtained in the Western part of Turkey. These socio-economic problems were compounded by ideologies (whether Marxist-Leninist or nationalist) with which the Kurdish separatist movement has been furnished. The attainment of an independent Kurdish identity and state has been encouraged by ideology and some of the Kurds living in Turkey have struggled against the ideological bases of the Turkish state at various times during this century. From the late 19th century to 1923 there were 15 Kurdish uprisings in southeast Turkey.[24]

With the formation of the Turkish Republic in 1923, Kurdish uprisings increased. During the 'consolidation' years from 1923 to 1937, there were another 22 uprisings.[25] That 17 of the 18 military engagements by the Turkish military during 1924-1938 were launched in south-eastern Turkey (Olson, 1989, p. 161) is a clear indication of the scale of the problem. Thus, since its birth the Turkish Republic has perceived Kurdish national-awareness as a threat to its own territorial integrity (Gunter, 1990, p. 23. Seyfi Tashan also saw the 'Kurdish Problem' as a serious threat to Turkey's territorial integrity, Tashan, 1987, pp. 32-40). Over the years, the 'Kurdish Problem' did not disappear, but continued to increase. Particularly within the last decade, there has been serious and growing guerilla activity by the PKK, which aims to establish an independent Kurdish state, involving the Kurdish populated areas of Turkey. The PKK, which is mostly active in Turkey, is an illegal Kurdish movement that has been fighting for 'the Kurds' independence' from Turkey, which it has described as 'imperialist' and whose policies in the area have been called 'exclusive war'. The PKK is believed to be a guerilla party aiming at 'revolution' for 'National Liberation' from 'Turkish Colonialism' (Serxwebun, 1987, pp. 279-84.

For a similar perspective on Turkey's policy and the Kurdish resistance, see also Burkay, 1986).

The sources of the 'Kurdish Problem' cannot be confined to the domestic factors, nor attributed to external ones alone, it is a transnational issue. This dimension of the 'Kurdish Problem' leads to intervention in the 'Kurdish Problem' by non-regional countries, and is shown by the form of interactions among the regional states directly affected by this transnational threat. Although the Kurds in Turkey revolted against the established order, this was not unique to Turkey, and the other 'host' countries experienced the same problems. Moreover, the concern of non-regional states with the 'Kurdish Problem' has broadened the issue to a wider forum of international politics, giving an international aspect to the 'Kurdish Problem', and attracting the attention of both regional and global actors (on international dimensions of the Kurdish Problem, see, for example, Olson, 1989, especially Chapter 6). According to S. N. Eden, there has been external intervention in the Kurdish Problem from three groups of states: the West, the 'East', and the Middle Eastern countries (Eden, 1990).

The most conspicuous evidence of the external concern with the Kurdish Problem in Turkey can be seen in the abortive Treaty of Sevres (1920). According to this Treaty, which sealed the end of the Ottoman Empire, the Allies of the First World War (Britain, the USA and France) aimed to set up a Kurdish state in the region. This was not to be successful because nationalist Turks were able to supersede the Treaty by the conclusion of the Treaty of Lausanne. However, this did not mean an end to outside intervention in the Kurdish Problem, as, for example, is illustrated by the Sheikh Said Rebellion of 1925 (Olson, 1989, p. 132). Robert Olson has argued that Great Britain changed its policy of establishing a 'Kurdish National Home' in the area as a result of this, and withdrew support for the Sheikh Said Rebellion after Turkey agreed to relinquish the province of Mosul and Kirkuk to British-mandated Iraq in the Turco-British Agreement of 1926 (Olson, 1989, pp. 132 and 148. On British intervention in the Sheikh Said Rebellion, see also Boravali, 1987). With that Treaty, Turkey and Great

Britain agreed to a joint approach to the 'Kurdish Problem'. In addition, Turkey sought similar cooperation with another neighbour, Iran. The Turkish-Persian Treaty (1926) was an attempt by Turkey to reverse Iran's policy for an autonomous Kurdish state in the area (Olson, 1989, p. 139). The USA, too, had been concerned with the 'Kurdish Problem',[26] and during the Iran-Iraq war both Iran and Iraq used the Kurds as a 'fifth column' to undermine their opponents (Boravali, 1987, p. 37; Gunter, 1992, Chapter 6).

In an attempt to solve this complex problem, Turkish governments have pursued domestic and foreign policy strategies in response to the socio-economic problems, and have sought to improve the living-standards of the people in the area to encourage their integration into Turkish society. It was believed that if the people in the region could be integrated into the mainstream of the society through 'economic interdependence', even beyond the Turkish borders, there would have been less fighting and disturbance. Even if the achievement of integration was sufficient to resolve the problem of socio-economic 'backwardness', however, this would not help to resolve the same problem in the neighbouring countries, Iraq, Iran and Syria. Of these states with significant Kurdish populations, Iraq has suffered the most from the Kurdish rebellion, mainly because it has the greatest number of Kurds outside Turkey (Robins, 1991, p. 59). Iraqi governments, be they royal, military, or Ba'athist, have struggled to cope with the Kurdish insurgence led by the Talabani and Barzani factions, which still exists in northern Iraq (for a concise history of Iraq's relations with the Kurds, see Harris, 1977).

The Talabani and Barzani factions have not been not so active in Turkish territory, but mainly confine their activities to northern Iraq and the border area between Iran and Iraq. However, their struggle for an independent state, even within Iraq, was not accepted by Turkey because of the potential consequences: Iraq would be fragmented into parts and success might encourage similar attempts by Kurdish separatists in Turkey.

The trans-territorial cooperation of these groups has proved a major military problem for the region. This cooperation enabled both the Barzani factions in the northern Iraq and the PKK in Turkey to operate in each other's 'sphere of influence', so that through guerilla tactics, the PKK was able to launch attacks in Turkey, while the Barzani was fighting against the Iraqi regime. This led to a 'convergence of interest' (Robins, 1991, p. 59) which convinced Turkey and Iraq to cooperate against Kurdish guerillas, and in order to confine Kurdish separatism (and to prevent the Kurdish insurgence in Iraq from spilling into Turkey) Turkey has courted regimes of all political hues in Baghdad that sought to do the same. It has continued to pursue security cooperation with Iraq, regardless of other problems,[27] and it has already been pointed out that the Saadabad Pact (1937) and the Baghdad Pact (1954-58) were partly a product of this kind of cooperation (Yalcintas, 1986; Gresh and Vidal, 1990, p. 110; Boravali, 1987; Ataov, 1989)

This political-military cooperation has extended to bilateral cooperation under the so-called 'hot pursuit' principle. As far back as 1930-1931, a Kurdish insurgency led by Sheikh Ahmad Barzani was curbed by a joint Iraqi-Turkish campaign (Hiro, 1990, p. 13; Vali, 1971, p. 301). In 1978 the two countries concluded a secret agreement, and a subsequent accord in 1984, which allowed each side to pursue 'subversive elements' up to nine miles inside each country's territory (Hiro, 1990, p. 149). During the Iran-Iraq war, Turkey and Iraq continued to cooperate on Kurdish issues, but at that time the 'Kurdish Problem' gained new features, as a result of the Iranian support for the Kurds in Iraq and as a result of increasing Kurdish insurgence by the PKK after 1984 (Hiro, 1990, passim). The Turkish government, despite its neutrality in the Iran-Iraq war, cooperated with Iraq to prevent the 'Kurdish Problem' from spilling over from Iraq into Turkey, and in compliance with the aforementioned agreement, Turkish troops entered eighteen miles into northern Iraq in May 1983 to destroy the bases of the Kurdish guerillas occupied by the Kurdistan Democratic Party (KDP) (Hiro, 1990, p. 149; *Keesing's Archives*, p. 32585. See also Boravali, 1987, pp. 38-9). Further border operations were mounted within Iraq, in October 1984, in August 1986, and March 1987, under the same 'hot pursuit' agreement (*Keesing's Archives*, p. 35135; Gunter, 1992, p. 42).

The water issue between Turkey and Iraq

The third issue which links the interests of the two countries is that of the trans-border waters. The Euphrates and Tigris rivers flow from Turkey through Iraq and Syria to the Persian Gulf. Whereas the oil pipelines and the 'Kurdish Problem' were instruments for cooperation, the Water Problem proved to be a thorny issue prior to the Iraqi invasion of Kuwait.

Turkish-Iraqi relations showed a deteriorating trend, especially after the end of the Iran-Iraq War in 1988. The most striking example of this trend was seen in the negotiations about the sharing of the two trans-border waters between Turkey, Iraq, and Syria. By 1990, Turkey had completed part of its 'Ataturk' dam, a reservoir needed to hold the waters of the Euphrates. On 13 January 1990, Turkey impounded the waters of the Euphrates in order to fill the reservoir of the Ataturk Dam (for example, *Cumhuriyet*, 15 January 1990, 14; *Tercuman*, 15 January 1990; *Facts on File*, 19 January 1990, p. 36; *Keesing's Archives*, p. 37201; *Newspot*, 18 January 1990, 11; *Briefing*, 15 January 1990). This action aimed to hold back 75% of its waters for a month, reducing its flow from 500 cubic metres per second down to 120 cubic metres per second. But no sooner had Turkey announced this (December 1989) than Iraq and Syria began to express their anxieties over Turkey's decision, by sending messages to the Turkish President, demanding a reduction of the period to less than one month.[28] Turkey's reply was quite reassuring, and a delegation led by Foreign Ministry Undersecretary for Economic Affairs, Necati Utkan, and State Hydraulic Works Deputy Director, Ozden Bilen, was sent to neighbouring countries to explain Turkey's policy (*Briefing*, 15 January 1990, p. 5). Furthermore, President Ozal stated that 'Turkey had taken into account the needs and concerns of [the] neighbours [not to] use the control of water to coerce or threaten them' (quoted in *Facts on File*, 19 January

1990, p. 36 and *Keesing's Archives*, p. 37201). Ozal also assured them that the Water Problem was not a threat to the neighbouring countries, and that the temporary cut was already compensated, as Turkey had released twice the amount of the water before the cut (*Newspot*, 18 January 1990).

Until the Iraqi invasion of Kuwait, there was an escalation of this dispute between Turkey and Iraq, and a series of meetings at various levels were concluded without any agreement. The central issue was whether this was a matter of political compromise or of technical cooperation among the three countries. At the Technical Committee meeting in Ankara on 7-12 March 1990, Turkey insisted that the Water Problem was a technical question and required technical cooperation amongst the three countries. In that context, to accomplish a 'just, rational, and optimal' use of all the water sources in the oasis, Turkish officials presented a three-phase plan, according to which the three countries were to conduct joint studies. The data to be collected in these studies were to be analysed by engineers from each of the three countries. The aim of the technical cooperation was to reduce the wastage of water to the minimum (*Cumhuriyet*, 15 March 1990; *Briefing*, 26 March 1990, pp. 17-18). The next trilateral meeting at the ministries level was held in Ankara on 26-27 June 1990 without any agreement (*Cumhuriyet*, 26, 27 and 28 June 1990; *Hurriyet*, 28 June 1990).

Due to the discrepancy in the views of these countries, the tension mounted when Turkish-Iraqi officials met in Baghdad on May 5-7, 1990. During this meeting, the dispute intensified to the point at which the planned Turkish-Iraqi negotiations in the Joint Economic Committee were halted in disagreement. On that occasion, whereas the Turkish side advocated a separate agreement for the Waters Issue, the Iraqi side insisted that Turkey should guarantee supply of 700 cubic metres of water per second, rather than the promised 500 cubic metres per second. It was also proposed that these terms should be included in the protocol to be signed at the end of the Joint Economic Committee talks (*Cumhuriyet*, 6 May 1990; *Hurriyet*, 8 May 1990). Following this disagreement the meeting was called off for a while, and resumed only after intervention by the two Prime Ministers, Taha Yasin Ramadan of Iraq and Yildirim Akbulut of Turkey. Although the Joint Economic Committee meeting was concluded with a protocol, in which there was no mention of fixed water supply by Turkey, the Iraqi attitude took another form when its President, Saddam Hussein, ironically ridiculed Turkey's global position in the wake of the changes in the East-West conflict. This, he claimed, would mean an end to Turkey's privileged place in NATO, and the ending of US support for Turkey.[29]   Prime Minister Akbulut did not interpret Saddam Hussein's statement as an indication of 'hostile' intent, but neither did he see it as a 'friendly gesture' (see Prime Minister Yildirim Akbulut's interview on Ankara TRT Television in Turkish, 1800 GMT, 20 December 1990, Foreign Broadcast Information Service Western Europe-90-246, 21 December 1990, p. 27).

As a result of this growing tension between Turkey and Iraq, each side began to direct accusations against the other. Both sides launched diplomatic skirmishes on this critical issue. Prime Minister of Iraq, Taha Yasin Ramadan, explicitly linked an improvement in Turkey-Iraq relations to the resolution of the Water Problem. Otherwise, 'if the problem continued like this', he was reported to have declared, 'Turkish-Arab relations would be badly affected' (referring to Iraqi Prime Minister Taha Yasin Ramadan's statement in the London-based Sartul-ul Evsat in Arabic, 'Arab Front Against Turkey', *Hurriyet*, 19 May 1990 and *Cumhuriyet*, 19 May 1990). For, as Iraqi Minister, Abdulvahhab Mahmut El-Sabah, also stated, the Ba'ath Party of Iraq had responsibilities to the whole Arab world (the Iraqi minister speaks to the journalists after the trilateral meeting in Ankara in late June 1990, *Cumhuriyet*, 29 June 1990). Iraqi Petroleum Minister, Isam El Celebi, was reported to have portrayed the dispute over the Euphrates water as a very serious matter and as detrimental to the balance and stability of the region, which, given Turkey's neglect of the settlement of the problem through negotiations, could obstruct the improvement of relations and cooperation between Turkey and Iraq.[30]   After the meeting in June 1990, the Iraqi Agriculture Minister held Turkey responsible for the failure of the trilateral talks and deemed Turkey's proposals on the Water Problem incompatible with international law and norms. Turkey was accused of having an intention 'to prolong negotiations, to procrastinate and prevaricate, to waste time'.[31] The Iraqi journal El-Tavra was reported to have reacted severely to Turkey's decision to impound the water for a month and demanded that Turkey shorten the filling period. El-Tavra was also reported to have accused Turkey of manufacturing obstacles to an agreement for sharing the Euphrates water among the three involved countries.[32]

The attitude of some media towards Turkey was also critical. One Arab newspaper perceived Turkey's decision as 'a threat not only to Syria and Iraq but against the Arab world as a whole'. Another argued that 'it was obvious that there were political reasons behind what Turkey demonstrated the suspension of water as technical matter'. Still another argued that 'the water problem might unify two unfriendly Arab countries to exert pressure on Turkey'. El-Ahram of Egypt, stressing that control of water is one of the most important weapons of the present age, portrayed the use of Euphrates' water as a weapon being directed against the Arab World. El-Ahram continued that the Turkey-Iraq-Syria border was replete with sensitive issues, of which water was the foremost. Other issues, El-Ahram indicated, included ethnic minority problems [referring to the 'Kurdish problem'], political and ideological discrepancies, and military tension (*Cumhuriyet*, 14 March 1990, reporting from the Arab newspapers). The Agreement between Syria and Iraq, which was concluded in Tunis, on the sharing of the Euphrates waters, was seen as a watershed in Iraq-Syria relations against Turkey's policy towards the Middle East (*Hurriyet*, 19 April 1990).

A little later, the disputes between Turkey and Iraq seemed to have gained another dimension when the Arab League Summit gave outright support to Iraq, its statement reading: 'the Arab League Council denounces the continuing media and political campaign against Iraq and biased scientific and technological embargo imposed on it'. The Council also stressed 'its effective solidarity with Iraq in adopting all the measures necessary to guarantee and protect its national security', and 'warned against the continuation of hostile campaigns against Iraq's national security' (*INA* in Arabic, 1340 GMT, 16 July 1990; *Summary of World Broadcasts*, Middle East/0819, A/4, 18 July 1990).

Turkish and foreign media interpreted the resolutions, adopted by the Arab League Summits on 30 May 1990, and on 16 July 1990, as demonstrating increasing Arab enmity towards Turkey. Semih Idiz of Cumhuriyet, and the BBC World Service, had predicted that the Arab League Summit would mount pressure on Turkey on the Water Issue in support of Iraq.[33] The BBC World Service subsequently reported that 'Turkey was criticised in the Arab League Summit in Baghdad on 30 May 1990' (the BBC World Service in Turkish, 31 May 1990, 2245-2330 (Turkish time) in *Dis Basin ve Turkiye*, 1 June 1990, B.N. 103, pp. 5-6).

Since there was no mention of Turkey in the Arab League's critical statement, it is questionable whether this was intended. Although the media interpreted this as a criticism of Turkey, it is also possible that it might have been directed against the Western World as, at that time, there was a growing dispute between Iraq and some Western countries, precipitated by the so-called 'Supergun Affair'. This affair attracted the increasing attention of the Western media, which accused Iraq of manufacturing 'superguns' to threaten the regional 'balance of power'. A campaign by the Western countries was initiated to stop Iraq from upgrading its already-formidable armed forces with the acquisition of the 'supergun' and nuclear weapons. Turkey, too, participated in this Western campaign.

The Water Issue and the 'Supergun Affair'

The tension caused by the Water Problem was compounded by the Turkish involvement in the 'Supergun Affair'. On April 19, when Turkish customs officials in Haydarpasa, Istanbul, impounded a 49-tonne pipe, Turkey inextricably became involved in the dispute between the United

Kingdom and Iraq, and the impounded pipe, which reportedly had been detected by the joint operation of the Turkish Intelligence Organisation (MIT) and the Israeli Intelligence Agency (MOSSAD), was sent back to Britain[34]. Subsequently, customs officials in Kapikule, Edirne, halted three more trucks heading to Iraq (*Cumhuriyet*, 30 April 1990 and 1 May 1990; *Briefing*, 7 May 1990, p. 14). Turkey also sent these pipes back to Britain (*Cumhuriyet*, 4 May 1990; *Hurriyet*, 4 May 1990). The latter case prompted Iraqi officials to summon the Turkish Ambassador to Baghdad for explanation. The Iraqi Treasury and Commerce Minister, Mehdi Saleh, warned Turkey not to take part in the affair between Iraq and Britain, to avoid a further deterioration in the relations between the two countries (interview with Iraqi Minister in *Hurriyet*, 4 May 1990. See *Briefing*, 7 May 1990, pp. 14-15).

Turkey's stance on the 'Supergun Affair' was an additional, provocative factor in the cooling of relations between Turkey and Iraq. It is noticeable that the Turkish-Iraqi Joint Economic Cooperation meeting in Baghdad on 5-7 May was held in the shadow of Turkey's repatriation of Iraqi pipes to Britain on 4 May. Observers in Ankara reported that, in response to Turkey's involvement in the 'Supergun Affair' and Turkey's Water Policy, Iraq had adopted an hostile attitude towards Turkey.

Some argued that there were those who wished to disrupt Turkey's relations with Iraq and Syria, to detach it from its neighbours, and who stimulated artificial threat-perception within Turkey. Turkey had, therefore, to exercise caution in relation to such artificial threat-perceptions (Ali Sirmen, 'Tehdid Algilamasi' (Threat Perception) *Cumhuriyet*, 7 April 1990). Another view contended that '[Turkey's] water never became a political leverage over its neighbours. Indeed, there are those who want to disturb Turkey-Arab relations, and put the improvement of those relations into disarray. Those groups who have been working for 50-60 years to prevent Turkey's orientation towards the Middle East, are now producing distorted news' (State Minister Kamuran Inan's statement in *Cumhuriyet*, 8 June 1990). It was also believed that the 'Turkey-Iraq-Syria water crisis' was a conspiracy to construct artificial breaking points, which could lead to a decline in Turkish-Middle Eastern economic and trade relations (Erol Manisali's statement in *Hurriyet*, 1 May 1990). Some went as far as to argue that the Water Problem was a fabrication of the Western sources to make divisions between Turkey and the Arab world and, among others, to preclude Turkey from being a 'great power' in the Middle East (Emin Ozdas speaking to *Tercuman*, 24 July 1990). There were those from the Iraqi side who believed that 'the allegations about the "Supergun Affair" marked a new conspiracy by Israel and the West against the Islamic World' (Iraqi Ambassador to Ankara, Tariq Abdulcabbar Cevad, speaking to *Turkiye*, 1 May 1990). Such nationalist approaches to the tension between Turkey and Iraq arising from the Water Issue and the 'Supergun Affair' may have been attempts to prevent the escalation of the existing tensions outlined above.

Whether or not the Water Dispute between Turkey and Iraq could have been resolved if the negotiations had continued after July 1990 is, of course, a hypothetical question. Anyway, Iraq's invasion of Kuwait on 2 August, 1990 changed the agenda of Turkish-Iraqi relations; while the invasion, which undermined the security of the countries in the Gulf region and the Middle East, led to an unprecedented international reaction.

It is unnecessary to discuss whether Turkey's reaction to the crisis was an important matter for the success of both the economic sanctions and the war against Iraq. Above all, in the view of Turkey's role in NATO, it was expected to support its allies by suspending the operation of the Turkish-Iraqi oil pipelines and other economic relations between the countries.

Turkey once more chose the side of the Western Alliance, suspending its relations with its neighbour. Turkey's choice produced two kinds of adverse consequences: economic losses because of sanctions and uncertainty and instability in Turkey's south-eastern region due to an emerging 'power vacuum' after Iraq's defeat in the Gulf War. So far as the security outcome is concerned, given the 'security interdependence' between the two countries, Turkey's decision had negative and positive effects. The rest of this chapter will focus on these negative and positive security outcomes of Turkey's decision, which illustrate some of the wider problems facing Turkey as a Western ally in the Middle East.

The Negative implications of the Gulf War on Turkey's security

During the Gulf War, there was a clearcut potential threat to Turkey: it might have lost its sovereignty over the Kurdish populated south-east Anatolian region. This potential threat was a product of not only the suspension of Turkish-Iraqi relations, but also the fragmentation of Iraq after its defeat in the War.

Another issue was the potential deterioration of the 'Kurdish problem' in Turkey due to the disruption of security cooperation after the Iraqi invasion of Kuwait. Due to the subsequent Turkish response, much of the control established over the Kurds was lost.[35]

As Ozal commented:

We are against the establishment of a new state within Iraq. In fact we have always supported the preservation of Iraq's territorial integrity. ...This is the spirit behind all our work and policy. A situation that we do not want must not be created. A Kurdish state must not be established.[36]

The reason for this objection was explained by himself: 'A Kurdish state is impossible...since in any case it [would] encompass Turkey because we have many more Kurdish citizens than Iraq'.[37]

This fear was not without foundation, because there were initiatives by Kurdish groups both in Turkey and Iraq to gain advantage from the crisis. The Gulf crisis was seen by the Kurds as an important, probably unique, opportunity to be exploited fully to achieve their aims.[38] As a Kurdish activist asserted, 'the Kurds have been struggling against the Iraqi regime since 1945... While Saddam is confronted by the entire world, the Kurds will move with all their strength'.[39] It was conceivable that the Kurds would attempt to intensify and extend their struggle for independence in the event of the war leaving a regional power vacuum.

In Iraq, the separatist Peshmerge fighters of the Democratic Party of Kurdistan (the DPK), led by Mas'ud Barzani, and the Kurdish fighters of the Patriotic Union of Kurdistan (the PUK) led by Jalal Talabani, were put on alert in order for offensive action against the Iraqi regime. Meanwhile, Kurdish sources reported that 40,000 armed Kurds, from the two separatist Kurdish organisations which had established an alliance, called The Iraq Kurdistan Front,[40] were planning to attack pro-Iraqi groups and to take control of Kurdish cities (Istanbul *Gunaydin* in Turkish, 31 December 1990, in *Foreign Broadcast Information Service*, Western Europe 91-004, 7 January 1991, pp. 38-9).   Having joined forces, the Iraqi Kurds made plans to capture seven cities in the northern Iraq. This was to be achieved by DPK leader Barzani's forces moving from the Bahdinan region, while PUK forces would come from the Soren region (Seyfettin Ozgezer and Omer Buyuktimur, 'Iraqi Kurds Prepare for War', Istanbul *Gunaydin* in Turkish, 6 October 1990, in *Foreign Broadcast Information Service*, WEU-90-199, 15 October 1990, pp. 32-33).   Talabani, the leader of the PUK, also tried to establish a wide-ranging front to include all the opposition forces in Iraq. He believed that the multi-factional front would be the only political alternative for the Kurds after Saddam's regime has been removed, and might have even formed a 'government in exile' (Istanbul *Hurriyet* in Turkish, 27 September 1990, *Foreign Broadcast Information Service*, Western Europe-90-192, 3 October 1990, p. 44). Talabani was reported to have stated that six Kurdish factions, from the region, had held a meeting in Damascus, Syria, and agreed to the attempt to overthrow Saddam Hussein (Emin Tanriyar and Muserref Seckin, 'Where is Turkey Running To?', Istanbul *Nokta* in Turkish, 2 September 1990, pp. 19-23 in *Foreign Broadcast Information Service*-Western Europe-90-222, 16 September 1990, pp. 38-9).

The Kurdish Worker's Party (the PKK) in Turkey was also stimulated to seek opportunities from the war. The intensification of the Kurdish struggle against Turkish state was instigated by the PKK. In a communique issued on 23 August 1990, by the National Liberation Front of Kurdistan Activities Office in Diyarbakir, the PKK called on the Kurds to unite against 'the enemy' [Turkey], and only follow the PKK's orders in the event of a war. The communique called upon the Kurds in Turkey to '...join the guerilla forces in [their] area and turn [their] guns against the enemy's war machine, against the collaborators, and against informers who sell themselves for a few cents'. It also called for an end to all internal disputes: 'All enmities and differences should be put aside...This is not the time for individuals, groups, tribes to feud among themselves. It is a time for hard work and self-sacrifice to bring our people's approaching independence and freedom close...'.[41]

The Kurds also pursued diplomatic/political and military tactics with the interested states. PUK leader Jelal Talabani's visit to Washington in mid-August 1990 was an attempt to secure America's military and financial support for the Kurds in return for Kurdish support for the American strategy and a promise to intensify Kurdish resistance against the Iraqi regime (*Gunes*, 16 August 1990; *Milliyet*, 16 August; Emin Tanriyar and Muserref Seckin, 'Where is Turkey Running To?', Istanbul *Nokta* in Turkish, 2 September 1990, pp. 19-23 in *Foreign Broadcast Information Service*-Western Europe-90-222, 16 September 1990, pp. 38-9). His final aim was clear: an autonomous Kurdish region for the Kurds in the northern Iraq in the post-war era.

An alternative risk for Turkey was the possibility that the Iraqis might have used Kurdish fighters as a proxy against them (*Cumhuriyet*, 8 August 1990), conceivably as a retaliation to Turkey's decision. The greatest danger was the disintegration of Iraq into several parts during and after the war, and occupation of the fragmented parts by the neighbouring countries. Ozal observed that to limit the chance of a 'change' in Iraq's territorial integrity was one of the cental aspects of Turkey's stance in the Gulf crisis and that all the possibilities of the change had been discussed in the meetings of the National Security Council, the General Staff, the Defence Ministry, and the Foreign Ministry (President Ozal, interviews with selected writers from the Turkish press at the Presidential Palace, Ankara, 18 August 1990, in *Sabah* [Turkish daily newspaper], 25 January 1991). Believing that changes in the region would occur after the war, he anticipated that the post-crisis era might bring about the dismemberment of Iraq, out of which there could emerge instability, threatening Turkey's territorial integrity. He was aware of the impact of the international crises: 'Each crisis brings the danger of split...the only thing not to do in a crisis situation is to live in the status quo' (Ozal, 1991, p. 332).

Turkey's main objective was that Iraq's territorial integrity should not be violated; it was against a fundamental change in the territorial boundaries of Iraq. As Ozal stated, 'Turkey was in favour of a democratic regime in Iraq, one that will safeguard the Arabs, Kurds, Turkomans, and others in the country (President Ozal, interviewed by London-based Al-Hayat, 17 February 1991, in *Dis Basin ve Turkiye*, 25 February 1991, B.N.22, pp.1-5; and in *Foreign Broadcast Information Service*-Western Europe-91-033, 19 February 1991, pp.52-53; also in *Cumhuriyet*, 18 February 1991). To the Turkish Foreign Ministry, it was preferable to keep the Ba'ath regime intact, rather than a division of Iraq into small states, due to the fear that if the Ba'ath regime in Iraq was to be toppled, the Kurds (as the second biggest force in Iraq) could dominate a subsequent regime,[42] and hence pose a threat to Turkey's security (the information was based on the Foreign Minister sources. Yasemin Congar, 'Saddam Gitsin, BAAS Kalsin' [Let Go Saddam, the Ba'ath May Stay], *Cumhuriyet*, 21 August 1990).

A 'power vacuum' in Iraq might result in the creation of an independent Kurdish state by the Gulf allies and/or in intervention by Iran and Syria.[43] Ozal worried:

In the case of a power vacuum in Iraq, Turkey will face a serious refugee problem. More important than that is that if there is an attempt to establish an independent Kurdish state in northern Iraq, Iran or Syria might take advantage of such a vacuum and try to occupy parts of Iraq (President Ozal, interviewed by London-based Al-Hayat, 17 February 1991, in *Dis Basin ve Turkiye*, 25 February 1991, B.N.22, pp.1-5).

These states might become involved not merely to secure their particular interests in Iraq, but also to prevent the interference of others: a response to a form of 'security dilemma.' In a Council of Ministers meeting, in mid-August 1990, chaired by Ozal, the US's traditional support to the Kurds was also discussed. There was a danger of the use of the Kurds by the USA as a 'fifth column' against the Iraqi regime.

Fragmentation was not expected by Turkey alone, it was one of the prominent 'predictions', in the US, about post-war Iraq. William Safire, an American journalist in *The New York Times*, speculated that, when the war was over, the boundaries of Iraq would be redrawn to penalise the aggressor. In a divided Iraq, he continued, Iraq's assets, especially oil, would be divided amongst an independent Kurdistan, a helpful Turkey, and those nations which had sacrificed the most. According to Sami Kohen, a Turkish columnist in Turkish daily newspaper *Milliyet*, Safire was well-informed of the views of the US Administration and in close touch with high-ranking officials, strategists, and foreign policy makers in Washington (Sami Kohen, 'Scenarios of the Gulf Crisis', Istanbul *Milliyet* in Turkish, 8 November 1990, in *Foreign Broadcast Information Service*-Western Europe-90-221, 15 November 1990, p. 39). A similar claim was made by a Turkish ex-intelligence officer, Mahir Kaynak. He argued that 'the US was planning to set up a Kurdish installed government in northern Iraq', a threat identified by Turkish foreign policy-makers for the last seventy years (Mahir Kaynak's statement, appearing in *Kayan Havai*, an Iranian magazine, No. 915, 31 January 1991, pp. 1 and 30).

Thus, the constraints on Turkey were twofold. First, Kurdish separatism (either alone or with the help of other countries) might intensify, with an uprising leading to the possible fragmentation of Iraq and consequent implications for Turkey's territorial integrity. Second, given the possibility of the fragmentation of Iraqi territory and the resultant 'power vacuum', neighbouring states could intervene in Iraq. These fears proved groundless, as the Western Alliance negated these attempts. That is, Turkey's involvement on the side of the Western Alliance brought about the preemption of the creation of a Kurdish state in the region and of the fragmentation of Iraqi territory in such a way as to create new states. The preemption of this threat was a welcome result of pro-Western Turkish foreign policy during the Gulf War.

The quick decision-making on 7 August to impose sanctions against Iraq was the first, and the most critical step, in this direction. In order to participate in the post-war settlement of the region, it was argued that Turkey had to play an active role in the crisis.[44]

The objective behind this cooperation with the Gulf Coalition was, to a great extent, to eliminate the dangers for Turkey's national and territorial security (the information was based on Government sources, *Gunaydin*, 20 August 1990). If Turkey had remained 'neutral', it was argued, it would have not had a chance to participate in the Gulf War diplomacy (the information was based on Government sources, *Gunaydin*, 20 August 1990).

Ozal expressed the apprehensions and motivations, that convinced him to take the side of the Gulf Coalition:

Without doubt, the Gulf crisis just next to us closely concerns our country. Therefore, we should never lose sight of the impact on our country of not only the developments in the region during the crisis, but also the potential changes to emerge after the crisis. That is why we should pursue a dynamic foreign policy to earn a position which will help to be influential on these developments and changes. In other words, in this Gulf crisis, one cannot expect us to adopt a hesitant, indecisive, and wait-the-other-to-decide attitude. Otherwise, it is obvious that we almost lose possibility of being an influential country in an issue in which Turkey has lofty interests.[45]

Turkey's situation is very important. We are very closely concerned with the Gulf crisis. Each and every development in Iraq and in the Middle East is of vital importance for Turkey. We are neighbours of the countries in the Middle East, particularly Iraq, we always pointed out this out. The changes that [may] take place must not conflict with Turkey's interests. In view of this, Turkey cannot remain indifferent to the changes. In fact, Turkey must be entitled to comment on the changes that [might] take place either in the direction of peace or in the direction of war. Turkey must influence any change in the Middle East. A significant change in Iraq must not conflict with Turkey's *security* [italic added]. This is the minimum precondition. How can this be achieved? Only by showing that Turkey has a role in the crisis. If Turkey were to withdraw to a corner and refrain from involving itself, then it would not be entitled to speak...Any change that will take place in Iraq must not be against Turkey (President Ozal, interviewed by Altemur Kilic of *Tercuman*, *Tercuman*, 8 December 1990).

Some observers saw such a view of the Turkish position as evidence of imperialistic design. As has been seen above, they believed that Turkey coveted northern Iraq and was looking for an opportunity to overthrow the status quo in the area, thereby assuming the oil-rich region of Mosul and Kirkuk. The deployment of the Turkish troops on the Turkish-Iraq border was shown as an evidence of this imperialist policy. However, Turkey's policy during the war was primarily aimed at the protection of the regional status quo.

Diplomacy for maintaining the 'status quo'

Responding to these allegations, Ozal contended that '...We will not go to war unless we are attacked by Iraq. We don't want any single centimetre in their territory. Will Turkey take Mosul and Kirkuk? No, it will not'. However, his stance was not without reservations. Apart from an Iraqi attack on Turkey, which would precipitate a Turkish 'self-defence', he outlined two additional preconditions for Turkey to become involved in such a war: 'if somebody attempts to establish a Kurdish state in that case we would intervene' and lastly, 'if a third country attempts to carve up the northern Iraq, in which case Turkey would also intervene'.[46]

Despite these assurances by Ozal, followers of the realist school of

International Relations might counter with the argument that, in the wake of an opportunity created by a power vacuum in northern Iraq, even Turkey might have pursued an expansionist policy. Such a view can, however, be undermined by still another proposition of the realist school: that whether a country will pursue an 'imperialist foreign policy' depends upon the existing 'balance of power' in the particular situation. Ozal himself noted that, 'if [Turkey] were to covet land from a country [Iraq], then other countries could act similarly against Turkey' (President Ozal, interviewed by Altemur Kilic of *Tercuman*, *Tercuman*, 8 December 1990).

Since Turkey's unilateral concern to preserve the status quo would not be sufficient, Turkish leaders consistently pursued diplomacy both in the Western and Middle Eastern capitals to prevent such a development (for the importance of these diplomatic moves, see Nur Batur, 'Baris Icin Diplomasi Atagi' [A Diplomatic Initiative for Peace], *Milliyet*, 22 August 1990). Indeed, Ozal's earlier telephone conversations with the leaders of Syria and Iran, and his agreement with them on a stance against Iraq, were part of such attempts about the status quo in the region after a potential regime-change in Iraq.[47] During the crisis and the war, contacts with, and diplomatic visits to, these countries continued. The basic theme of these visits was to reach an agreement with them to maintain the status quo ante.[48] Against the possibility of a violation of Iraqi territory by Syria and Iran, Ozal warned them that, 'Turkey would not tolerate it' (President Ozal, interviewed by Arnoud Brorchgrave, editor of the *Washington Times*, appearing in *Gunes*, 12 January 1991. Also, the *Financial Times*, 1 January 1991), but 'intervene in the situation'.[49] It is also important to note that, by acting in the same camp with Syria and by monitoring Iranian policy closely throughout the war, Turkey tried to control both diplomatically. Ozal's agenda during his visit to the Gulf countries on 15-19 October 1990 included not only the issue of compensating Turkey's economic losses, but also the 'Kurdish Problem'. He was, for instance, reported to have been worried by the visit to Saudi Arabia by the PUK leader, who sought financial and political support from the Coalition members (on the alleged Saudi support to Talabani see Vahab Yazaroglu, 'Saudi Support for Kurds', *Milliyet*, 31 October 1990, also in *Foreign Broadcast Information Service*-Western Europe-90-219, 13 November 1990, p. 43). Ozal asked these Arab states, especially Syria, not to give support to the Kurds (Mehmet Oztoprak, 'Ozal's Gulf Tour: Meaningful Signals to US', Istanbul *Gunaydin* in Turkish, 21 October 1990, in *Foreign Broadcast Information Service*-Western Europe-90-205, 23 October 1990, pp. 38-39).

When the war against Iraq began on 17 January 1991, and the increased possibility of Iraq's fragmentation grew, the responses from Iran and Syria to Turkey's messages, looked quite cooperative. They both expressed their wishes to maintain Iraq's territorial integrity.[50] Simultaneously, the Turkish Foreign Minister was dispatched to Iran, Syria, Saudi Arabia, and Egypt, in an effort to evaluate likely post-war developments in the region (Ankara *Anatolia* in English, 0957 GMT, 11 February 1991, in *Foreign Broadcast Information Service*-Western Europe-91-028, 11 February 1991, p. 38). During his visits to these countries, Foreign Minister Alptemocin sought to agree with these countries that Iraq's territorial integrity should not be violated.[51] Ozal was satisfied that Iran and Syria did not wish any change in Iraq's territory.[52]

Turkey undertook similar diplomatic initiatives with the Western members of the Gulf Coalition. In a statement to Spanish Television, Ozal reiterated Turkey's opposition to an independent Kurdish state in northern Iraq. Promising that Turkey had no ambitions against Iraqi territory, he also reiterated his wish to see the preservation of the status quo ante of the regional borders (President Ozal, statement, appearing in Ankara *Anatolia* in English, 1005 GMT, 17 February 1991 in *Foreign Broadcast Information Service*-Western Europe-91-033, 19 February 1991, p.55, also in *Cumhuriyet*, 18 February 1991, and *Sabah*, 18 February 1991). In his statement to the *Financial Times*, Ozal also warned 'the US and the other countries', arguing that 'it was not in the interests of the US or other countries to back Kurdish separatism in northern Iraq'.[53]

The response to Turkey's demands from the Western states was crucial. The US Ambassador to Ankara, Morton Abromowitz, stated that the USA was against the creation of an independent Kurdish state in the region (*Gunaydin*, 14 September 1990). In his speech in February 1991 to the Senate Foreign Affairs Committee, Secretary of State Baker allayed Turkey's fears, stating that the USA was against the fragmentation of Iraq. Similar assurances came from Britain: responding to reports in Turkish newspapers that Britain supported the independence of the Kurds, the British Embassy in Teheran announced that Britain was not in favour of a Kurdish state in the region (Teheran *IRNA* in English, 1627 GMT, 14 February 1991, in *Foreign Broadcast Information Service*-Western Europe-091-033, 19 February 1991, p.57).

As far as diplomatic support was concerned, it was also important that a planned Kurdish conference, to be held in Switzerland, was blocked during the Gulf crisis by the Turkish government through its diplomatic initiatives in Washington, Bonn, Paris, and Stockholm (Yasemin Congar, 'Kurt Konferansi Ertelendi' [The Kurdish Conference was cancelled], *Cumhuriyet*, 3 November 1990). This marked a diplomatic success, by halting the conference which had been precipitated by Talabani's visits to the Western capitals (Yasemin Congar, 'Kurt Konferansi Ertelendi' [The Kurdish Conference was cancelled], *Cumhuriyet*, 3 November 1990 and Ankara *Anatolia* in French, 0830 GMT, 7 November 1990, in *Foreign Broadcast Information Service*-Western Europe-90-216, 7 November 1990, p. 44). Towards the end of the war, Ozal's special envoy, Kamuran Inan, paid a visit to France, Britain, and Spain where he not only explained Turkey's stance in the war, but also tried to avert Western support for the Kurdish independence movement (*Gunaydin*, 12 February 1991. See also Kamuran Inan, interviewed by Xavier Gautier of *Le Figaro* in French, 31 January 1991, in *Foreign Broadcast Information Service*-Western Europe-91-028, 11 February 1991, pp. 41-3).

Military Cooperation

Turkey's military involvement in the War against Iraq occurred in two different ways. The first was the deployment of the Allied Mobile Force-Air (AMF-A) in Erhac, Malatya, the southeastern town of Turkey, alongside Turkey's own deployment of ground and air forces in the region, especially in Diyarbakir, in the border between Turkey and Iraq. Starting from early January 1991, a squadron of 42 aircraft and 575 personnel from Germany, Belgium and Italy was deployed in Erhac.[54] Additional NATO support to Turkey assumed the form of the dispatch of Patriot missiles from the Netherlands and the USA in the eve of the War (Ankara Turkish Television, 1800 GMT, 11 January 1991, in *Summary of World Broadcast*, ME/0969, A/18, 14 January 1991). The second, and most important, aspect of Turkey's involvement in the War was the permission to the US forces to use military bases, especially the Incirlik air base, from the beginning of the war.[55]

However, it is important to make distinction between Turkey's own deployment of forces in the south-eastern region and the deployment of AMF-A in the Turkish-Iraq border and the use of the Incirlik air base. The deployment of the Turkish forces in the area was directed against a potential Kurdish insurgency, and against any aggression against Turkish territory. The deployment of AMF-A and the use of the Incirlik air base, however, should be seen within the strategy of war against Iraq and with Turkey's perceived role in the Middle East.

The first demand by the US Administration to deploy forces in the region was made in September 1990. The US Secretary of State asked the NATO allies to contribute to the UN efforts in the military isolation of Iraq.[56] A more specific demand to Turkey came from US Secretary of Defence Richard Cheney in November 1990, who asked the Turkish Government to make additional military deployments along Turkey's southern border with Iraq (Smith, 1990). At that time, Turkey was not willing to admit the NATO forces into the Turkish-Iraqi border (*Milliyet*, 8 November 1990); rather, Turkey was deploying its own troops in the region to a total of 120,000 men by the start of the war on 17 January

1991. By late December 1990, Turkey made the request to deploy the AMF-A to be on the border.[57]

The deployment of the AMF-A in Turkey was the first operational deployment in the history of NATO (Howe, 1991, p. 251). The AMF-A was not so strong to deter an Iraqi retaliation against Turkey, but the NATO allies stated that the Alliance would defend Turkey if there was a need.[58] AMF-A was a symbolic force 'to show that the NATO will support Turkey if there is an attack to Turkey' (President Ozal, interviewed by the CNN, 17 January 1991, in *Dis Basin ve Turkiye*, 18 January 1991, B.N.12; *Cumhuriyet*, 18 January 1991, *Milliyet*, 18 January 1991. Also quoted in Cevizoglu, 1991, p. 51). AMF-A was to tie down Iraqi forces in the north, and to further encircle Iraq (on US war strategy and Turkey's position in it, see Smith, 1990). As the UN deadline of '17 January' for Iraq's withdrawal from Kuwait approached, it became clear that the primary US strategy was that of military operation against Iraq. Allied strategy aimed at drawing some of its troops from southern Iraq to the north, and the US looked for forces to act as a 'fifth column' in the north, to engage Iraqi forces so as to weaken Iraqi resistance in the south.

There were two alternative forces useful for this strategy. The first alternative was the deployment of the Turkish troops on the Iraqi border. General Norman Schwarzkopf, the Commander of the Operation Desert Shield, asked the US Administration to use Turkish territory to draw more Iraqi troops to the north (Smith, 1990). The AMF-A also served this objective.

Alternatively, if Turkey had refused to cooperate with the Allies in the deployment of the NATO forces in Turkey, this could, however, be supplemented by Kurdish activists. Thus, Turkey was in a competition with the Kurdish alternative, but to give a chance to the Kurds to act as a 'fifth column' against Iraq would mean giving overt support to the formation of the Kurdish military forces and to their standing Army in the north.

Turkey effectively ruled out the possibility of using the Kurdish forces against Iraq not only by deploying its own forces in the area, but also by calling AMF-A into the area. AMF-A also acted as a deterrence against the neighbouring countries that might have planned to enter Iraq in the case of fragmentation.

The Turkish daily newspaper, *Cumhuriyet*, pointed to an agreement between Ozal and the visiting US Secretary of State, which was a US assurance to preserve the status quo in the region, in return for Turkey's support for the military operation against Iraq (*Cumhuriyet*, 17 January 1991). Turkey's permission for the US planes to use Incirlik airbase was linked to the US assurance that Iraq's territorial integrity was not to be fragmented. Ozal, himself, was quoted as saying that 'President Bush asked me to permit the use of the bases...Raising the possibility of an Iranian or Syrian encouragement to Iraq [meaning the fragmentation of Iraq], Turkey would without hesitant enter Iraq in such a situation. Bush supported my view' (*Sabah*, 25 January 1991).

In allowing this permission, an additional motivation should be considered: Ozal was delighted to see that Iraq's military power was destroyed by the Coalition allies and that Iraq's threat to Turkey in the Water Issue had been eliminated. He asserted that Iraq was a threat to Turkey. On 23 January 1991, when Turkey had already participated in the war against Iraq by opening the Incirlik air base, Ozal argued that '...We are a country of 57 million; we are a NATO member. Yet Iraq has weapons we do not have' (President Ozal, statement, appearing in *Anatolia* in Turkish, 1812 GMT, 23 January 1990, in *Summary of World Broadcast*, ME\0979, A/20, 25 January 1991), and that Iraq's army had to be destroyed to the extent that it would be no threat to Turkey.[59] As an explanation of this threat, Ozal also pointed to the pre-crisis Turkish-Iraqi disputes: despite the fact that Turkey made significant assistance to Iraq during its war against Iran, Iraq showed an enmity towards Turkey in the Water Problem. Iraq demonstrated an aggressive attitude against Turkey's friendly policy. Ozal was glad to see that 'the thing which had to be carried out by Turkey, was [instead] done by some other countries...' (President Ozal's talks with the Turkish Deputies in the Parliament, quoted in *Tercuman*, 16 January 1991).

Turkey gained credit with the West for the post-war era. An incident at the end of the war illustrates this aspect of situation. During the War, President Bush had encouraged 'the Iraqi people' 'to take matters in their hands to force Saddam Hussein, the dictator, aside'.[60] When the Kurds in the northern Iraq attempted at the end of the War to do what President Bush had suggested, they encountered a heavy response from the Iraqi army, to the extent that their uprising met a bloody fate. Failing in their uprising against the Iraqi army, a huge number (around 2 million) Kurds fled from the Iraqi military onslaught towards the mountainous region of Turkey from mid-April 1991 onwards. Turkey faced a major refugee problem, with far-reaching impact on its own 'Kurdish Problem' in south-eastern Anatolia (on the Kurd's debacle as a result of the Iraqi military assault, see *Time*, 15 April 1991). Such a large number of Kurdish refugees could also have led to the formation of an enlarged political coalition with the Kurds in Turkey. It could result in the fragmentation of Iraq, the fear Turkey had from the beginning of the crisis.

Bush did not seem to live up to his commitments to support the Kurds, and the Shiites in the south of Iraq, in their attempt to gain independence. Indeed, Bush was reluctant to deploy American troops inside Iraq territory because of domestic and international considerations.[61] He acted very slowly, coming under serious criticism both from American and international public opinion (*Time*, 15 April 1991). However, Bush eventually changed his policy and decided to launch 'Operation Provide Comfort' in order to help the refugees return back to Iraq.[62]

President Ozal was, perhaps, one of the influences on President Bush's change of mind. As well as blocking the Kurdish refugees from entering Turkish towns in huge numbers, Ozal criticised Bush for his failure to launch an operation to prevent this tragedy. Subsequently, he floated the idea that there should be security enclaves within Iraq to enable the refugees to return to their homes without fear of Iraqi oppression.[63] For their security, Ozal proposed that the USA and other Allies should deploy troops to the northern Iraq. After a telephone conversation between the two Presidents, what is now called 'the

Operation Poised Hammer' force was deployed in northern Iraq.[64] The refugee problem was partly resolved, as Kurdish refugees returned to the tent camps, in what were later called 'the safe havens', built in northern Iraq by the allied forces. This was a considerable relief for Turkey.

The final point about the military/security cooperation is that one must assess the gap between the 'expectations' of the Turkish decision-maker and the reality at the end of the Gulf War. The opportunities provided to Turkey during the Gulf War did not mean that Turkish cooperation with the Gulf allies eradicated the 'Kurdish problem' and secured Turkey's security forever. Although Turkey attained its objective of maintaining the territorial integrity of Iraq, the suspension of cooperation with Iraq against the Kurds, and Iraq's loss of control over the Kurds in the region, has reinforced the movement towards an independent Kurdish state. While the Kurds in Iraq have established what is called 'de facto statehood' (Gunter, 1990, Chapter 10), the PKK in Turkey has increased its activities against Turkey's soldiers and the people in the region. Indeed, the 'Kurdish problem' in Turkey and Iraq has worsened as the campaign of the Kurds has been able to exploit the collapse of Iraq's power after the war (Hale, 1992, p. 689). The Kurds in Iraq have enjoyed a much easier environment, in the so-called 'safe haven' above the 36th parallel, and been able to create the basis of an independent Kurdistan (on the developments about the Kurdish political, economic, military preparations in the northern Iraq, see *Time*, 1 June 1992 and 28 September 1992), ironically protected by the Operation Poised Hammer based in the Incirlik air base in Turkey. Another gap between the 'expectations' and the 'reality' can be seen in the post-war Iraq. What was 'expected' - that the Saddam Hussein regime would be overthrown at the end of the war and replaced by a democratic government - did not happen. It is important to note that there were allegations that Saddam Hussein's regime has been assisting PKK activities in Iraq (Gunter, 1990, pp. 112-3), and so its activities in Turkey.

One fact should not be overlooked, however: if Turkey had not allied with the Western allies against Iraq, or chosen one of the other two options, the 'Kurdish problem' might have been much worse from the Turkish point of view than at present. The Kurds might well have been used as a 'fifth column', leading to the deterioration of the situation in the region. Thus, by acting as it did, Turkey prevented this from occurring, at least during the period of the Gulf War. Nor should the post-war fruits of the cooperation between Turkey and the Western members of the Gulf allies be overlooked. When Turkey subsequently launched a series of cross-border military operations against the PKK, both within Turkey and in the territory of Iraq, similar to these previously undertaken in cooperation with Iraq in the 1980s, Turkey's military actions were not criticised so much by the Western countries. There was even evidence of support by the US officials for Turkey's cross-border operation in Iraq in October 1992. On 17 November 1992, both the US State Department and the Pentagon declared that they remained against the fragmentation of Iraqi territory. Even Germany's condemnation of Turkey's alleged violation of the human rights of the Kurds did not last long.[65] The visit to Turkey by German Chancellor Helmut Kohl was an indicative of Germany's support for Turkey.[66] Germany also became the first European country to ban PKK activities: an important indication of cooperation (for example, *Newspot*, 2 December 1993)

Notes

1. On Turkey's importance for the Middle East region see McGhee (1990), especially pp. 60-62, and 65-7. McGhee, as the then US Ambassador to Turkey, played the most critical role in Turkey's membership to NATO. In his book, McGhee discloses the process of Turkey's membership to NATO. His conversations with the Turkish leaders, President Celal Bayar and Prime Minister Adnan Menderes illuminate the motivations in the US and Turkish decision-makers to make Turkey a member of NATO. See also Harris, 1972, (pp. 44-5).

2. The US Department of State Bulletin is the official monthly record

of the United States foreign policy.

3.   The main motivation behind this pact was as security concern arising from Italian threat in the Middle East. For example, Ulman (1966, pp. 241-71).

4.   The information gathered from table 49, *T.C. Petrol Isleri Genel Mudurlugu Dergisi* [*Journal of Turkish Oil Affairs General Directory* hereafter], Petroleum Activities in 1990, No.33, p.139; and table 6, in *OECD Economic Surveys: Turkey*, November 1978, pp. 12-13.

5.   The Turkish government granted on June 6, 1974 to the Turkish Petroleum Syndicate (TPAO) three licences to drill for oil in the Aegean Sea between the Greek island of Limnos and the Turkish islands of Imroz and Bozcaada. Upon this allocation to TPAO, the US Dorchester Gas Corporation was given permission for oil explorations in the area covering 175,000 hectares. *Keesing's Contemporary Archives* [American news digest], [*Keesing's* hereafter], pp.26667-8, and 27011.

6.   *BOTAS* [Pipelines Transportation Co.] *Annual Report 1990* (Ankara: Desen Ofset, no date). The agreement between Iraq and Turkey in 1973 necessitated the establishment of 'Boru Hatlari Ile Petrol Tasimacilik A.S.' (BOTAS) [the Pipelines Transportation Co.], as supervisory organ for the operation of the pipelines. See also, *Journal of Turkish Oil Affairs General Directory*, No.33, p.83; *Cumhuriyet*, 7 August 1990, including the terms of the Agreement.

7.   *BOTAS Annual Report 1990*. *The Journal of Turkish Oil Affairs General Directory* gave a higher amount for the transported oil in 1989, that was 82,908 million tonnes: *Journal of Turkish Oil Affairs General Directory, ibid.* p.84.

8.   According to the BOTAS's 1990 Investment Program, the company was planning to start soon building the third pipeline from Iraq to Turkey. For this purpose, BOTAS had already earmarked TL500 million for the feasibility study of the project. *Hurriyet* [Turkish daily newspaper], 29 January 1990; and *Milliyet*

[Turkish daily newspaper], 29 January 1990; *Newspot*, 1 February 1990. *Newspot*, published by the semi-official (Turkish) General Directorate of Press and Information, is a weekly (now fortnightly) newspaper in English.

9.   The rest of Turkey's oil came from other Middle Eastern countries: Libya, Iran, Algeria, Saudi Arabia, and around 6% from the Soviet Union, and China. Table [Turkey's import, production, and consumption of oil], in *Cumhuriyet*, 21 August 1990 .

10. Interview with Oktay Vural, May 1992, Ankara. Oktay was the General-Director of BOTAS [Pipelines Corporation Co.] during the Gulf crisis. He was involved in the decision-making process to close the oil pipelines.

11. In 1987-1988, for instance, while some 72% of Turkey's total exports to the Middle East went to three countries, Iraq, Saudi Arabia, and Iran, some 92% of Turkey's imports from the Middle East came from these countries. Guven (1990, p. 190); Kalaycioglu (1988, p. 87).

12. As early as 1983, Iraqi Deputy Prime and Foreign Minister, Tariq Aziz, came to Turkey to ask financial assistance for Iraqi imports from Turkey. *Briefing* [Turkish weekly journal in English], 21 February 1983, p.ll, and 4 December 1989, p.12; *Keesing's*, p.33042. See also, Ankara Radio in Turkish, no date no time, *Summary of World Broadcast*, [*SWB* hereafter], Middle East [ME hereafter]/W, 1400 GMT, 29 July 1986; *Hurriyet*, 11 April 1988.

13. In material terms, Turkish workers in the Middle East transferred a total of TL29 billion between 1967 and 1989, with a steady annual increase during the 1980s. Irbec, *op.cit.*, p. 105.

14. In quantitative terms, the number of Turkish workers going to Iraq decreased from 10,467 per annum in 1981 down to 3,717 per annum in 1988, whereas their number in Saudi Arabia increasingly raised from 342 in 1967 per annum up to 34,645 in 1988 per annum. Table 41, taken from Turkish Job Centre, in Irbec, *op.cit.*, p. 106.

15. Some of these banks are Al-Baraka, Faisal Finance,

Saudi-American Bank, Arab-Turk Bankasi, Bahreyn and Kuveyt Bankasi, Habib Bank, Bank Mellat. Irbec, *op.cit.*, pp. 74-7.

16. According to this agreement, both countries were to cooperate in joint ventures to be financed by Kuwait to increase investment in Turkey. *Dis Isleri Bakanligi Bulteni* [Turkish Foreign Ministry Bulletin], 23-26 September 1985, p.26. The Bulletin is now out of publication.

17. Kuwait, occupying the eleventh position in the list of overall foreign investment in Turkey, was a shareholder in seven joint ventures such as Akdeniz Fertilizer Complex with 47.25%, Kuveyt-Evkaf Finance Institute with 59%. *The Middle East Economic Digest*, Vol.34, No.33, 24 August 1990, p.23. *Hurriyet*, 3 August 1990; *Gunes* [Turkish daily newspaper, now out of publication], 10 August 1990; table 28, in *HDTM*, Turkey's Main Economic Indicators, April 1991, p.47. See also, Devlet Planlama Teskilati Yabanci Sermaye Baskanligi, Yabanci Sermaye Raporu, 1987-1989, June 1990.

18. The $822.5 million from the IDB, $333 million from Saudi Development Fund, $127 million from Kuwaiti-Arab Economic Fund, $40 million from special OPEC fund, $27 million from Abu Dhabi Arab Economic Development Fund. Irbec, *op.cit.*, p.159.

19. Among its neighbours, Iraq has, according to Turkkaya Ataov, been an exceptional country with which Turkey had little, if any, problem; regardless of Iraq's regime, orientation, and policies, Turkish-Iraqi relations have, throughout, been good. Despite temporary and minor disputes resulting from the use of rivers and the Turkish minorities in Iraq, Ataov argues, Turkey-Iraq relations were based on solid, realistic and friendly grounds. Ataov (1989).

20. Interview with Candan Karlitekin, May 1992, Ankara. Karlitekin is Head of the Research Department of the Turkish Eximbank.

21. This section will examine the 'Kurdish problem' as far as its importance to Turkish-Iraqi relations is concerned. Therefore, it will be a background for the discussion of the 'Kurdish problem' during the Gulf crisis later in this chapter.

22. The Kurdish people are dispersed into four Middle Eastern countries as well as to the ex-Soviet Union. See Bradshaw (1991).
23. There is no certain record about the population of the Kurds living in Turkey. It varies from 3 to 10 million. Gresh and Vidal (1990, p. 111).
24. Vedat (1980). Some of the uprisings in this period are as follows: Babanzade Abdurrahman Pasa Isyani (1806), Bedirhan Isyani (1831), Seyh Ubeydullah Isyani (1880), Seyh Selim ile Sabahattin ve Ali Isyani (1912), Kocgiri Isyani (1920). See also Hidir Goktas, Kurtler: Isyan-Tenkil (Istanbul: Alan Yayincilik, 1991).
25. Vedat, *ibid.* See also Aktas, *ibid.* Some of those uprisings in this period are as follows: Nasturi Rebellion (1924), Zilan Rebellion (1925), Sheikh Said Rebellion (1925), Semdinli Rebellion (1925), Reskotan and Reman Isyani (1925), Pervani Rebellion (1926), Guyan Rebellion and Colemerik Raid (1926), Hoca Rebellion (1926), Kocogu Rebellion (1926), Hakkari Beytussebab Rebellion (1926), Agri Rebellion (1926), Bicar Rebellion (1927), Zilanli Resul Aga Rebellion (1926), Zeylan Rebellion (1930), Tutakli Ali Can Rebellion (1930), Oramar Rebellion (1930), Buban Rebellion (1934), Abdulkuddus Rebellion (1935), Abdurrahman Rebellion (1935), Sason Rebellion (1935), Dersim Rebellion (1937).
26. The US supported the Iranian Shah in his intervention in the Kurdish problem in Iraq especially before the Iran-Iraq Treaty in 1975. On the US Kurdish policy see Yavuz, *op.cit.*; and Gunter (1992, pp. 26-9).
27. For example, Harris, *op.cit.*, p.70; Kurkcuoglu (1972, pp. 12 and 24n). Kurkcuoglu noted that Turkey-Iraqi relations and cooperation persisted even in the face of Iraq's very radical and pro-Soviet tendencies after 1958. And Ataov, *op.cit.*
28. Syria and Iraq's reaction to Turkey's decision came even before the implementation of the decision. *Briefing*, 25 December 1989, p.9; *Facts on File*, 19 January 1990, p.36. On their reaction after January 13, also *Tercuman*, 15 January 1990; *Keesing's*, p.37201.

29. Yildirim Akbulut was interviewed on the Turkish Television program '32.GUN', Ankara TRT Television in Turkish, 1800 GMT, 20 December 1990, *Foreign Broadcast Information Service* [*FBIS* hereafter]-Western Europe [WEU hereafter]-90-246, 21 December 1990, p.27. See also, Derya Sazak, 'Akbulut-Saddam Gorusmesi', *Milliyet*, 30 August 1990. This incident was mentioned by those interviewed: Mehmet Kececiler, May 1992, Ankara. Kececiler was State Minister for Petroleum Affairs during the Gulf crisis. He was one of the most heavily involved statesmen in the decision-making process. And Cemil Cicek, May 1992, Ankara. Cicek was State Minister during the Gulf crisis.

30. Iraqi Oil Minister Isam El Celebi, interviewed by the official Iraq journal *Elif-Be*, 'Iraq accuses Turkey in the dispute on the use the Euphrates Water', 6 June 1990, *Dis Basin ve Turkiye*, 7 June 1990, B.N.106, p.3, and 11 June 1990, B.N.108, pp.4-5.

31. Iraqi Agriculture Minister Abd al-Wahhab Mahmud's statement, quoted in the text of dispatch datelined by Baghdad, 4 July 1990, (ME/0793 i), and Wakh in Arabic, 1445 GMT, 4 July 1990, *SWB*, ME/0809 A/5, 6 July 1990. On the accusation by the Iraqi and Syrians of Turkey of being selfish, and opportunist to use the water for its own purposes only see, *The Christian Science Monitor*, 2 July 1990, Sam Cohen writing from Istanbul, *Dis Basin ve Turkiye*, 9 July 1990, B.N.120, p.8-9.

32. Iraqi official journal of Ba'ath Party, Al-Tavra, was also reported to have argued that Turkey's decision would affect the life of the people living around the Euphrates River, and inhibiting some industrial projects in Iraq, *Gunes*, 15 January 1990; *Tercuman*, 15 January 1990; *Milliyet*, 15 January 1990.

33. Semih Idiz in *Cumhuriyet* predicted that the Arab League Summit would support Iraqi claims against Turkey, *Cumhuriyet*, 22 May 1990; the BBC World Service in Turkish, 25 May 1992, 1900-1930 (Turkish Time) in *Dis Basin ve Turkiye*, 28 May 1990, B.N.99, pp.12-13.

34. *Briefing*, 7 May 1990, pp.14-15; *Cumhuriyet* reported that even

MI-5 and MI-6 of Britain and KIP of Greece cooperated with MOSSAD and MIT, *Cumhuriyet*, 23 April 1990; and *Hurriyet*, 24 April 1990.

35.   *Cumhuriyet*, 8 August 1990. Also, Yalcin Dogan, columnist in Turkish daily newspaper *Milliyet*, whose view was based on inside information from the deliberations during the decision-making process, noted the decision-makers were concerned that 'the PKK might get advantage of the war against Iraq' to increase its separatist activities.   Yalcin Dogan, 'Amerika'nin Harekati, Turkiye'nin Petrolu...' [America's Action, Turkey's Oil...], *Milliyet*, 4 August 1990.   And Cengiz Candar, 'Turkiye Tarafsiz Kalamayacak' [Turkey Unable to Remain Neutral], *Gunes* [Turkish daily newspaper, now out of publication], 8 August 1990. Turan Yavuz noted that with the closure of the oil pipelines, and Turkey's pro-US policy, the 'Kurdish problem' came to the top of the agenda of the Turkish government. Yavuz, *op.cit.*, p.128.

36.   President Ozal, interviewed by Altemur Kilic of *Tercuman*, *Tercuman*, 8 December 1990, also appearing in, *FBIS*-WEU-90-239, 12 December 1990, p.39-40. And, for example, President Ozal, talks with selected writers from the Turkish press at the Presidential Palace, Ankara, 18 August 1990, in *Sabah* [Turkish daily newspaper], 25 January 1991.

37.   President Ozal, interviewed by Xavier Batalla, Barcelona Lavanguardia in Spanish, 27 January 1991, pp.8-9, in *FBIS*-WEU-91- 021, 31 January 1991, pp.45-47.

38.   Yavuz pointed to two different views among the Kurds on their position in the Gulf crisis. Some advocated a pro-Iraqi policy; some preferred to intensify their struggle for independence, and thus advocated a pro-US policy. Yavuz, *op.cit.*, pp.124-125.

39.   Seyfettin Ozgezer and Omer Buyuktimur, 'Iraqi Kurds Prepare for War', Istanbul *Gunaydin* in Turkish, 6 October 1990, in *FBIS*-WEU-90-199, 15 October 1990, p.32-33. The article was based on an interview with an anonymous Kurdish activist in northern Iraq.

40. The alliance among the DPK of Barzani, the PUK of Talabani, and other six Kurdish groups was formed in July 1987. Gunter (1992, pp. 39-40).

41. Bonn Berxweden in Turkish, 15 September 1990, in *FBIS*-WEU-90- 203, 19 October 1990, p.42. On the seriousness of instability in the Kurdish-inhabited Turkey, see Claus Ther, 'Intifada in Kurdistan: Little is heard about the Anatolian Kurdish Guerillas- Turkey wants to enter the EC clean', *Vienna Der Standard* in German, 13 August 1990, *FBIS*-WEU-90-193, 4 October 1990, p.43.

42. The information was based on the Government sources. Emin Pazarci, 'Dort Endisemiz Var' [We Have Four Worries], *Tercuman*, 24 December 1990. In a similar report appearing in Turkish daily newspaper *Milliyet*, Turkey's concerns in the wake of approaching war were analysed: the apprehensions were not different from those in the beginning of the crisis: Istanbul *Milliyet* in Turkish, 3 January 1991, in *FBIS*-WEU-91-004, 7 January 1991, p.39.

43. President Ozal, interviewed by Al-Hayat, *op.cit.* Professor Haluk Ulman noted that President Ozal's policy was based on two assumptions: first, Saddam Hussein will be overthrown; and second, the West will be re-shaping the Middle East from scratch after the crisis, in which Turkey must have an active policy to have a 'say'. In view of this, President Ozal played an opportunist policy, rather than a policy of caution. Haluk Ulma, 'Iki Hayati Varsayim...', *Gunaydin* [Turkish daily newspaper], 20 August 1990. The same view was expressed by Uluc Gurkan, 'Roma'dan ABD'ye', *Gunes*, 21 August 1990.

44. For example, President Ozal, talks with selected writers from Turkish press at the Presidential Palace, 18 August 1990, in *op.cit.* There President Ozal portrayed Turkey's decision in a similar fashion. He said that:
To have a 'word' in the developments which might lead to a 'Kurdish State' in the northern Iraq, Turkey must have a right to

say something about the developments in the region because they closely concern Turkey. We want to prevent the creation of the Kurdish state. If Turkey were not in the coalition, the things would proceed outside Turkey's knowledge, and against Turkey's interests.

45. President Ozal, address at the Turkish Grand National Assembly, 1 September 1990, T.B.M.M. Tutanak Dergisi [Turkish Grand National Assembly Records] [TGNA Records hereafter], 1 September 1990, lst.sess., Term 18, Vol.47, the Legislative Year 4, p.13. Also, President Ozal, interviewed by Ugur Dundar, Ankara Turkish Television, 1900 GMT, 18 January 1991, in *SWB*, Middle East [ME hereafter]/0976, E/24-27, 22 January 1991; President Ozal, interviewed by Nicholas Witchell of the British Television BBC-1, 0833 GMT, on 22 August 1990, in *Newspot*, 23 August 1990, p.2, and in *Dis Basin ve Turkiye*, 23 August 1990, B.N.153, pp.1-3. *Newspot*, published by the semi-official (Turkish) General Directorate of Press and Information, is a weekly (now fortnightly) newspaper in English. And President Ozal, interviewed by PBS-TV, 22 August 1990, in *Dis Basin ve Turkiye*, 24 August 1990, B.N.154, pp.1-5.

46. President Ozal, interviewed by Matthias Nass and Michael Schweli of German weekly *Die Zeit*, 22 February 1991, in *Dis Basin ve Turkiye*, 22 February 1991, B.N.21, pp.1-8; and in *FBIS*-WEU-91- 038, 26 February 1991, p.17. President Ozal had another interesting view on the territorial integrity of Iraq and Turkey's ambitions: on the question of Mosul being part of the Lausanne Treaty, but its loss following the 1925 Ankara Agreement to Britain, and whether he would abrogate the 1925 Agreement, President Ozal said that

'I don't give importance to the land and resources. Look at the Japanese example. A third of Turkey with 130 million population. The important thing is the human factor...We abandoned these lands after the war...Today natural resources are not so important'. He reiterated that except for the creation of a Kurdish state,

Turkey would not intervene in Iraq even in the vacuum. *Ibid.*

47. Cengiz Candar, 'Turkiye Tarafsiz Kalamayacak' [Turkey unable to remain neutral], *Gunes*, 8 August 1990. Candar argued that if Saddam was broken down, there would emerge a power vacuum in the Iraq where the factions would fight each other. At the end, he argued that Turkey could have found herself in a war alongside Iraq, Iran, and Syria. This was the point which made Turkey the central actor in the crisis.

48. President Ozal's diplomacy with the regional countries, especially with Iran and Syria, is noteworthy: after his visit to Syria in October where the two countries agreed on the maintenance of the Iraq's borders, President Ozal visited Iran in November, where he argued that Turkey, Iran and Syria had parallel views on the status quo, or on the inviolability of Iraq's borders. *Hurriyet* [Turkish daily newspaper], 13 November 1990; *Gunaydin*, 14 November 1990. *Milliyet*, 13 December 1990.

49. President Ozal was quoted to have said that 'If Iraq is defeated and penetrated by Iranian or Syrian troops, Turkey would enter Iraq.' *Gunes*, 13 January 1991.

50. On Iranian President Rafsanjani's special envoy A. Mo'ayyeri's visit to Turkey: Teheran *IRNA* in English, 1928 GMT, 21 January 1991, in *FBIS*-WEU-91-014, 22 January 1991, p.56; and his press conference in Ankara, in Teheran *IRNA* in English, 2218 GMT, 21 January 1991, in *FBIS*-WEU-91-014, 22 January 1991, p.57. Also, Ankara *Anatolia* in English, 1630 GMT, 21 January 1991, Ankara TRT Television Network in Turkish, 1800 GMT, 21 January 1991, in *FBIS*-WEU-91-014, 22 January 1991, p.56. In addition, Iranian Ambassador To Turkey, Mohammed Reza Baqeri, also stated that:
'We know that Turkey does not covet any Iraqi land and that it will not open a second front in the Gulf war...We are opposed to the establishment of a Kurdish state in the region...so are other regional countries.', quoted in Ankara *Anatolia* in Turkish, 1410 GMT, 9 February 1991, in *FBIS*-WEU-91-028, 11 February 1991,

p.41.

51. Apparently, Alptemocin's visits to Iran and Syria may have been prompted by the comments in Iranian Radio on Turkey's designs on the Iraqi territory as much as Turkey's suspicion on Iranian design on Iraq. Alptemocin's signals to Iranian officials in Teheran, Iranian Agency, 6 February 1991, in SWB, ME/0991, i(b), 8 February 1991, and *SWB*, ME/0992, i, 9 February 1991. On Alptemocin's visit to Syria on 11 February, and the talks about the Iraq's territorial integrity: *SWB*, ME/0994, (i), 12 February 1991; *SWB*, ME/0995, i(b), 13 February 1991; and Turkish Television in Turkish, 1700 GMT, and 1800 GMT, 12 February 1991, in *SWB*, ME/0996, A16, 14 February 1991.

52. President Ozal, statement, appearing in Ankara *Anatolia* in English, 1005 GMT, 17 February 1991 in *FBIS*-WEU-91-033, 19 February 1991, p.55, also in *Cumhuriyet*, 18 February 1991, and *Sabah*, 18 February 1991. Also President Ozal, address to the World Economic Forum, in Ankara Turkish Radio, 2100 GMT, 3 February 1991, in *SWB*, ME/0990, A/22, 7 February 1991, and in Ankara Domestic Service in Turkish, 2100 GMT, 3 February 1991, in *FBIS*-WEU-91-023, 4 February 1991, pp.49-50.

53. President Ozal, interviewed by Jim Bodgener of the *Financial Times*, the *Financial Times*, 21 August 1990. Turkish Ambassador to Washington, Nuzhet Kandemir, also whispered to the American Administration, stating that a peaceful solution of the crisis was to Turkey's preference if only to maintain status quo in the Iraqi borders. *Gunaydin*, 19 October 1990.

54. The announcement by Turkish Foreign Minister A. K. Alptemocin at a news conference at the Turkish Grand National Assembly on December 21, 1990, of the deployment, Ankara TRT Television Network in Turkish, 1700 GMT, 21 December 1990, in *FBIS*-WEU-90-247, 24 December 1990, p.41. On the deployment of the forces see, for example, Ankara *Anatolia* in English, 1550 GMT, 3 January 1991, in *FBIS*-WEU-91-003, 4 January 1991, p.29; Ankara Turkish Television, 1800 GMT, 8 January 1991, in

SWB, ME/0966, A/7, 10 January 1991.

55. The permission was granted by the Parliament on January 17, 1991. *TGNA Records*, 17 January 1991, the Government's motion in p.328, and the voting in p.332. And few hours after the permission by the Parliament, the Council of Ministers meeting made the decision to allow the foreign forces to use the Turkish bases, Ankara TRT Television Network in Turkish, 2000 GMT, 17 January 1991, *FBIS*-WEU-91-013, 18 January 1991, p.73. Previously, alongside the permission, additional 48 U.S. war planes had been sent to Incirlik on 15 January 1991. Ankara *Anatolia* in Turkish, 1535 GMT, 15 January 1991, in *SWB*, ME/0972, A/10, 17 January 1991. And the planes taking off from Incirlik started to bomb Iraq from 18 January, Jerusalem Voice of Israel and IDF Radio Networks in Hebrew, 1300 GMT, 18 January 1991, in *FBIS*-WEU-91- 014, 22 January 1991, p.55.

56. On the demand by US Secretary of State Baker from the NATO allies, in NATO Foreign Minister meeting in Brussels 10 September 1990, *Gunes*, 11 September 1990; *Cumhuriyet*, 11 September 1990; *Milliyet*, 11 September 1990.

57. The UN Security Council Resolution 678 asked Iraq to evacuate Kuwait by 15 January 1991. Otherwise, Resolution 678 allowed to 'use all necessary means' against Iraq.

58. NATO Foreign Ministers meeting in Brussels assured Turkey that in accordance with Article 5 of the North Atlantic Treaty, they would come to Turkey's assistance if there was to be an attack from Iraq. See among many others, for instance, *Cumhuriyet*, 11 August 1990; *Gunes*, 11 August 1990; *Milliyet*, 11 August 1990; and *NATO Review*, 'European Security: Lessons Learned From the Gulf War', *NATO Review*, No.3, June 1991, p.7.

59. President Ozal, interviewed by London-based Al-Hayat, 17 February 1991, in *Dis Basin ve Turkiye*, 25 February 1991, B.N.22, p.1-5; in *FBIS*-WEU-91-033, 19 February 1991, pp.52-53; also in *Cumhuriyet*, 18 February 1991; and in *Anatolia* in Turkish, 1525 GMT, 17 February 1991, *SWB*, ME/1001, A/12,

20 February 1990.

60.   President Bush's Remarks to Raytheon Missile Systems Plant Employees, 15 February 1991, Weekly Compilation of Presidential Documents, p.177, cited in Dannreuther (1991-1992, p. 53).

61.   For the reasons why President Bush was hesitant to react to the Kurdish tragedy see George J. Church, 'The Course of Conscience', *Time*, 15 April 1991, pp.22-24. On the emergence, US response, and Turkey's dilemma about the refugee problem in April 1991 see also Yavuz, *op.cit.*, especially Chapter 8.

62.   The Operation Provide Comfort, launched from 20 April, included not only humanitarian but also military involvement of the US troops as well as those from the UK, France, the Netherlands, and Italy. *Time*, 22 April 1991, and 29 April 1990.

63.   In his statement to Iranian news agency IRNA, President Ozal was quoted to have said that:
'The Kurdish refugees fleeing from the oppression in Iraq to Turkey and Iraq could go back their home only if they are protected by a strong military Allied force to be deployed in the region.'
President Ozal reiterated that Turkey was against the fragmentation of Iraq, which would exacerbate the problem. *Cumhuriyet* (European Edition), 3-9 May 1991. Also cited in Yavuz, *op.cit.*, p.193; and *Time*, 22 April 1991.

64.   On Ozal-Bush telephone conversations see Turan Yavuz, 'ABD'nin Kurt Karti' [US's Kurdish Card], *Milliyet*, 2 October 1992; and Yavuz, *op.cit.* A similar argument was made by Lally Weymouth, 'Turkey's Help Should be Reciprocated', *The International Herald Tribune*, 22 May 1991. The same incident was discussed by William Hale, 'Turkey, the Middle East and the Gulf crisis', *International Affairs*, Vol.68, No.4, 1992, p.687-688. President Ozal supported the deployment of the 'Hammer Force' in Turkey, President Ozal, address to the Conference on 'Turkey's National Security and Integrity', organised by the Business World Foundation, appearing in *Milliyet*, 22 December 1992.

65.   When Turkish forces launched a 'hot pursuit' operation to bomb the PKK camps up to 20 miles within northern Iraq in October 1991, unlike other Western countries, Germany criticised the Turkish action as a violation of human rights and political standards set by the Conference on Security and Co-operation in Europe. The *Financial Times*, 15 October 1991.

66.   During his visit to Turkey, Helmut Kohl affirmed that Turkey has the sovereign right to take all measures against terrorism in Turkey in compliance with the law. *Hurriyet*, 21 May 1993; *Cumhuriyet*, 21 May 1993; *Sabah*, 21 May 1993.

Bibliography

Ataov, T. (1989), 'Iki Dogu Komsumuz: Irak ve Iran', *Siyasal Bilgiler Fakultesi Dergisi*, Vol.44, No.2, January-Jun

Ayanoglu, E. (1990), 1980 *Sonrasi Yurtdisi Muteahhitlik Hizmetlerindeki Gelisme ve Teknonloji Ihracati*, HDTM IGEME, Ankara

Boravali, A-F. (1987), 'Kurdish Insurgencies, the Gulf War, and Turkey's Changing Role', *Conflict Quarterly*, Vol.7, Fall

Bradshaw, D. (1991), 'After the Gulf War: The Kurds', *The World Today*, Vol.47.5, May

Burkay, K. (1986), *Kurdistan'in Somurgelestirilmesi ve Kurt Ulusal Hareketleri*, 2nd edn, Ozgurluk Yolu Yay.

Cevizoglu, M. H. (1991), *Korfez Savasi ve Ozal Diplomasisi: Belqesel*, Form Yayinlari, Istanbul

Dannreuther, R. (1991-1992), *The Gulf Conflict: A Political and Strategic Analysis*, Adelphi Papers 264, Brassey's for the International Institute for Strategic Studies, Winter, London

Demirer, M. A. (1985), 'Economic Relations with the Middle East', in Harris, 1985

Devlet Istatistik Enstitusu [State Statistical Institute] (DIE) (1991), *Haziran 1991'de Turk Ekonomisi*. Istatistik ve Yorumlari, June

Eden, N. (1990), *Sark Meselesinin Dis Boyutu*, Erciyes University, Kayseri

Gresh, A. and Vidal, D. (1990), *A to Z Middle East*, Zed Books Ltd., London

Gunter, M. (1990), *The Kurds in Turkey: A Political Dilemma*,Westview Press, Oxford

Gunter, M. (1992), *The Kurds of Iraq: Tragedy and Hope*, St.Martin's Press, New York

Guven, T. (1990), 'Turkiye'nin OrtaDogu Ulkeleri ile Ekonomik ve Ticari Iliskilerinin Son 10 Yili', in HDTM, *Turkiye Ekonomisi ve Dis*

Ticaretindeki Son Gelismeler, HDTM Ekonomik Arastirmalar ve Degerlendirmeler Genel Mudurulugu, Ankara

Hale, W. (1992), 'Turkey, the Middle East and the Gulf crisis', *International Affairs*, Vol.68, No.4

Harris, G. S. (ed.) (1985), *The Middle East in Turkish-American Relations*, The Heritage Foundation, Washington D.C.

Harris, G. S. (1972), *Troubled Alliance: Turkish-American Problems in Historical Perspective. 1945-1971*, American Enterprise Institute, Washington D.C.

Harris, G. S. (1977), 'The Kurdish Conflict in Iraq', in Suhrke and Noble, 1977

Hiro, D.(1990), *The Longest War: The Iran-Iraq Military Conflict*, Paladin, London

Howe, J. T. (1991), 'NATO and the Gulf Crisis', *Survival*, Vol.33, No.3, May/June

Irbec, Y. Z. (1990), Turkiye'nin Dis Ekonomik Iliskilerinde Islam Ulkeleri, Turkiye Odalar ve Borsalar Birligi Yayinlari 141, Ankara

Kalaycioglu, S. (1988), 'Turkey's Economic Relations with the Arab World and the Role of Arab Banks in the Turkish Economy', *Studies on Turkish-Arab Relations*, Annual 3

Kaplan, L. L. (1988), *The NATO and the United States: Enduring Alliance*, Twayne Publishers, Boston

Karaosmanoglu, A. L. (ed.) (1987), *Turkiye'nin Savunmasi*, Foreign Policy Institute, Ankara

Kurkcuoglu, O. (1972), Turkiye'nin Arab Orta Dogusuna Karsi Politikasi, *Ankara Universitesi Siyasal Bilgiler Fakultesi Yayinlari* 340, Ankara

McGhee, G. (1990), *The US-Turkish-NATO-Middle East Connection: How the Truman Doctrine Contained the Soviets in the Middle East*, The Macmillan Press, London

Mango, A. (1989), 'Turkey and the Middle Eastern Market', in Manisali, 1989

Manisali, E. (1987), 'Economic Complementaries and Potentials for Cooperation Between Turkey and the Arab Countries', *Studies on*

Turkish-Arab Relations, Annual 2,

Manisali, E. (ed.) (1989), *Turkey's Place in the Middle East,* The Middle East Business and Banking Publications, Istanbul

Mudurlugu, H. v. D. T. (HDTM) (1987), *Ulke Raporlari: Irak'in Genel Ekonomik Durumu ve Turkiye ile Ticari Iliskileri. 1987 Yili Raporu,* HDTM Ekonomik Arastirmalar ve Degerlendirmeler Genel

Mudurlugu (the HDTM Economic Research and Evaluations Department) (1990), *Turkiye Ekonomisi ve Dis Ticaretindeki Son Gelismeler,* HDTM Ekonomik Arastirmalar ve Degerlendirmeler

Mudurlugu, Ankara (1989), *Turkiye-Islam Ulkeleri Dis Ticareti,* HDTM Ekonomik Arastirmalar ve Degerlendirmeler Genel Mudurlugu, November

Olson, R. (1989), *The Emergence of Kurdish Nationalism and the Sheikh Said Rebellion, 1880-1925,* University of Texas Press, Austin

Robins, P. (1991), *Turkey and the Middle East,* Pinter Publications for Royal Institute of International Affairs, London

Serxwebun, W. (1987), *Kurdistan'da 'Ozel Harp': Emperyalizmin 'Ozel Savas''i ve Turk Ordusnun Kurdistan'da Yuruttugu Savasin Niteligi Uzerine,* Herausberger, Koln

Suhrke, A. and Noble, L. G. (eds), (1977), *Ethnic Conflicts in International Relations,* Praeger Publishers, London

Tashan, S. (1987), 'Turkiye'nin Tehdid Algilamari', in Karaosmanoglu, 1987

Turkish Constructors Association (1990), *A Study on International Contractinq Services,* Turkish Constructors Association, Ankara

Ulman, H. (1966), 'Turk Dis Politikasina Yon Veren Etkenler, 1923-1968', *Ankara Universitesi Siyasal Bilgiler Fakultesi Dergisi,* September

Vali, F. A. (1971), *Bridge Across the Bosphorus: The Foreign Policy of Turkey,* The Johns Hopkins Press, Baltimore and London

Vedat, S. (1980), *Turkiye'de Kurtculuk Hareketi ve Isyanlari,* Vol.1, Kon Yayinlari, Ankar

Whetten, L. L. (1984), 'Turkey's Role in the Atlantic Alliance', *Atlantic Quarterly,* Vol.2, Part 3

Yalcintas, N. (1986), 'Economic Relations between Turkey and Islamic Countries', *Studies on Turkish-Arab Relations, Annual* 1

7 China and post-Cold War security in the Asia-Pacific region

KEN DARK

Introduction

I intend to examine themes in Asia-Pacific security, rather than attempt to review all relevant aspects of this complex region. The geographical limits of an 'Asia-Pacific Region' have been set differently by different analysts, so first it is useful to begin by providing a definition of what is meant by this term. Here, the Asia-Pacific region is defined as comprising the western part of the 'Pacific Rim': a region which I see as composed of all the states surrounding the Pacific Ocean and its neighbouring seas (such as the South China Sea and the sea of Japan). The Asia-Pacific region is, therefore, the western part of this area, comprising four sub-regions in East Asia, South East Asia, Australasia and the Pacific islands of Polynesia and Melanesia. The eastern part of the 'Pacific Rim', principally comprising the Americas, can be conveniently divided from this region by taking Hawaii as the central point dividing the eastern part of the region from the west. Geopolitically, this makes sense, as Hawaii is both part of the USA and one of the Polynesian islands.

By encompassing only the western part of the Pacific basin, this region may be seen as geographically distinct from the much-discussed 'Pacific Rim' (which is, itself, variously defined: for alternative treatments of these regions, see Drakakis-Smith, 1992; Rogman, 1991; Shibusawa *et al*, 1991; Segal, 1990c). Likewise, one can distinguish geographically the Asia-Pacific region from Asia by the inclusion of Australasia and the Pacific islands.

The Region is not culturally homogenous, but, in political and economic terms - and, as we shall see, in terms of some of its security problems - the region can be examined as a whole and shares access to the Pacific and the economic and diplomatic ties which have developed around its shores (Thompson, 1994). Since the end of the Cold War the economic importance of this region and its security have been the centre of much attention in the West, for example the alarmist *Time* essay of 31 July 1995 by Charles Krauthammer. Many commentators have concentrated on the role of China in this region (for example, *The Economist*, 7 October 1995, pp. 93-4; Shambaugh, 1994) and the supposed `threat' which it constitutes to Western interests (for a recent discussion of the security of East Asia, see: Buzan and Segal, 1994). The development of post-Cold War Chinese military and economic roles in the Pacific has not, however, been the only characteristic which highlights the unusual significance of the region for international security. The Asia-Pacific region contains two of the small group of surviving communist states (even if, in China's case, adherence to Marxist ideology might seem to some no more than nominal). These two states are also the only communist regimes in the 1990s which have a nuclear weapons capability.

Of course, another notable aspect of the region has been the much-discussed rise to economic prominence of the so-called 'Asian Tigers' and the shift in patterns of economic growth, long centred on the West, to east Asia (Thompson, 1994, pp. 222-7). While the implications of this sudden economic and technological development of the region have been widely discussed in relation to international political economy and developmental issues, the risk they pose to international security has, perhaps, received not only less, but arguably insufficient, attention (for example, Dixon, 1991; Harding, 1987; Mackerras *et al*, 1994, pp. 63-101).

The economic development of China since the 1980s has, of course, been a rapidly changing aspect of the area (on China's economic transformation, see, for example, Mackerras *et al*, 1994, pp. 102-49 and 180-91; Cable and Ferdinand, 1994). Unlike economic changes in the former Soviet Union, the move away from central planning to a market-based economy has not been accompanied by equivalent social and political reforms (Moise, 1994, pp. 213-32). The size of the Chinese economy and the vast population of the People's Republic of China suggest that it is with China that any discussion of the relationship between international security and the international political economy of this region may usefully begin. So, the discussion here will start by examining the case of China and then look at the remainder of the region, moving roughly north to south from the two Koreas to Australasia. Finally, some conclusions about the character of post-Cold War security in the region as a whole will be suggested.

China and international security in the Asia-Pacific region

It is difficult to discuss the character of contemporary China without realising its pivotal role in contemporary international security (see, for example, Songiao, 1994). By far the largest state in the Asia-Pacific region, with potentially the largest economy and rapid economic growth, it has doubled its military spending in the last decade. At the same time, it has both serious domestic political and social problems and a major demographic problem faced by its booming population (Moise, 1994, pp. 213-35; Chan, 1989; Goldman, 1994; Bannister, 1987).

Chinese armed forces far exceed those of its neighbours, other than Russia, in the Asia-Pacific region, both numerically and in terms of nuclear capability (Segal, 1985; Neaman, 1994, pp. 165, and 170-73; Neaman, 1995, pp. 169, 171 and 176-9). This military advantage is being developed by the modernisation of China's armed forces, including its nuclear forces (Neaman, 1994, p. 165). China continues to undertake nuclear weapons tests, which suggests the continuing development of Chinese nuclear weapons capabilities (Neaman, 1994, p. 165; Neaman, 1995, p. 169, see also p. 171). It seems that new ballistic-missile systems are being developed which will be operational by the end of the twentieth century, although China does not have multiple warheads for use in conjunction with such weapons at present (Neaman, 1994, pp. 165). There are, however, approximately seven Chinese ICBMs that have been tested with MIRV warheads (Neaman, 1995, p. 176).

The size of Chinese conventional and nuclear forces is, therefore, formidable in its regional context and the Chinese army of over two million is also modernising its conventional forces (Neaman, 1994, p. 166; Neaman, 1995, pp. 270-5, for both modernisation and military expenditure). It is capable of support by over four thousand fighter aircraft and a fleet including over 50 submarines and 50 surface craft (Neaman, 1995, pp. 177-8; also see Lewis and Litai, 1994). But large armies - or even stocks of nuclear warheads - do not constitute a threat to regional security unless there is the will to use them and political cause for them to be employed (on Chinese foreign policy, see Segal 1990b; Hu, 1995).

When one examines Chinese attitudes to neighbouring states and the distribution of Chinese interests in the Asia-Pacific region, the threat posed by China's forces initially appears slight (Hu, 1995). China is well served by regional stability, in the status quo it has the prospect of becoming regionally dominant, at least in east Asia (Pye, 1994). In military terms, none of its neighbours pose a direct threat to the existence or prosperity of the Chinese state. Nor is there evidence that China's neighbours are remotely likely to intervene to attempt to topple the communist government.

To the west, China has a secure, if somewhat permeable, boundary with the new states of Central Asia, and its long-contested border with Russia (Stephan, 1995) is more likely to cause local tensions and bursts of geopolitical diplomacy than inter-state warfare (*Times Higher*, 13

January 1995, pp. 13-14; Segal, 1990a). So, although China has disputes with Russia and other states to its west, it is very unlikely to be drawn into war by aggression from this direction (on FSU/Asia-Pacific relations, see Thakur and Theyer, 1993).

A threat of Chinese expansion into the Pacific seems harder to evaluate. The existing disputes with neighbouring states to the east, notably Taiwan, and recent Chinese claims in the South China Sea, may be sources of future tension (on the current disputes, see Valencia, 1995; Thompson, 1994, pp. 244-5; Leifer, 1995; Bearman, 1995, pp. 166-7; Hickey, 1992; Garver, 1992.)

More worrying, perhaps, is the recent Chinese tendency to disregard the protest of Taiwan over its missile-testing programme and there are hints of expansionist intentions toward Central Asia. The settlement of large numbers of Chinese citizens in Central Asia and across national borders, therefore, could be seen as having security consequences for the region. China's expanding population far exceeds that of surrounding states and demographic factors operating within China could be seen as posing a potential threat to its neighbours, although Chinese migration has not posed such a threat in the past (there are, of course, cross-border communities already, for instance see Benson and Svanberg, 1988).

The Western response to such expansionist trends has tended to be extremely restrained and the USA seems to be switching its emphasis from supporting Taiwan to gaining economic and other involvement in the People's Republic (Lee, 1989; Moise, 1994, pp. 230-1). Western disinterest in restricting Chinese piecemeal expansion and regional hegemony may also be suggested by the decreasing degree of support for Tibet in the West (Moise, 1994, pp. 227-8). The Chinese control of Tibetan territory seems relatively uncontested compared to other analogous disputes, while the ability of states with a large Buddhist population to assist the independence of Tibet seems both slight and not especially forthcoming (on China's disregard for Western attitudes; Baker, 1993). Consequently, there seems no significant possibility of either local or outside pressure leading to Tibetan independence while the current situation prevails (Mackerras *et al* 1994, pp. 41-3 and 253-4). More likely is increased Chinese immigration, due to demographic pressures in China, and the more intense assimilation into mainstream Chinese culture of the Tibetan population. While under such circumstances it seems very unlikely that Tibet could become a major source of instability within China or a threat to Chinese interests overseas, this may hint at the possible fate of other politically marginal territories, when seen from the Western point of view, into which China might expand if opportunity arose.

The greatest threat to international security posed by China may be of Chinese expansion into Central Asia, rather than territorial conquest or acquisition through mass immigration in the Asia-Pacific region. However, there are very large Chinese populations in many of the south-east Asian states (Suryadinata, 1989; see also Grant, 1993). For instance, Malaysia has between 30-35% of its population of Chinese descent and in Brunei approximately 30% of the population is of Chinese descent. As Chinese contacts dominate the economy of some south-east Asian states, for example Indonesia and Malaysia, and these are likely to intensify as the Chinese economy moves into a more vigorous stage of development, then areas of south-east Asia could be drawn into an economically dependent relationship with China, despite their own economic wealth (on the political 'vacuum', see Roy, 1995). Obviously a wealthy dependency is more valuable to a core state and this trend might be intensified by recent attempts to claim neighbouring parts of the ocean as Chinese territorial waters (Leifer, 1995). It is, therefore, possible, to imagine a dependent periphery surrounding China developing very rapidly in south-east Asia and Central Asia, and the possibility of North Korean dependence must also be admitted if relations with the West and with South Korea do not improve.

A negative aspect of Chinese economic development - from some points of view - may, therefore, be Chinese dominance in east Asia (Pye, 1994). This might be a serious problem for China's neighbours if it is accompanied by political totalitarianism, rather than political liberalisation, and if the repopulation of peripheral territories by China's large population becomes a feature of East Asian migration patterns: the Chinese population is already approximately 20% of the total world population (Wang and Hull, 1991).

If Central Asia collapsed into inter-state war or civil war within one of the new Central Asian states was to draw in Chinese military intervention, this might increase the chance of such developments occurring. Whether Russia would be willing to permit Chinese intervention in the 'Near Abroad' is, however, doubtful. The Chinese diplomatic and military links forged with Iran and Pakistan over the last decade might be seen not in terms of Chinese attempts to outflank India in geo-strategic terms, but to eliminate opposition from strongly-Muslim neighbouring states to the annexation or resettlement of Central Asia.

Again, one faces several problems in proposing such a hypothesis. If China were to expand - however peacefully - into Central Asia, Western diplomatic opposition, and possibly even economic measures, could be expected, and not only Russian but Turkish (and possibly Arab) political opposition, and perhaps economic action, anticipated.

The overseas Chinese are not unified in their support for Beijing and Deng Xiaoping has attempted to distance the People's Republic from them, so suggesting that these are not seen as possible allies in Chinese expansionism (Ramanathan, 1994; Hodder, 1992, p. 54). The practicalities of expansion into either Central Asia or the Pacific may, therefore, present such problems as to preclude Chinese moves in this direction. It also seems uncertain whether China's ambitions in these areas are political or economic: if the latter, they may be achievable without conflict with either the West or Russia.

The developments visible inside China are not likely to bring about stability (Austin, 1995; Segal and Goodman, 1994. See also, Betts, 1993/94). Overpopulation and economic growth have led to demographic and economic disparities between social groups and areas (Grant, 1995; Segal, 1994; Sugimoto, 1994). Westernisation and the development of 'consumerist' attitudes have further divided society and intensified existing urban:rural contrasts (Segal 1994; Goldman, 1994; Cannon and Jenkins, 1990).

Divisions are also visible along cultural and ethnic grounds, no longer submerged by Marxist ideology, a factor seen by many as significant in the break-up of the former Soviet Union (Sugimoto, 1994). Recent rapid growth in two religious groups, Christians and Muslims, has led both to further changes in value systems and the emergence of new interest groups (Pas, 1989). The potential for east Asian societies to witness a rapid growth in the number of Christian believers has been evidenced in the case of South Korea, where the population included a small Christian minority at the time of the Korean War, but (if present trends continue) will almost certainly have a Christian majority in the early part of the twenty-first century (for instance, O'Brien and Palmer, 1993, pp. 79 and 124). In South Korea, the process of Conversion and economic growth occurred to some extent in parallel. In China, although the scale of the country and problems of communication may make this a longer process, the speed at which religious change is happening suggests that an analogous transformation may be under way.

Whereas the rapid increase in the number of Christians in China seems a country-wide change, growth in support for Islam is a more regionalised characteristic (Brown, 1986; Gladrey, 1991). This has been most noticeable in those provinces close to Central Asia, which are among those least affected by economic growth. The Christian population tends to be closely connected with economic growth, however, and the incorporation of Hong Kong and its even more Christianised population into southern China may speed up Christianisation, at least locally.

Consequently, China in the early twenty-first century may contain several distinctive communities in cultural and religious terms, and these may be unevenly distributed over the country. The fragility of communist party control and pressures produced inside China by these changes (on this, see Joffe, 1995), and by economic and demographic pressures in the context of a loss of legitimacy on the part of any form of unifying Marxist ideology, may lead to political fragmentation (Austin, 1995; Grant, 1995; Chan, 1989). Were China to fragment, plainly the separation of the more Westernised, economically developed and urbanised areas from those with primarily agricultural economies relatively untouched by both Westernisation and urbanism, might be expected. This might, in part, serve to separate the more Christianised zones from those with larger Muslim populations, although Christianity has made rapid progress among rural populations in the last two decades. The area with the largest number of Muslims may be expected to be situated close to Central Asia with which they could well share some cultural and economic characteristics.

The possibility of China fragmenting into successor states does not necessarily reduce the risk posed by China's military might to regional stability. Civil war in China could resemble inter-state warfare elsewhere, given the size of the country and its geopolitics, while other areas of the Asia-Pacific region might be drawn into such a conflict. Nor need successor states be less expansionist than the current Chinese government.

The greatest danger faced by its neighbours and by the West if China either adopts a more expansionist and regionally hegemonic policy, or if it breaks up, is that posed by its nuclear weapons. Any analysis of the security of the Asia-Pacific region must, as a consequence, take account of this and the danger of nuclear war resulting from the other communist regime in the region, North Korea.

The threat of nuclear war in East Asia

While China's nuclear arsenal is regionally unparalleled, other than by that of Russia, it is also probably unusable against many of its neighbours, even in total war. For example, Japan and Australia have allies with even more formidable nuclear capabilities in North America and Europe. Russia still maintains nuclear superiority over China (Neaman, 1995, pp. 113-4). Consequently, on these grounds alone, China is unlikely to be involved in a war that it could not easily win using conventional weapons - given its vast superiority in conventional forces over all its neighbours except for Russia - so is unlikely to resort to nuclear warfare, even if war occurred. As there is no serious prospect of direct Chinese-American war in the Pacific, the only risk of nuclear war involving China is, therefore, in a Russian-Chinese conflict, or if China was drawn into a conflict involving one of the states to its south, such as India, Pakistan, or the states of south-east Asia (on the South Asian area; Gupta, 1995; Hewitt, 1993; Bearman, 1995, pp. 191-202).

The risk of China initiating a nuclear war is, therefore, probably slight and is far lessened by the observation that it is hard to imagine any form of conventional inter-state warfare directly destroying the Chinese state. Nuclear war would, therefore, not be a profitable strategy for China, and there is no indication that weapons being developed are for purposes other than deterrence.

North Korea is, perhaps, more likely to use such nuclear weapons as it possesses but, if so, in a limited fashion against either Japan or South Korea (Neaman, 1995, pp. 260-1, p. 165 on North Korean nuclear capability). Recent developments, following the crisis in 1994, may mean that nuclear disarmament and non-proliferation agreements will produce a non-nuclear North Korea (Bearman, 1995, pp. 13 and 174-83). If political tensions with South Korea are reduced and the economic advantages of reunification and cooperation prevail, then the danger of nuclear conflict in the Korean peninsula may cease. This would certainly be in the interests of both South Korea and Japan, as it is hard to imagine North Korea retaining its communist ideology or acting as a competitor in the international economy in relation to these states (on their economic development; Mackerras, 1992, pp. 387-409). The possibility for South Korean business to encompass the North Korean workforce, and the potential for Westernisation following enhanced economic contacts may suggest that current disputes are unlikely to be maintained long into the twenty-first century.

The danger of a new Korean war may encourage diplomatic efforts toward resolving the North-South conflict in Korea on the part of both China and the USA. The danger of any such conflict escalating into regional war would only be likely if China, Russia or the USA entered into it. Despite US involvement in South Korea's security, the awareness of the implications of such escalation may limit its likelihood and deter North Korea from aggression against the South. It is hard to see how a new Korean war could be won by the North, unless China were to disregard its own interests and become involved.

It is, therefore, unlikely that a nuclear war will be fought in east Asia despite the recent increase in tension in Korea and China's developing nuclear arsenal. This does not mean that one should see it as less of a priority to reduce China's nuclear weapons capabilities, particularly ICBM and SLBM forces, and it does not lessen the importance of eliminating the North Korean nuclear capacity. What is to be stressed is the continuing danger inherent in nuclear states becoming involved in neighbouring crises and especially the importance of keeping China, Russia and the USA out of any situation which might escalate into direct war between these states.

Another potential nuclear state is Japan (on Japan's international relations, see Buzan, 1995; Akaha, 1995; Katzenstein and Okawara, 1993; Inoguchi, 1991 and 1993). The success of the Japanese economy has prompted increased involvement in global politics and changes in Japanese attitudes to security issues (Mahbubani, 1992; Sasae, 1994). While, in technological and economic terms, Japan could develop a nuclear weapons capability, its security is ensured at present by its close relationship with Western states, especially the USA (on the USA and Japan; Sasae, 1994). Although there have been recent indications of political and economic problems between Japan and its Western allies (Sasae, 1994; Yabunka, 1991; Ogura, 1993), it seems unlikely that Japan itself would instigate a war in the Pacific (Friedman and Lebhard, 1991, is implausibly pessimistic). Nor does it seem plausible that Japan will develop its own nuclear weapons unless under threat from its neighbours and devoid of Western assistance (Sorrell, 1993. On Western foreign affairs; Nye, 1992-1993; Oxnam, 1992-1993).

The emergence of new nuclear states in the Asia-Pacific region is, however, likely. The booming economies of south-east Asia and the transfer of Western technologies into this area may lead to the development of a nuclear weapons capability in one or more of the south-east Asian states (Carus, 1990). There is also the possibility that, in south-east Asia, biological or chemical weapons of mass destruction may be developed. Although the risk of war involving China seems low and Chinese military force is more likely to be used (like Chinese economic strength) as a diplomatic tool in order to secure Chinese interests and to establish Chinese preeminence in East Asia, there may be greater risks of major war in south-east Asia. This area, therefore, forms the next topic to be examined here.

The risk of war in south-east Asia

As decades of scholarly research have not provided a clearcut answer to the question 'why do wars occur?', it is extremely difficult to preempt which factors are likely to cause a major war when reviewing the contemporary situation in south-east Asia. There are, however, some worrying indications that the area is potentially at risk of two, or more, of its states becoming involved in a major war (on the security problems of the area: McGregor, 1993).

Some characteristics of the international relations of contemporary south-east Asia highlight these indications (Neher, 1994). The area contains states with shared borders and booming economies (Dixon, 1991; Dwyer, 1990), each of which has a developed technological sector including high technology potentially applicable to military purposes (on south-east Asia force modernisation, see Thayer, 1990). These states are disparate in cultural and political systems but are characterised by authoritarian, in some cases military, governments. These governments are not especially concerned with issues of Western public opinion, human rights, American and western European notions of democracy and adherence to the norms of international law (Dutt, 1985; Kidron and Segal, 1991, pp. 62-3 and 138).

For example, Thailand has a bureaucratic and censorious administration with notable economic inadequacies and relatively high military spending compared to neighbouring Malaysia. The population of Thailand (26 million) is considerably larger than that of Malaysia (17.9 million), although both have successful economies (Kidron and Segal, 1991, pp. 113-15; Mackerras, 1992, p. 485). Even in economic terms, however, they are dissimilar, with Malaysia having a less export-driven economy and being barely able to produce sufficient food for its own population, whereas Thailand has a flourishing agricultural economy (Neher, 1994, pp. 52-5 and 135-7; Kidron and Segal, 1991, pp. 124-5). While Thailand uses three times more fuel than it produces, however, Malaysia produces surplus fuel (Kidron and Segal, 1991, pp. 123-4). Although there is no immediate threat to Malaysia from Thailand, these disparities - combined with the clear military supremacy of Thailand, which has forces approximately twice as large as those of Malaysia - may form a basis for future aggression (Neaman, 1995, pp. 187-8 and 195-7).

There are also cultural differences that might antagonise political and economic grievances between the two states. Whereas Thailand has a Buddhist state-religion and greater democracy than Malaysia (a Muslim state), it has less tolerance of deviation from social norms (Neher, 1994, pp. 57 and 132; Kidron and Segal, 1991, pp. 66-7, 72-3, 78-9 and 140-44). The Malaysian distaste for democracy might easily become used to legitimate conflict with Thailand (Neher, 1994, pp. 51-2 and 133-5; Kidron and Segal, 1991, pp. 60-61).

An even more dangerous example of these disparities is provided by Indonesia, which is the most populous Muslim state of all (Neher, 1994, p. 105; O'Brien and Palmer, 1993, pp. 22-23). Like Malaysia, the Indonesians do not have an export-driven economy and more is imported than is exported. Indonesia shares with Malaysia a distaste for liberal democracy and personal freedom and makes efforts to enforce conformity among its population (Neher, 1994, pp. 113-5; Kidron and Segal, 1991, pp. 60-61 and 66-7). Similar to Malaysia, also, is its difficulty in producing enough food for its needs, and this is an acute problem given its geographical constraints on habitation and its rising population (Mackerras, 1992, pp. 25 and 472; Kidron and Segal, 1991, pp. 16-17 and 28-9). Indonesia has proved less successful in gaining world markets for its products than the other states of south-east Asia, although, unlike Thailand, it is self-sufficient in respect to fuel requirements (Kidron and Segal, 1991, pp. 18-19, 26-7 and 32-3). Indonesia has, however, sufficient internal population pressure (the current population is larger than that of several neighbouring states combined, being 189.4 million) to prompt geopolitical expansion. It is hard to see how it can obtain resources to support its population without acquiring new territory or rapid technological development.

The situation is aggravated by the fact that all of these states are, in 1995, making territorial and other claims against each other (Kidron and Segal, 1991, pp. 12-13). In the case of Indonesia and Malaysia, this includes a substantial claim on maritime resources, which may lead to future conflict. Already these states have been involved in armed conflicts arising from such claims, including the Indonesian invasion of East Timor. All of these states have been accused by Western observers of using oppressive measures and political violence. All have been accused of obstructing human rights investigators and holding political prisoners. These latter points do not suggest special concern for international law or Western attitudes to sovereignty.

This pattern is, perhaps, made more alarming when one compares Indonesia to some of its neighbours in military terms. For example, Indonesia has an army of 214,000 compared to Malaysia's 90,000 and Thailand's 150,000 (on relative force sizes: Neaman, 1995, pp. 179-81, 187-8 and 195-7).

Consequently, national disparities and contrasting political cultures may be seen as giving rise to a situation in which inter-state warfare might easily occur. It is possible to recognise economic and demographic factors that, in conjunction with cultural and religious differences and authoritarian regimes, might be a basis for war in south-east Asia.

Although there does not seem a significant risk of war between China and the West, and the risk of war between China and Russia is limited, there is a serious danger of war in south-east Asia during the coming decades. The scope and form of this would depend on several factors. Some are general: whether all-out or limited war was waged and the types of weapons used, but others, such as the relative capabilities of the specific states involved and their geographical proximity, might play an important part in determining the scale of the conflict. The extent to which non-proliferation controls prevent south-east Asian states from acquiring nuclear, biological or chemical weapons would, however, be a critical factor in prohibiting such a conflict from taking the form of a war employing weapons of mass destruction (Clarke, 1989; Nolan 1991. On proliferation outside of Europe and North America, see also Leifer, 1988; Nolan 1991).

Averting the threat: regional organisation in south-east Asia

Recently, a hopeful development in the regional politics of south-east Asia may lessen the chance of war (Acharya, 1993; Park, 1993; Evans, 1994; Anon, 1995). A possible framework for regional security cooperation has been developed through the Asian Regional Forum and APEC meetings held in the region in 1994 (Bearman, 1995, pp. 183-5). Annual meetings of the Asian Regional Forum may promote peaceful co-existence between the neighbouring states of south-east Asia, a hope endorsed by Thailand and Indonesia (although with some reservations) and at the APEC meeting by Malaysia (Bearman, 1995, pp. 183-5). The apparent willingness of these major states in south-east Asia to work together to secure regional peace is encouraging and a further meeting took place in Summer 1995 to build upon these foundations (Bearman, 1995, p. 15).

Such a regional security framework may offset the problems caused by national disparities and hostilities, as may a mutual fear of China to the north. As we have seen, there is a chance that south-east Asia, or at least some of its component states, could become dependencies (albeit in an informal and economic fashion) to a Chinese 'super-economy', were this to develop. Nor would it be wise to underestimate the level of awareness among the governments of south-east Asia, no matter how dissimilar from the West in their political ideologies, of the disastrous nature of a regional inter-state war and the importance of building new security and economic structures to manage their disputes.

The 'forgotten' Pacific states: Australasia and the Islands

Most assessments of Asia-Pacific security concentrate on Japan, China and (sometimes) south-east Asia. They tend to exclude Australasia and the Pacific Island states, including Papua New Guinea (although this is not a universal omission, Henningham, 1995; Sutton and Payne, 1993b). Yet, the post-Cold War transformation has changed the security interests and international political context of these states, too.

Australia has a complex security problem as discussed in the Australian Defence White Paper, *Defending Australia* (AGPS, Canberra, 1994, see also Evans, 1989; Fry, 1990). While there are no obvious threats from neighbours and relative geographical isolation from south-east Asia makes 'spillover' from neighbouring conflicts implausible, Australia is also distant from its principal allies in North America and Europe and has been downgrading its links with British and Commonwealth forces. Given the long and 'open' coastline to the north of the Continent, and the relative military weakness of Australian forces (Neaman, 1995, pp. 171 and 173-4) compared to those of east and south-east Asia, one may doubt whether Australian self-sufficiency in security matters is adequate to ensure the continued security of the state in the new post-Cold War situation.

It is doubtful whether the continuing military alliance with the USA alone is capable of insuring Australia against military threats from the north that could clash with other US interests. This is not, of course, to suggest that the USA is other than a reliable military ally for Australia, simply that US economic and political reorientation towards east Asia may construct new patterns of interest, bypassing Australasia, which is relatively unimportant to the US today, in economic or military terms. So, unless Australia can reformulate its relationship with the European or Commonwealth states, it must either develop a new importance to the USA or seek new alliances with the politically fundamentally different states of south-east and east Asia, unless it attempts a costly policy of self-sufficiency (Evans, 1995 on Australia/Asia-Pacific relations. On 'self-sufficiency' see, for example, Cheeseman, 1993). The possibility of securing Australia through an alliance with, for example, Indonesia, is very doubtful. Differences in political systems and economics coincide with fundamental religious and cultural differences (Mackerras, 1992, pp. 573-85). In any such alliance, Australia might expose itself to a greater degree of threat if, in a crisis situation, its interests diverged from those of its new allies. While attempts are under way to secure Australia's defence through the construction of regional security cooperation, it remains to be seen whether these will prove successful.

For Australia to defend itself against a potential threat from south-east Asia or China unaided, would require a massive programme of re-armament and the modernisation of its forces. Again, despite their limitations as indices of military strength, simple figures for Australia's armed forces illustrate the problem: the army is, in 1995, only 23,700 strong, and so is dwarfed by that of several of its neighbours, including Indonesia (Neaman, 1995, pp. 173). The airforce has fewer combat aircraft than Thailand, let alone China (Neaman, 1995, p. 174). The geopolitical situation, which in part provides Australia with some degree of security, leaves the long, and often sparsely-populated, northern coastline facing states with much more heavily armed forces (Babbage, 1990).

Although fear of attack from the north has long been part of the Australian culture, with the Cold War certainty of US military backing diminished there may be more basis to such worries than at any time in the past (Mackerras, 1992, pp. 611-20). To counter this, Australia has two potential advantages: the possibility of superiority in communication and information-technology and its relationship with a series of potential allies (some in the Pacific) who do not have developed economic or military interests linking them as strongly as the USA with east or south-east Asia.

Among Australia's potential allies in the Pacific, none (apart from the USA) has sufficient forces alone to deter Chinese or south-east Asian aggression, were this threatened. Among its allies outside the region, only France and the UK could provide a nuclear, and to a limited extent conventional, deterrent on this scale. Reliance on European support may be unpalatable to those engaged in Australian party politics, but it is perhaps the surest way of using existing contacts to secure Australia's defence into the twenty-first century (on Australian foreign policy; Mediansky and Palfreeman, 1990). The involvement of the UK and other Commonwealth states, including Canada, in Australia's security could also have a useful effect in relation to the USA. America may be more willing to engage in the defence of Australia if the interests of key 'Pacific Rim' or European allies were involved.

Similar problems apply to Australia's potentially most formidable ally in the South Pacific - New Zealand. New Zealand's own armed forces are of a high quality but numerically weak, even compared to those of Australia. For instance, in 1995, New Zealand had only 4,500 soldiers and 37 combat aircraft (Neaman, 1995, pp. 189-90).

As we have seen, the south-east Asian states and China may be far less reticent in the future about using military force or annexing neighbouring territory than they were during the Cold War. While such a threat to Australasia cannot be said to be 'likely', it is possible, and this should prompt reconsideration of Australian and New Zealand security policy and levels of armament.

The island states of the Pacific may be in an even more perilous situation were any of the Asian-Pacific states to pursue an expansionist policy (Sutton and Payne, 1993a and b; Ross, 1993). Papua New Guinea shares a mutual border with Indonesia, but (in 1995) with a low population (4,345,000) and an army of only 3,200 Papua New Guinea is militarily weak by comparison with its neighbour (Neaman, 1995, p. 190). Indonesia has shown its willingness to annex adjacent territory by force (Thompson, 1994, pp. 187-9 and 266) and despite the strong geostrategic situation of Papua New Guinea, especially with regard to the Highlands bordering Indonesia, and its proud military tradition, Papua New Guinea would probably not be capable of defending itself against a major Indonesian attack. Its safest security guarantees would seem to come from its links with Australasia, although the combined forces of all of its potential allies in the region might be no match for Indonesia in a total war.

There is, then, an important Australasian and Pacific island interest in promoting regional cooperation and peaceful development in south-east Asia. As in the case of south-east Asia itself, these could alleviate the potential threat of war, but there is also a strong impetus to strengthen existing links with European states and, perhaps, with the USA.

If one sees either China or any of the south-east Asian states as potentially willing to pursue an expansionist or military hegemonic strategy in the Pacific (on the political environment, see Ball, 1993; Mahbubani, 1995), then it is hard to avoid the conclusion that Australasia and the island states must seriously re-evaluate the question of assigning a regional military role to non-Pacific states or to the Commonwealth. The latter seems problematic for a range of reasons and there would seem to be four options open to them. The first is to persuade the USA that its interests do not lie with east (and south-east) Asia, rather with the South Pacific. Given overriding economic and US security considerations, this may be a very difficult task (Fukuyama and Oh, 1993). Second, there is the possibility of building a security structure through existing linkages with regional states. This has been embarked upon but would be a vast task, involving a high level of risk, although it might receive widespread regional support given the shared potential threats (on these; Huxley, 1993; Grinter and Kihl, 1987). It is difficult, however, to see how such a security agreement without a nuclear state such as the USA, France or Britain could deter an opponent with nuclear weapons. Britain and France, themselves, have economic interests in east and south-east Asia, but these are unlikely to have such an effect on foreign policy as those of the USA. Both Britain and France have deployed forces in the Asia-Pacific region in recent decades and have historical links and, to a lesser extent, sentimental connections in popular culture that prompt public interest in Australasia or the Pacific islands. This, therefore, introduces the next option open to Australasian and Pacific island governments: to reinvolve Britain in the security of

Australasia and the Pacific islands.

Britain is a traditional ally of many of these states and even today successfully maintains an ability to project force globally - albeit on a limited scale - as has been seen in the Falklands and the Gulf War. There is also the British strategic nuclear deterrent to take into account. Consequently, this suggestion has much to commend it in strategic terms, although it may seem politically problematical, especially to Australia (on the potential unpopularity of such an approach see, McCarthy, 1994, especially p. 53 and on current Australian foreign policy, Beaumont and Woodward, 1993).

The final option is to attempt to reinvolve France in the security of this region (on France and the Pacific, see Aldrich, 1993). France lacks the traditional links with Australasia that Britain maintains, and has recently not proved diplomatically successful in the Pacific (Neaman, 1995, p. 169). Yet it shares the ability to deploy force globally and provide a limited nuclear deterrent. The Pacific states may well find that either Britain or France (or both) would be willing to play such a part, given their greater post-Cold War freedom to act and their aspirations to global roles. If so, these states will have to be persuaded to play this role on an inter-governmental level: neither the EU nor NATO is a plausible framework for such a security relationship, although the political relationships developed within the Commonwealth could form a basis for security cooperation between Britain, Canada and the South Pacific states.

Conclusion

This discussion considers only some themes in Asia-Pacific security and necessarily leaves many uncertainties regarding them, as it is problematical to assess the significance of current trends in China, south-east Asia and elsewhere in the Asia-Pacific region (recently addressed by Dibb, 1995; Friedberg, 1993/4). While, plainly, the situation in North Korea has to be very carefully managed to avoid the dangers of escalation and inter-state war, it is, perhaps, not as great a direct threat to regional security as is often supposed. While it may have been overstressed in the past, it is difficult to assess the degree of threat posed by China. The processes of state-collapse may, in any case, overtake China before it could become a serious threat to its neighbours, even if it chose to adopt this role (Goldstone, 1995, for an alternative view, Huang, 1995). South-east Asia seems to constitute a far greater threat to regional security, and there is a risk of the proliferation of weapons of mass-destruction in this area.

There are, however, some hopeful developments in the construction of a regional security framework that may alleviate the danger of war in south-east Asia. Finally, Australasia and the island states, although at present relatively secure and unlikely to become drawn into a war in south-east Asia were this to occur, have a serious medium-term security problem, which is only soluble by a radical revision of security policy. It may be that it is time to reinvolve at least one, if not more, of the European states in providing for the security of the South Pacific and to build on Commonwealth-based shared identities in developing security co-operation, unless the USA is willing to intensify its involvement in this area.

The end of the Cold War has, therefore, brought about fundamental changes in all parts of the Asia-Pacific region in relation to their security. It seems that it is this region, not Europe, which now poses the greatest threat of major war.

Bibliography

Anon (1995), *The Pacific Review* 8.3

Acharya, Amitav (1993), *A New Regional Order in South-East Asia: ASEAN in the Post-Cold War Era*, Brassey's, London

Akaha, Tsuneo (1995), 'Japan's security agenda in the post-Cold War era', *The Pacific Review* 8.1

Aldrich, R. (1993), *France and the South Pacific since 1940*, Macmillan, London

Austin, Greg (1995), 'The strategic implications of China's public order crisis', *Survival* 37.2

Babbage, Ross (1990), *A Coast Too Long: Defending Australia Beyond the 1980s*, Allen and Unwin, Sydney

Ball, Desmond (1993), 'Strategic culture in the Asia-Pacific region', *Security Studies* 3.1

Baker, Philip (1993), 'China: human rights and the law', *The Pacific Review* 6.3

Bannister, J. (1987), *China's Changing Population*, Stanford University Press, Cambridge, Mass.

Bearman, Sidney (ed.) (1995), *Strategic Survey 1994/95*, Oxford University Press, London

Beaumont, Joan and Woodward, Gary (1993),'Perspectives on Australian foreign policy', *Australian Journal of International Affairs* 48.1

Benson, L. and Svanberg, I. (eds) (1988), *The Kazaks of China: Essays on an Ethnic Minority*, Alonquist and Wiskett, Stockholm

Betts, Richard K. (1993-94), 'Wealth, power and instability. East Asia and the United States after the end of the Cold War', *International Security* 18.3

Brown, G. Thompson (1986), *Christianity in the People's Republic of China*, rev. edn., John Knox Press, Edinburgh

Buzan, Barry (1995), 'Japan's defence problematique', *The Pacific Review* 8.1

Buzan, Barry and Segal, Gerald (1994) 'Rethinking East Asian security', *Survival* 36.2

Cable, Vincent and Ferdinand, Peter (1994), 'China: enter as a giant', *International Affairs* 70.2

Cannon, T. and Jenkins, A. (eds) (1990), *The Geography of contemporary China: The Impact of Deng Xiaoping's Decade*, Routledge, London

Carus, W. Seth (1990), *Ballistic Missiles in the Third World: Threat and Response*, Praeger. New York

Chan, Anita (1989), 'The challenge to the social fabric', in Goodman and Segal, 1989

Cheeseman, Graeme (1993), *The Search for Self-Reliance: Australian Defence Since Vietnam*, Longman Cheshire, Melbourne

Clarke, Magnus (1989), 'Ballistic Missiles in the Third World and the Proliferation of Strategic Defence Technology', *Arms Control* 10.2

Dibb, Paul (1995), *Towards a New Balance of Power in Asia*, Oxford University Press, Oxford

Dixon, C. (1991), *South East Asia in the World Economy,* Cambridge University Press, Cambridge

Drakakis-Smith, D. (1992), *Pacific Asia*, Routledge, London

Dutt, A. K. (ed.) (1985), *Southeast Asia: realm of contrasts*, Westview, Boulder

Dwyer, D. (ed.) (1990), *Southeast Asia: geographical perspectives*, Longman Press, Harlow

Evans, Gareth (1989), *Australia's Regional Security*, Commonwealth of Australia, Canberra

Evans, Gareth (1995), 'Australia in East Asia and the Asia-Pacific: beyond the looking glass', *Australian Journal of International Affairs* 49.1

Evans, Paul M. (1994), 'Building security: the Council for Security Cooperation in the Asia Pacific (CSCAP)', *The Pacific Review* 7.2

Friedberg, Aaron L. (1993/4), 'Ripe for rivalry: prospects for peace in a multipolar Asia', *International Security* 18.3

Fry, Greg (1990), *Australia's Regional Security*, Allen and Unwin, Sydney

Fukuyama, Francis and Oh, Kongdan (1993), *The US-Japan Security Relationship After the End of the Cold War*, RAND, Santa Monica

Garver, John W. (1992), 'China's push through the South China Sea: the interaction of bureaucratic and national interests', *China Quarterly* 132

Gladney, D. C. (1991), 'Muslim Chinese: Ethnic nationalism in the People's Republic', *Council on East Asian Studies*, Harvard University Press, Harvard

Goldman, Merle (1994), 'Dissent in China after 1989', *The Oxford International Review* 6.1

Goldstone, J. A. (1995), 'The coming Chinese collapse', *Foreign Policy* 99

Goodman, David and Segal, Gerald (eds) (1989), *China at Forty, Mid Life Crisis?*, Oxford University Press, Oxford

Grant, R. L. (1993), *China and Southeast Asia*, Westview, Boulder

Grant, R. L. (1995), 'Political and economic reform in China', *The World Today* 51.2

Grinter, L. E. and Kihl, Y. W. (eds) (1987), *East Asian Conflict Zones*, St Martin's Press, London

Gupta, Shekhar (1995), *India Redefines its Role*, Oxford University Press, Oxford

Harding, Harry (1987), *China's Second Revolution: Reform After Mao*, The Brookings Institution, Washington

Henningham, S. (1995), *The Pacific Island States*, Longman, London

Hewitt, V. M. (1993), *The International Politics of South Asia*, MCPS, Manchester

Hodder, Rupert (1992), *The West Pacific Rim. An Introduction*, Belhaven Press, London

Hu, Weixing (1995), 'China's security agenda after the Cold War', *The Pacific Review* 8.1

Huang, Yasheng (1995), 'Why China will not collapse', *Foreign Policy* 99

Huxley, Tim (1993), *Insecurity in the ASEAN Region*, RUSI, London

Inoguchi, Takashi (1991), *Japan's International Relations*, Pinter London

Inoguchi, Takashi (1993), *Japan's Foreign Policy in an Era of Global Change*, Pinter, London

Joffe, Ellis (1995), 'The PLA and the Chinese economy: the effect of involvement', *Survival* 37.2

Katzenstein, Peter J. and Okawara, Nabuo (1993), 'Japan's national security: structures norms, and policies', *International Security* 17

Kidron, Michael and Segal, Ronald (1991), *The New State of the World Atlas*, Simon and Schuster, London

Krauthammer, Charles (1995), 'Why America must contain China', *Time* 146.5

Lee, Lai To (1989), 'Taiwan and the reunification of China', in Goodman and Segal, 1989

Leifer, M. (1988), *ASEAN and the Security of South-East Asia*, Routledge, London

Leifer, Michael (1995), 'Chinese economic reform and security policy: the South China Sea Connection', *Survival* 37.2

Lewis, John Wilson and Litai, Xue (1994), *China's Strategic Seapower*, Stanford University Press, Cambridge

McCarthy, John (1994), 'The great betrayal reconsidered: an Australian perspective', *Australian Journal of International Affairs* 48.1

McGregor, Charles (1993), 'Southeast Asia's new security challenges', *The Pacific Review* 6.3

Mackerras, Colin (ed.) (1992), *Eastern Asia. An Introductory History*, Longman Cheshire, Melbourne

Mackerras, Colin, Taneja, Pradeep and Young, Graham (1994), *China Since 1978*, Longman Cheshire, Melbourne

Mahbubani, Kishore (1992), 'Japan adrift', *Foreign Policy* 88

Mahbubani, Kishore (1995), 'The Pacific impulse', *Survival* 37.1

Mediansky, F. A. and Palfreeman, A. C. (eds) (1990), *In Pursuit of National* Interest: Australian Foreign Policy in the 1990s, Pergamon, Sydney

Moise, Edwin E. (1994), *Modern China: a History*, 2nd edn., Longman Press, Harlow

Neaman, Rachel (ed.) (1994), *The Military Balance 1994-1995*, Brassey's, London

Neher, Clark D. (1994), *Southeast Asia in the New International Era*, Westview Press, Boulder

Nolan, Janne (1991), *Trappings of Power: Ballistic Missiles in the Third World*, Brookings, Washington

Nye, Joseph S. Jnr. (1992-1993), 'Coping with Japan', *Foreign Policy* 89

O'Brien, J. and Palmer, M. (1993), *The State of Religion Atlas*, Simon and Schuster, London

Ogura, Kazuo (1993), *Japan-US Economic Frictions: Official Accounts, Realities Behind*, Shinbun-Sha, Tokyo

Oxnam, Robert B. (1992-1993), 'Asia/Pacific challenges', *Foreign Affairs* 72.1

Park, Hee Kwon (1993), 'Multilateral security cooperation', *The Pacific Review* 6.3

Pas, Julian F. (ed.) (1989), *The Turning of the Tide: Religion in China Today*, Oxford University Press, Oxford

Pye, Lucien W. (1994), 'China: a superpower?', *The Oxford International Review* 6.1

Ramanathanm Indira (1994), *China and the Ethnic Chinese in Malaysia and Indonesia*, Sangam Books, London

Reiss, Edward (1992), *The Strategic Defence Initiative*, Cambridge University Press, Cambridge

Rogman, G. (ed.) (1991), *The East Asian Region*, Princeton University Press, Princeton

Ross, Ken (1993), *Regional Security in the South Pacific: The Quarter Century 1970-95*, Australia National University, Canberra

Roy, Denny (1995), 'Assessing the Asia-Pacific "Power Vacuum"', *Survival* 37.3

Sasae, Kenichiro (1994), *Rethinking Japan-US Relations*, Brassey's, London

Segal, G. (1985), *Defending China*, Oxford University Press, Oxford

Segal, G. (1990a), *The Soviet Union and the Pacific*, Unwin Hyman, Boston, Mass.

Segal, G. (ed.) (1990b), *Chinese Politics and Foreign Policy Reform*, Kegan Paul Int., London

Segal, G. (1990c), *Rethinking the Pacific*, Clarendon Press, Oxford

Segal, Gerald (1994), *China Changes Shape: Regionalism and Foreign Policy*, Brassey's, London

Segal, G. and Goodman, S. G. (eds) (1994), *China Deconstructs*, Routledge, London

Shambaugh, David (1994), 'Growing strong: China's challenge to Asian security', *Survival* 36.2

Shibusawa, M. *et al* (1991), *Pacific Asia in the 1990s*, Routledge, London

Simpkin, R. E. (1985), *Race to the Swift: Thoughts on Twenty-First Century Warfare*, Brassey's, London

Songqiao, Zhao (1994), *Geography of China. Environment, Resources, Population, and Development*, John Wiley, New York

Sorrell, Mark (1993), *The Wary Warriors: Future Directions in Japanese Security Policies*, RAND, Santa Monica

Stephan, J. J. (1995), *The Russian Far East*, Cambridge University Press, Cambridge

Sugimoto, Takashi (1994), 'The political stability of ethnic regions in China', *Asia-Pacific Review* 1.1

Suryadinata, L. (1989), *The Ethnic Chinese in the ASEAN States*, ISEAS, Singapore

Sutton, P. and Payne, A. (1993a), 'Lilliput under threat: the security problems of small island and enclave developing states', *Political Studies* 41

Sutton, P. and Payne, A. (1993b), *Size and Survival*, Cass, Ilford

Thakur, Ramesh and Thayer, Carlyle A. (eds) (1993), *Reshaping Regional Relations: Asia-Pacific and the Former Soviet Union*, Westview Press, Boulder

Thayer, Carlyle A. (1990), *Trends in Force Modernisation in South-east Asia*, Canberra Peace Research Centre, Research Centre of Pacific

Studies, ANU

Thompson, Roger (1994), *The Pacific Basin Since 1945*, Longman, London

Toffler, Alvin and Heiddi (1990), *Powershift*, Little and Co., Boston, Mass.

Valencia, Mark J. (1995), *China and the South China Sea Disputes*, Oxford University Press, Oxford

Wang, Jiye and Hull, Terence H. (eds) (1991), *Population and Development Planning in China*, Allen and Unwin, Sydney

Yabunka, Mitzoi (1991), *Economic Negotiations with the US: Real Picture or Fictions*, The Simul Press, Tokyo

8 Some problems confronting British security policy makers

DAVID HIGGINBOTTOM

Introduction

'The limits and extent of planning in Britain for national security have been controversial for the past couple of hundred years' (Cecil, 1931, p. 218). Whilst one can understand the logic of Lord Salisbury's view, it is to be remembered that the next fifty years after his remarks saw Britain involved in wars that threatened its interests all over the globe. More recent discussions of these security interests have produced some counter-intuitive - if not illogical - opinions. For instance, a book produced in 1985, whilst containing a wealth of useful factual information and coherent argument, suggested that significant reductions in defence spending would not reduce the level of national security (Chalmers, 1985, p. 161). This chapter seeks to highlight a few of the problems that now confront - and will continue to confront - British security policy makers in the post-Soviet world, by looking at both long-term trends in British security and some current problems facing defence policy-makers.

First, I shall discuss some general themes that may assist

understanding of the arguments deployed later. Then I shall outline the major, 'overall', problems and then a few of the more specific problems which flow from these. This will enable the identification of threats to British national security and permit conclusions as to what might be done to meet these threats.

Achieving state-security

It is my contention that there are some longstanding regularities regarding state security. To achieve any form of security, all states constantly indulge in a three pillar policy in the conduct of their external affairs.

The first pillar is diplomacy, by which states attempt to try to persuade other states not to breach their security. The second is 'intelligence-gathering', which is conducted both overtly and covertly, with the latter means usually perceived as the most valuable option by governments. This state intelligence-gathering seeks to ascertain two things: is the state's security potentially threatened by any other state or states and if so, is this potential threat likely to acted upon. Finally, each state has the third pillar - military force - which has the task of both dissuading potential aggressors and providing the capability of actually preventing aggression. The most effective means of achieving adequate military force is to concentrate upon the latter task because, by so doing, the former is also achieved. 'Bluffs' can always be called and often are.

Normally, states rely for the achievement of security upon a combination of these three pillars operating. No one pillar necessarily occupies the prime position, whether in peace or war. The level of effort put into the three pillars at any one time depends largely upon national economics and national threat-perception. This chapter will concentrate upon the third pillar, although each has an important part to play in ensuring state security.

In addition to attention to these three pillars of national security, states also carry out security assessments in two forms: assessments of threat and of risk. Both forms of assessment are usually, at present, conducted with the short-term (one or two years ahead) and the longer-term (fifteen years or more ahead) in mind. Threat-assessment consists of attempts to determine challenges to sovereignty, whilst risk-assessment determines what threats can be countered with the (usually finite) resources available. No state, even the USA, can hope to cover every perceived threat.

Nevertheless, apparently obvious threats that turn into painful realities sometimes appear to come as a surprise to policy makers. The former Yugoslavia provides us with a very salutary example of this. The events of the early 1990s seem to have taken a number of governments by surprise, even in Western Europe, but the threat was plainly visible for years before the event. For instance, Larabee (1977) wrote, 'the prospect of a Yugoslavia without Tito is particularly unsettling because the country has a long history of political instability and ethnic conflict'.

It is my view that the collapse of the Soviet Union, and with it the bipolar world, has not (at least, yet) increased either world or regional stability, or 'state security', but has reduced both. The relaxation of the discipline imposed on states by the Cold War has allowed many tensions between, and within, states to surface that were formerly kept in check.

War in the twentieth century

War and armed conflict have two quite clearly different natures in the sense of International Law. 'War' is used to describe military operations conducted between and within states.

Again, a long-term regularity might be seen to apply to war: despite technological innovations, the twentieth century can be claimed to have brought no fundamental change to the nature of war, what causes it and how it is resolved. Sun Tzu's treatise (Griffith, 1971) is widely perceived by strategists to be as valid today as it was when written over two thousand years ago. The only significant twentieth-century change is that the sum of human technological knowledge in all spheres of life has increased dramatically, and at an ever-increasing speed. This enhanced knowledge plainly affects the prosecution of war, and it makes the matter in every respect more complex. But it does not change the fundamental nature of war, its causes and the means of its resolution. Two examples will suffice to show that technology does not simply speed up warfare, but complicates its prosecution (Burt, 1976; Macksey, 1986).

In 1944 during the three-month Battle of Normandy, 21 Army Group required a daily re-supply by air from Britain of about 50 tons of maps, but it is highly unlikely that anyone at all in the English army that fought at Agincourt actually had anything resembling a modern map! A contemporary British armoured regiment fighting at intense rates would require a re-supply in every twenty-four hour period of about 1000 tons of assorted stores, fuel, lubricating oil, ammunition, spare engines and power trains, gun barrels and the like (RUSI, 1991, p. 8). As tanks do not simply trundle down roads, re-supply vehicles must be able to go across country too. This limits their payload to about 5-7 tons. Thus, many supply vehicles are needed and these also require fuel, lubricating oil, spare parts and manpower to operate and maintain them. Despite these impressive logistic requirements, the military function of tanks is, arguably, no different from that of the armoured medieval knight, whose daily logistic requirement was probably in the weight-order of a few kilograms. In a sense, the tank and the knight are merely 'engines of war', which have the task of destroying the opposing force's 'engines of war', but the tank represents a far greater logistical commitment.

The generalisation that the nature of war has not changed must, however, be tempered by a realisation that these technological changes have altered the pace of war: modern war tends to start with much less warning time, and it tends to be of shorter duration than in the past. Conventional war seems, however, neither more, nor less, destructive in a relative sense than in the past despite this, given the changed scales of time and of the state-actors involved. For example, it is still generally held that the greatest human slaughter in a given time in battle was achieved at Cannae in 216 BC (Dupuy and Dupuy, 1970, p. 65), and it is widely accepted that the most destructive war in terms of human life and property in which the USA was involved was the American Civil War of the nineteenth century, not World War II or subsequent conflicts.

These phenomena, together with the technological advances, highlight four critical issues which have to be constantly borne in mind by security policy makers, and especially those of technologically advanced states. First, increased logistical complexity means that preparation time is increased: one cannot produce armed forces 'out of thin air', in large part because of what has been called 'the training time penalty'. For example, a raw recruit cannot be turned into a simple infantryman today in less than six months. That is, if he (and such a recruit is still likely to be male in Western states) is to have much chance of surviving in combat, he will need six months training. Second, wars now tend to be 'come as you are parties': the days of raising *ab initio* 'citizen armies' are over and professional armies hold sway. Third, the most vulnerable part of any state's armed forces is still the human element. For example, the fastest way to render a modern high technology air-force ineffective is not to waste time indulging in aerial combat, it is to concentrate on neutralising the air-crew before they reach their aircraft. Without trained crew, unless there are readily available reserves, expensive aircraft or other technologically-advanced weapons systems become useless. The final point is that, regrettable as it is, war still seems to be regarded as of utility by much of the human race.

Armed forces and states

A long-term regularity is also visible when examining the role of armed forces. As has been stated, the existence of effective armed forces is one of the three pillars of any state's security policy. For a state to have effective armed forces there are also three requirements. The first, already mentioned, is to possess military equipment and personnel. The second is to have a productive economic base to furnish military hardware. Third, there has to be effective research and development arrangements that update both the armed forces and the industrial base.

If these three requirements are met, and if each operates in conjunction with the others in a cooperative way, then at modest cost (in terms of the GNP of any Western state) it is possible to produce high quality armed forces. This is not a new feature of warfare and an example may be taken from British history: the 'longbow of Gwent' (Bryant, 1965). Taken into military use by the English during the time of Edward I, this weapon was rapidly developed in its effective capacity. The 'productive economic base' to produce it was set up and, as a result of the Statute of Winchester (in 1285), effectively trained manpower existed. Thus, by the time of Edward III, the existence of this weapon and the ability to produce both it and bowmen enabled the English to possess a relatively small army compared to that of other European kingdoms, but one which was among the most formidable in Europe, a situation that lasted for well over a hundred years. That is, military capacity was equivalent to human and material resources, combined with technology and training.

British security policy

A final long-term regularity concerns British security policy itself. An examination of British security policies over several centuries suggests some clearly discernible long-term trends still of relevance today. The first is that Britain, apart from the prosecution of some of its colonial wars, has long sought security by means of inter-state alliances. Again and again, either it became involved in war because it belonged to an alliance, or it formed an alliance to meet the demands of an ongoing war. Thus, in the post-Soviet era, the reliance by Britain on a security alliance (such as NATO) seems commonplace in terms of British history and need not diminish national sovereignty any more than have previous alliances.

Another long-term trend is that of manning its armed forces with what might be termed 'long service regulars', or 'volunteers'. Even in the conduct of the First World War, the British used conscription relatively sparingly. Conscripts were not used in the First World War until 1917, and even then conscription was selective, rather than universal. This latter condition existed only in the Second World War and in the post-war period of 'National Service'. So, 'universal' conscription was atypical.

Finally, whilst it seems that - speaking historically - in the matter of threat-assessment the British are fairly competent, they are less so in the matter of risk-assessment. For example, over a period of nearly a quarter of a century, successive British governments took considerable risks with the plain military threat posed by Argentina to the Falkland Isles (Higginbottom, 1996). These unsatisfactory risk-assessments, carried out over many years, may have contributed significantly to the events which culminated in the Argentine invasion of 1982.

Nor does it seem that British attitudes to security policy have overcome this tendency (note the review of HMSO, 1981). To give an example: an article in a major UK newspaper in 1994 discussed recent defence cuts in Britain (*Sunday Times*, 10 July 1994, p. 4.6), under the title 'Why we must plan for the wars we can win'. Unfortunately, British history shows clearly that it has often become involved in wars not because it could win them but simply because the British Government perceived no choice but to fight them.

PROBLEMS FOR BRITISH SECURITY POLICY-MAKERS TODAY
Securing Europe or securing Britain?

The question of whether UK security policy is aimed at the security of Britain as an independent, sovereign state, albeit in an alliance, or the security of some form of 'collective' political entity such as NATO or Europe, is plainly of key importance. Furthermore, it must be decided, in choosing the latter option, whether not only policy decisions but also the armed forces to back them up are to be collectively supplied. Put another way: are the armed forces of Britain to be completely unified into a NATO or 'European' armed force? This is a fundamental decision, for the manner in which it is answered inevitably leads to different roads ahead for the UK.

If the 'British' option is selected then it is hard to see any argument that could support the notion that Britain no longer needs armed forces capable of operating on (and under) the sea, on land and in the air. Lacking any one of these components the armed forces will be ineffective. However, if the integrated 'European' route is selected, then it is, perhaps, inevitable that the British Government will seek to cut expenditure on armed forces in favour of other forms of public spending. On a near-constant basis since 1953, successive British governments have produced defence 'reviews' that are, in practice, merely defence spending-cuts (Bellini and Pattie, 1977, p. 217). In the early stages of Britain's defence run-down after 1953, politicians had a reasonable excuse because 'Empire/Commonwealth' commitments were reduced, but from the mid-eighties onwards, politicians have not been cutting 'imperial' defence, rather the defence of the British isles itself. Possibly the two most controversial defence restructuring exercises in recent years were 'Options for Change' and, later, 'Front Line First'. Both seem perfectly reasonable compromises between political needs and military commitments. But from the military point of view - especially in the case of the latter - they were enfeebling. Perhaps, in the future, they will be regarded as no more sensible than the pre-Second World War 'Ten Year Rule'.

If Britain decides not to completely commit itself to the 'European' security option, then another problem confronts British policy makers. Bearing in mind that there seems a strong British political tradition of seeking security within an alliance-framework, then with whom will the British ally themselves? One obvious solution is to retain the Atlantic Alliance (in the shape of NATO), which has proved a most effective security guarantee for over forty years. Currently, NATO is only viable in a military sense with American military power, so the question arises as to whether the 'European' part of NATO can continue to enjoy the possibility of US military support: there are a number of reasons suggesting that it might not (interestingly preempted by Galtung, 1973, chapter 8).

The first of these is the widely-recognised run-down of the armed forces of the USA. The only matter of debate here is the extent of this run-down and its likely effects (for example, Cordesman, 1993). The second reason results from trends visible in aspects of US foreign policy. The State Department found themselves seriously at odds with the 'Europeans' in the matter of Bosnia in 1994, although it was disguised under the camouflage of 'NATO versus the UN' ((RUSI, 1995, p. 29), and (in March 1995) differences between the governments of the USA and Britain were glossed over with arguments about US domestic politics (*Daily Telegraph*, 11 March 1995, p. 22). The ability to evade differences of opinion does not alter the fact that there have been rifts in matters directly affecting security issues, while on the economic front there are signs of ever-increasing strain between the USA and Europe. For example, in March 1995 there was disagreement about the appointment of a new leader for the World Trade Organisation (*Daily Telegraph*, 16 March 1995, p. 10).

It appears that the USA may be becoming more 'isolationist', as it becomes economically and militarily ever weaker. Thus, the future of NATO in its present form - with genuine American commitment - is clearly in the balance and has been for some time: both before and after the Soviet collapse (RUSI, 1995, pp. 33-41. See also Rudrey and Reychler, 1988, esp. p. 18).

So, British security policy-makers currently have a dilemma. On the one hand they can decide to align themselves more strongly with Europe, for which no obvious basis exists outside NATO and the WEU, unless it is to form a unified EU force. Alternatively, they might select the 'Atlantic' option, also through NATO, which seems fraught with the risk of ineffectiveness. Neither of these options seems very attractive if one accepts the premise of US decline, and both highlight the importance of NATO to British security.

It could be argued that the British would get the best of both worlds if they maintained, or reconstructed, their own armed forces and then allied themselves to whichever actor appeared the strongest at any given moment. This would also simply be a continuation of tradition that appears to have stood Britain in good stead for centuries, but their ability to act in this way may be constrained by prior commitments, self-perceptions and diplomatic factors.

The problem of the 'Peace Dividend'

In the aftermath of the Soviet collapse it became fashionable for politicians in both Europe and America to announce a 'peace dividend'. This meant reducing public spending on all of the three pillars of national security already described. Presumably 'savings' were to be deployed in some other fashion, either in the shape of tax cuts or increased welfare. That this dividend was debatable is best exemplified by the position adopted by the British Liberal Democrat Party. In the 1992 General Election this party took the view that 'defence' spending could be halved by the year 2000. Subsequently, perhaps as a result of exposure to some realities of the post-Cold War world in relation to the former Yugoslavia the party's leader publicly declared that view mistaken (*Daily Telegraph*, 26 April 1994). Nor have the Conservative Party stressed the continuing need for strong defence. In February 1995, a 'defence' body suggested that it is now the Labour Party, rather than the Conservatives, who are warning the nation of the weakened state of Britain's armed forces (RUSI, February 1995, p. 11).

There has also been an effect on public perceptions of security. In Europe and North America a considerable body of citizens have allowed themselves to be persuaded that, at least as far as they are concerned, the prospect of war has ended. In democracies, such views might be expected to have a significant impact upon governmental decision-taking and scope for manoeuvre in security policy making. The problem, therefore, of misplaced British public notions of monetary 'peace dividends' and of changed perceptions of security is a serious one, which has to be faced by those responsible for British national security in the post-Soviet world. It might be supposed that spreading costs among EU members would cater for this, but the 'European' option also has significant problems.

Leaving aside the possibility that the collective funding of European defence and the loss of British Governmental control over British security policy could be claimed to mean the end of British sovereignty, the central problem that British security policy-makers have to face up to is, 'for how long will the EU exist'. Merely because the EU has been instituted, or because the 'federalists' might 'win' the political battles, does not necessarily mean that the EU will survive for long into the next millennium. The collapse of the Soviet Union shows quite clearly the speed with which modern states and federations can disintegrate.

Equipment procurement

The total capacity of the EU's defence industries far outweighs the demand from solely European forces, but there is much duplication in effort in both Research and Development and production. The Chief of Defence Procurement, in a presentation in 1992 (RUSI, October 1995, p. 75), went further and foresaw a greater 'international dimension'.

Any 'winding down' of defence industries almost certainly means a rise in that - generally disliked - characteristic, unemployment. There are plenty of examples that illustrate this; for example, one need only consider the demise of the Swan Hunter and Cammell Lairds shipyards. In March 1995, the British Government decided to purchase a mixed military helicopter fleet with part provided by a British firm and part by an American firm. The purely military 'objections' were obvious: the British product had, for instance, a smaller payload, and 'mixed' fleets demand mixed, and therefore larger, logistic-back up and a greater diversity of spare parts and properly trained maintenance personnel. Thus, on the one hand, 'unemployment' was not created but this benefit was probably wiped out by greater logistic demands at the expense of the military 'teeth' of the British forces. Likewise, 'downscaling' RAF engineer support in favour of a civilian equivalent (again, a decision on political grounds) was producing less than satisfactory maintenance results (*Daily Telegraph*, 20 June 1995, p. 5). All of this shows clearly how the perceived danger of unemployment can drive decision-making in security issues, even if these decisions might be more sensibly discussed in entirely military terms.

If a state purchases equipment from abroad, it needs to be sure that supply of replacements and spares will be forthcoming. When this is not the case then military options and operations can be jeopardised, as the Argentines found when the French reduced supply of the air-launched Exocet missile in 1982. The history of defence equipment collaboration with other nations in Europe is not as encouraging as might be hoped. An attempt in the 1970s/80s to produce a main battle tank foundered, probably on the grounds of diverging tactical doctrines, and the Germans eventually pulled out of the Eurofighter project, mainly (perhaps exclusively) on the grounds of costs (Tusa, 1992a, p. 13).

The problem of conscription

In the post-Soviet era some European countries have begun to have serious reservations about the utility of conscription. Belgium has abandoned it since 1993 (Fiorenza, 1992, p. 28), and the Netherlands and France appear to have accepted - as a result of the lessons of the Gulf War - that conscripts are of little value for military operations (Tusa, 1992b, p. 28). The Germans have recently announced 'Crisis Reaction Forces', which will consist of 80% regular personnel (RUSI, December 1994, p. 13).

This matter raises a problem for any form of 'united European armed forces': how long will one state that contributes troops be allowed to retain conscription whilst another does not? It is probably true to say that for Europe to have all-regular forces of sufficient manpower to meet all 'national' commitments, then the costs will soon be much greater than those of conscript-based armed forces. This might become a serious problem for states habitually reliant on conscription and prove highly unpopular in those states (such as the UK) that are not.

Paying equal shares

Currently, the NATO states do not spend the same proportion of GNP on defence. The range is about 1.2% to 4.8% of GNP (RUSI, October 1994, p. 39). In the context of NATO, a security alliance made up of independent states, this is acceptable, but the bulk of the NATO states are also in the EU and the same disparity in spending would occur, therefore, in relation to EU-based forces. In 1995 and 1998 Germany will increase its defence budget (RUSI, December 1994, p. 13). So, to a lesser extent will France in 1995 (RUSI, March 1995, p. 21). However, not only is there disparity in terms of GDP but also in terms of share of government spending: for example, defence will take up 13.5% of government spending in France for 1995 (RUSI, March 1995, p. 21) whilst the same figure in Britain is a mere 5.8%.

Any attempt at the production of a homogenous 'European Union' security policy inevitably means that, perhaps sooner rather than later, there will be great pressure on all member states to harmonise defence spending, probably in terms of proportion of GDP and/or proportion of government spending. This might mean some reduction by certain states with corresponding increase by others, but it may well be that some states - for example France, Germany and Greece - may not feel able to reduce their spending on defence unless they can clearly see a viable alternative in place for their national security.

The most significant problem is, perhaps, that the inevitable domestic political arguments about defence spending are likely to produce a 'smokescreen' that will hide the real problems of national differences in security issues.

National interests and European unification

Those committed to some form of politically federalised, or 'United', Europe seem to hold the opinion that nationalism will rapidly disappear following unification. They argue that this disappearance will, in some way, reduce European commitments worldwide. That this is not the case is suggested by the 'fishing' dispute that arose in March 1995 between Canada and Spain (and so, Europe), and which exposed divisions in attitudes to foreign affairs between Britain and the rest of the EU. It can, of course, be argued that, in Britain's case, any differences were simply the product of generalised anti-European sentiments and, given time, such emotions will wither away as younger generations of committed 'Europeans' reach adulthood and have the capacity to influence public opinion and vote in elections. There are, however, many indications that nationalism does not become absorbed by political inclusion in a larger entity. To give an example: Scotland has been a part of a unitary state for nearly three hundred years, but it is plain that nationalist sentiment is still prevalent.

If a long-established state of fifty-eight million or so is in danger of breaking up after more than three hundred years in existence, then it becomes likely that a new federation of nearly 350,000,000 or so might be somewhat more vulnerable to collapse. Nor is this liable to be a product of British anti-Europeanism alone.

Speaking in November 1992, the Chief of the French Defence Staff made it plain that French forces would be deployed anywhere in the world in defence of perceived French national interests (RUSI, February 1993, pp. 4-7). The same officer, speaking in March 1994, trying to see the problem somewhat more through 'European' eyes, did not preclude French deployments in pursuit of French interests (RUSI, April 1994, pp. 17-21). As for the other European states, the Chief of Staff of the German Federal Armed Forces, speaking in October 1994, explicitly made the point that the Bundeswehr must have in being combat-ready, readily available, forces, 'able to be employed under all geographical and climatic conditions' (RUSI, December 1994, pp. 8-13). This intention was stated in the context of NATO, WEU or UN operations rather than the EU, and it is a far-reaching change in Germany's position from that which it adopted even two years before. These states have shown a greater, not reduced, sense of extra-European national security interests in the post-Cold War world than was the case prior, for instance, to the Maastricht Treaty of 1992.

It is, of course, clear that Britain, too, still has national interests worldwide, which require troop deployments. Here, the Falklands 'War' of 1982 is an obvious case.

The public positions of these three states alone suggest a striking pattern. If the perceived overseas national interests of all member states are seen together, then it would seem that collectively they have interests that are to be found all over the globe. This raises the question of when does the national interest of one state in the EU run counter to that of another, and (if they act in accordance with a unity of interest) might the population of Europe collectively be willing to see the EU as a 'world policeman'.

EMERGING THREATS TO BRITISH INTERESTS AND SECURITY

While Britain faces at least as many threats in the post-Soviet period, in the post-Cold War situation the nature of the threats has changed drastically. I shall outline three key problems.

An economic war?

A global problem stems from the global economy. There is a danger that the world is now in the first stages of what may become an economic war (*The Economist*, 1-7 October 1994; Kennedy, 1994) produced by the extraordinary development of communications in the twentieth century and the globalisation of the international economy, which has set into motion a global desire for unprecedented material acquisition. New economic coalitions (of which the European Union and NAFTA are examples) are being built up in order to enable global economic growth, but result in economic regionalisation. Although these blocs currently co-exist in a peaceful way, this does not preclude the potential and possibility for a future collapse into conflict.

While it is most likely that inter-regional economic competition of this sort would take an economic or diplomatic form, as 'trade wars' and the like, these might escalate into armed conflict - if only by proxy - between rival blocs.

If the global economy regionalised into confined blocs, then states will seek national economic security and attempt to develop the capacity to assist 'friendly' states either within their own, or some other, region. Yet there are clear risks of the globalisation of this conflict. The notion that any state can pursue an isolationist policy in a 'globalised' international political economy is an unrealistic illusion, so that economic conflicts of this sort contain within them the dynamic of escalation.

Economic threats have, of course, been recognised for decades. Writing in 1980, ex-President Nixon explained lucidly how oil in the Persian Gulf region was the North Atlantic/Western European 'jugular' (Nixon, 1980, Chapter 4), while as early as 1977 Sir Fred Hoyle produced a clear and persuasive case that the only hope that states such as Britain have of securely meeting future energy needs lies in nuclear fuel (Hoyle, 1977). An IISS paper published in 1977 (Krapels, 1977) suggested that only sudden, severe and long-lasting reductions in oil supplies can be considered an immediate security threat to most states, but the paper also concludes in the context of the 1973 OPEC price rise, 'But for Europe the threat to oil supplies was not a small difficulty' (Krapels, 1977, p. 30). This highlights the continuing risks deriving from dependency on oil.

While as much as a third to one half of the world's land mass includes sedimentary basins (Pratt and Good, 1950, opp. p. 14), it is now clear that many of these basins do not contain oil. The essential fact from a security perspective is that it is known, rather than potential, reserves which matter in security calculations. Hoyle showed that the location of the bulk of proven reserves centred around what was then the USSR, the Arabian Peninsula and North Africa (Hoyle, 1977, p. 3). Further, he showed that if the 'poor' states in the world were not to remain 'poor', then the supply of usable energy worldwide would have to rise significantly (Hoyle, 1977, Chapter 4). This pattern of global economic growth is now happening, at least in some parts of the Asian-Pacific region, and there is increasing pressure upon all world energy sources, particularly oil.

Despite several attempts (for example Chapman, 1975) to show that it is possible for Britain to survive without oil, and despite the North Sea fields, it is clear that the British economy is still heavily dependent on oil imports, especially from the Middle East. In the immediate past, and for the immediate future, Britain was (and will be) a net exporter of oil (HMSO, 1995-6, Table 3.4 p. 39). However, Britain still has to import oil, in large part because the North Sea fields do not yield some grades of crude oil that are essential to the UK economy.

Whether Britain has security policies that are national or tied to a 'greater Europe', the need for oil is an essential fact of the national political economy. The UK economy, and hence 'living standards', depends to a great extent upon oil imports. This situation will hold good for at least fifteen or twenty years, even if 'Europe' started to develop a system of total nuclear-fuelled usable energy now. Unless the whole population of Britain is prepared to accept constantly reduced material standards of living, then it has a vested interest in oil continuing to flow from both the Middle East and North Africa. This has a continuing security importance for the UK. While military force may well be unnecessary to ensure economic security, securing this resource alone demonstrates why Britain must possess, or have access to, armed forces capable of operating in these regions for the foreseeable future. We cannot be sure that we have seen the last Gulf War.

Another example may make the case for a global capability - it is probable that a substantial oil field, estimated as 50% greater than the total British sector of the North Sea, lies within a 200 mile radius of the Falklands. Production, however, will not be achieved for five to seven years at least (*Keesings Archives*, 1993, p. 39775), and if Britain is to profit from this discovery, it must be prepared to defend the Falklands (which, I hardly need to remind the reader, has already been subject to one invasion) for decades to come.

Globally, the 'oil world' is in an unsettled state. In 1993 world production was 66 million barrels per day (*Keesings Archives*, 1994, R155), but this production mostly comes from only two sources, OPEC and non-OPEC states. In late 1993 the world price fell to US$14 per barrel. OPEC wished for a cut in world production to boost prices, but non-OPEC states disagreed (*Keesings Archives*, 1994, p. 39842). Even within OPEC there is division: in March 1994, the world oil price fell to US$13 per barrel, and an attempt at a coordinated cut in world production was thwarted by Saudi Arabia. The government of Iran was apparently 'infuriated' (*Keesings Archives*, 1994, pp. 39937-8).

The risks posed by an angered 'regional power' are clear. Iran is regarded as a 'pricing hawk' and is currently undertaking a significant re-armament programme (*Sunday Telegraph*, 15 January 1995, p. 20; *Daily Telegraph*, 23 March 1995, p. 13), which includes deployments that could easily close the Straits of Hormuz. It is too readily forgotten that the 1961 Iraq attempt to overrun Kuwait had to be staved off by a British military deployment, that in 1991 by a coalition including the UK (on the complex political and military situation in the Gulf, see Hollis, 1993), but the key point is straightforward: oil, itself, is a destabilising factor in many of the key production areas vital to British interests.

If Britain wishes to retain access to imported oil and, therefore, retain its current material standard of living then the events of 1961 and 1991, seen in the context of the rise of regional economic blocs, suggest that it must be prepared to fight to do so.

Nuclear, chemical and biological weapons proliferation

In late 1993, *The Economist* suggested that, if the number of states which possessed missiles with ranges of 600 miles (or over) and nuclear, chemical or biological (NBC) warheads continued to increase, then the hope of controlling proliferation would have collapsed (*The Economist*,

1993, p. 14). This statement highlighted the problem of the 'knock-on' effect of states acquiring NBC weapons and delivery systems. If one state acquires them, then their immediate neighbours - that is, those within range - will probably want them too, as the most widely-recognised deterrent to nuclear attack is the threat of nuclear counter-strike (see Vigeveno, 1983). That is, new 'nuclear states' will emerge in response to 'nuclear neighbours'.

In the case of nuclear weapons, it seems that fission devices in the 10-20KT range are still the most simple practical warheads to design (Greenwood, Rathjens and Rvina, 1976), but the real problem with such weapons from the point of view of a 'new nuclear state' is the production of a reliable delivery system. Without such a system nuclear warheads, and for that matter biological and chemical devices, are more 'showpieces' than of military or political utility. A reliable delivery system must have long-range and accuracy, and it is the acquisition of such delivery systems that makes a state a serious contender for classification as an 'NBC power'. It is also still the case that the optimum delivery system in terms of payload, range, accuracy and survivability, is the missile. In the 1990/91 Gulf War, Iraqi SCUDs proved to be a great problem for the Coalition forces. The campaign to neutralise them was mounted by some of the best troops available, supported by very sophisticated air-power in great strength, but it was only partially successful (Atkinson, 1994; de la Billiere, 1992).

An examination of one state with interests likely to lead it into conflict with the West - North Korea - demonstrates the realities of the threat posed by the proliferation of weapons of mass-destruction and of appropriate delivery systems. In 1994 there was Western concern that North Korea was developing a 'major nuclear weapons industry', an especially worrying development as it was the world's largest proliferator of ballistic missiles (RUSI, July 1994, pp. 51-3). For instance, North Korea produces a missile called 'Nodong', which has a payload of 500 kg and could deliver a 50KT nuclear warhead (or a VX chemical warhead). It has also acquired a commercial version of GPS Navstar (satellite navigation system), and the Nodong's circular error of probability is about 700m (HMSO, 1994b, p. 145). The range of the missile is about 2000km, but this may be being upgraded to 4000km (HMSO, 1994a, p. 132). Plainly, an NBC capability would be a formidable addition to this weapon's destructiveness, and might render North Korea a potential threat to its neighbours.

Likewise, Iran may be working on a joint nuclear warhead project with North Korea (HMSO, 1994b, p. 145) and it is quite clear that Iran has acquired a great deal of nuclear technology from many sources, especially, perhaps, from former Soviet republics (*Sunday Telegraph*, 15 January 1995, p. 20). It has also now certainly acquired Nodongs from North Korea (RUSI, May 1993, p. 40). There is some concern that Libya might attempt to acquire both missiles and nuclear warheads from North Korea (HMSO, 1994a).

The danger in this case is, therefore, of an anti-Western North Korea, with weapons of mass destruction that could be delivered reasonably accurately to, for example China, Japan, the Philippines, Malaya, Thailand, Burma and India, with an anti-Western Iran capable of doing the same to Israel and most of the Middle East, particularly the oil-rich states of the Gulf. Serious as these examples are, another anti-Western state, Libya, would, if equipped with such weapons, be able to deliver them to every capital city in Western and Central Europe, to say nothing of being another possible threat to the Middle East. This is, of course, a 'worst case' image but the image of nuclear proliferation to any area could, in itself, increase the pressure for further proliferation in virtually the entire Middle East and East Asian regions. Quite apart from threatening some of Britain's most important diplomatic and military allies and vital trading partners and the oil supply, new nuclear states in the Middle East could, conceivably, even threaten the British Isles themselves.

Terrorism

The last threat is one which has been around for some time. It is a well-known axiom that 'one man's terrorist is another man's freedom fighter'. This old aphorism serves to hide several points of special relevance here. The first is that terrorists (or for that matter 'freedom fighters') do not legally exist. The laws of most states define the acts normally associated with such individuals and organisations simply as 'criminal'. The methods that they employ put them beyond the pale of regular military action in terms of established international law, so rendering them 'criminal' in this sense too. Changes to international law in the past thirty years might, however, be construed as offering such individuals partial protection and so recognition and accommodation (Roberts and Guelff, 1982, pp. 441-12; De Lupis, 1987, pp. 50-3), and the definition of individuals as having 'combatant status' could be seen to give anyone engaged in military or quasi-military operations of any sort, protection under international law. An examination of the two 1977 Geneva Protocols and especially Protocol I Article 44, gives a definition of 'combatant status' that is not completely precise, but it is still sufficient to refute this view. It is unlikely that either 'terrorists' or 'freedom fighters' could meet all the obligations laid upon them by such international law. This being so, here they will be referred to by the word 'terrorist', to differentiate them from regular (legal) soldiers, and to indicate their 'criminal' status.

This interpretation also implies the realisation that, in this century (and particularly in the last half of the century), terrorism has been on the increase. Such activity is not only carried out by non-state groups such as the Provisional IRA, but is also used by groups sponsored by states. The Oliver North affair showed that Iran has undoubtedly been involved, to some extent, in this practice (RUSI, 1993, p. 294), and state-sponsored terrorism has also existed in Latin America (RUSI, September 1993, pp. 68-70). Despite the ever-shifting reference frames needed in its evaluations, it seems that the Lockerbie Pan Am bombing probably implicates Libya in this sort of behaviour, too.

During the bipolar era of the Cold War it might have been possible for the world community to reduce the level of terrorist activity, or even to control state-terrorism entirely. This course was not achieved, perhaps because the two main protagonists elected to support various terrorist groups (as defined here), sometimes in the prosecution of the war, sometimes for domestic political reasons. With the ending of the bipolarity and the emergence of the new multipolar world, it will prove even harder to control terrorism. Further, some recent political successes by terrorist groups may have reinforced their belief in the utility of terrorism. It is plain that the scope and scale of communication worldwide is ever increasing and this affects all forms of 'military operations' (see, Rados, 1992, pp. 183-91), especially terrorist campaigns, because it reinforces the view that terrorists need not obey international norms.

For a variety of reasons, neither states nor international organisations can control this phenomenon and it is, therefore, difficult to avoid the conclusion that the activities of various forms of terrorist groups will not only continue but also become more, and not less, prevalent. A case could be made that there is some real danger that most 'war' in the immediate and medium-term future will be prosecuted by terrorist means, as defined here.

Further, it needs to be taken into account that some terrorist campaigns develop into 'war' in the classic and legal senses. Such campaigns are beyond the abilities of the police to control and require the use of armed forces, as in the case of the South African 'border war' (for a detailed exposition see, Steenkamp, 1989). The armed forces required by any future British security policy should, therefore, be capable of conducting operations against terrorist groups and they must be capable not only of defeating terrorists but also of peacekeeping in terrorist situations, by standing between such people and those whom they attack.

CONCLUSION

Britain needs to retain effective, well-equipped and well-trained armed forces for the foreseeable future. This responsibility may be met on a strictly national basis, or by the use of the traditional British policy of security through alliance. This might be achieved in the 'European' context, whether this be through some form of collective policy of separate states or by a 'European' national policy. Put another way, the British people are going to have to furnish both human resources and money to maintain adequate armed forces for a long time to come and this will have to be done irrespective of what other 'needs' arise, no matter how compelling they seem to be.

Whatever approach is selected, serious problems for policy-makers will arise. The length of this chapter precludes attention to many other security problems that exist, but there should be no doubt that there are many.

There is one further point. To be effective, 'British' armed forces - from whatever source - need the following characteristics: they will need to be readily available, because in the event of any operational deployment there is unlikely to be time to hesitate, they must be capable of projection worldwide and, finally, they must be capable of operating in low-intensity, limited, and general, war situations and in an NBC environment.

This being so, the current tendency to cut defence spending, no matter how well-intentioned or skilfully presented in 'Options for Change' or 'Front line first', may be misguided. No serious alternatives to a viable NATO or WEU exist, and some might argue that both of these organisations face significant difficulties in the 1990s. Perhaps this is the biggest problem of all that faces British security policy makers.

Bibliography

Atkinson, R. (1994), *Crusade-The Untold Story of the Gulf War*, Harper Collins, New York

Bellini, J. and Pattie G. (1977), 'British Defence Options - A Gaullist Perspective, *Survival*, September/October

Bryant, A. (1965), *The Age of Chivalry*, The Reprint Society Ltd

Burt, R. (1976), *New Weapon Technologies*, Adelphi Paper 126, London

Cecil, G. (1931), *Robert, Marquis of Salisbury*, London

Chalmers, M. (1985), *Paying for defence*, Pluto Press Ltd, London

Chapman, P. (1975), *Fuels Paradise*, Pelican Books, London

Cordesman, A. H. (1993), *US Defence Policy: Resources and Capabilities*, RUSI

Cyprus Press and Information Office, Cyprus: *The Way to Full EC Membership*, Second Edition, Republic of Cyprus

De la Billiere, General Sir Peter (1991), *RUSI Journal* Winter

De la Billiere, General Sir Peter (1992), *Storm Command*, Harper Collins, London

De Lupis, I. D. (1987), *The Law of War*, Cambridge University Press, Cambridge

Dupuy R. E. and Dupuy T. N. (1970), *The Encyclopedia of Military History*, The Military Book Society, Oxford

Fiorenza, N. (1992), 'End of Conscription, deep troop cuts ahead for Belgium', *Armed Forces Journal International*, October

Galtung, J. (1973), *The European Community: A Superpower in the Making*, George Allen and Unwin, St Leonards, NSW

Greenwood T., Rathjens, G. N. and Rvina, J. (1976), *Nuclear Power and Weapons Proliferation*, Adelphi Paper 130, London

Griffith, S. B. (1971), *Sun Tzu-The Art of War*, Oxford University Press, Oxford

Higginbottom, D. L. (1996), 'Stress, Communications and Decision Taking in International Relations', PhD dissertation, University of Reading

HMSO (1981), *UK Defence Programme-The Way Forward*, June, Cmnd 8288

HMSO (1994a), Foreign Affairs Committee quoted *Minutes of Evidence* 7 December 1994 p132

HMSO (1994b), Foreign Affairs Committee-UK Policy on Weapons Proliferation and Control in the Post-Cold War Era, *Minutes of Evidence* 14 December

HM Treasury (1995-6), *Financial Statement and Budget Report 1995-96*, HMSO, London

Hollis, R. (1993), *Gulf Security: No Consensus*, RUSI

Hoyle, F. (1977), *Energy or Extinction?*, Heinemann Educational Books Ltd, Oxford

Kennedy, P. (1994), *Preparing for the Twenty First Century*, Fontana Press, London

Krapels, E. N. (1977), *Oil and Security*, IISS Summer, Adelphi Paper 136, London

Larabee, F. S. (1977), *Balkan Security*, IISS Summer, Adelphi Paper 135, London

Machsey, K. (1986), *Technology in War - The impact of science on weapon development and modern battle*, BCA

Mao Tse Tung (1966), *Selected Military Writings*, Foreign Language Press, Peking

Nixon, R. (1980), *The Real War*, Sidgwick & Jackson Ltd, London

Pratt, W. E. and Good, D. (1950), *World Geography of Petroleum*, American Geographical Society

Roberts, A. and Guelff, R. (1982), *Documents on the Laws of War*, Clarendon Press, Oxford

Rados, A. (1992), *War and the Power of Television*, RUSI and Brassey's Defence Yearbook

Rudrey, R. and Reychler, L. (1988), *European Security beyond the Year 2000*, Praeger, New York

RUSI (1972), *Journal* October

  (1993), *International Security Review*

  (1993), *Journal* February

  (1993), *Newsbrief* May, Vol. 13 No. 5

  (1993), *Newsbrief,* September, Vol. 13 No. 9

  (1994), *Journal* April

  (1994), Journal October

  (1994), *Journal* December

  (1994), *Newsbrief* July, Vol. 14 No. 7

  (1995), *International Security Review 1995*

  (1995), *Newsbrief* January 1995 Vol. 15 No. 1

  (1995), *Newsbrief* February, Vol. 15 No. 2

  (1995), *Newsbrief* March Vol. 15 No. 3

Steenkamp, W. (1989), *South Africa's Border War 1966-1989*, Ashanti Publishing (Pty) Ltd, Johannesburg

Tusa, F. (1992a), 'Germany Hints: slash EFA costs and fighter will become a new option', *Armed Forces Journal International*, December

Tusa, F. (1992b), 'Europeans uncertain about future of reserves, Utility of conscription', *Armed Forces Journal International*, October

Vigeveno, G. (1983), *The Bomb and European Security*, C. Hurst and Company, London

Index